ONN DUGGAN is a native of Wexford Town. A retired teacher and
Head of History at Avondale Community College in Rathdrum, County
ow, he holds a Master's Degree in Modern History. Historian in residence
land's Own magazine, he has contributed in excess of 400 articles to the
ine, and is the main contributor to the very successful and popular Cen-
Annual since 2016. He has been commissioned to write a special issue
life of Michael Collins, to be published on the centenary of his death in
t 2022. Eamonn has also contributed to various academic and historical
y publications. In 2014, he delivered the annual Ivy Day oration in com-
ration of Charles Stewart Parnell.

We Go
Into Actio
Today
at Noon ..

EAM
forme
Wick
for *I*
maga
tenar
on th
Augu
socie
mem

We Go Into Action Today at Noon ...

First-hand Accounts from Ireland's Revolutionary Years 1913–22

Eamonn Duggan

THE O'BRIEN PRESS
DUBLIN

First published 2021 by The O'Brien Press Ltd.
12 Terenure Road East, Rathgar, Dublin 6, D06 HD27, Ireland.
Tel: +353 1 4923333 Fax: +353 1 4922777
Email: books@obrien.ie
Website: www.obrien.ie
The O'Brien Press is a member of Publishing Ireland.

ISBN 978-1-78849-271-3

10 9 8 7 6 5 4 3 2 1
25 24 23 22 21

Printed and bound by ScandBook UAB, Lithuania.
The paper in this book is produced using pulp from managed forests.

Published in:

DUBLIN
UNESCO
City of Literature

This book, which became a labour of love, is dedicated to two people.
To Jill, your encouragement and patience helped me see
the project through to its conclusion; and to my late Dad,
who I know in my heart would have approved of it.

Contents

Introduction   page 9

Chapter 1   The Witness Statements Archive   17

Chapter 2   The Truth About the Rising   21

Chapter 3   Cork Awaits the Call to Arms   30

Chapter 4   An Influential Monsignor   37

Chapter 5   The Curious Tale of 198 Parnell Street   52

Chapter 6   Procuring Arms and Gathering Intelligence   59

Chapter 7   Tipperary Republicans Lead the Way   68

Chapter 8   Ambushes and Attacks in the Rebel County   80

Chapter 9   The Brave Republican Women   93

Chapter 10   Father Aloysius: Chaplain to the Republican Heroes   104

Chapter 11   Frank Thornton: An Extraordinary Life in
             Irish Republicanism   117

Chapter 12   Vincent Byrne: Committed to the Republic and the Squad   135

Chapter 13   Seán Moylan: Committed Republican and Outstanding
             Military Leader   156

Chapter 14   Tadhg Kennedy: A Proud Kerryman and a True Patriot   183

Chapter 15   Eamon (Ned) Broy: An Extraordinary Policeman and
             Courageous Republican   199

Chapter 16   Cumann na mBan: The Unsung Heroines of the War of
             Independence   217

Chapter 17   Áine Ceannt: The Quintessential Republican Woman   231

Postscript: The Legacy of the Civil War and the Road to Recovery   246

Introduction

Charles Stewart Parnell passed from this world in October 1891, marking the end of a political era in Ireland that had been dominated by the very emotive issue of home rule. The Irish Parliamentary Party that Parnell led from 1882 imploded during the months prior to his death, mainly because of the sensational Kitty O'Shea scandal, a divorce case that rocked Victorian Britain. Without its charismatic leader, the party was rudderless, devoid of direction until the turn of the century.

During the last decade of the nineteenth century and the first six years of the twentieth century, political activity in Ireland came to a standstill. The Conservative Party and their sometime allies the Liberal Unionists were not interested in restoring the Dublin parliament, lost to Ireland since the Act of Union in 1801, and the issue of home rule disappeared off the Westminster political agenda.

With little possibility of achieving home rule, Irish nationalists found themselves with time on their hands to discuss how their country should proceed in the short term. The enthusiasm for self-determination, in some form or other, was not diminished, but they had little choice but to bide their time until the political landscape in Westminster changed sufficiently to allow the 'Irish question' to re-emerge as a live political issue.

In the meantime, the political void had to be filled and a national debate quickly began as to how that intention might be achieved. It was clear to many nationalists that they needed to be in a better place if they were to avail of the next opportunity to stake their claim to self-determination. In order to get to that place, they began to press for an Irish cultural revival. It became apparent that a distinction had to be drawn between the Irish and the British peoples, in terms of traditions, culture, language and pastimes. There would be little point in pursuing political independence in the future if the people of Ireland were prepared to accept British traditions as integral to their lives. The onus, therefore, would be placed on clearly identifying Ireland as a separate nation, with its own distinct heritage, culture, language and history, in no way similar to those of her neighbour and oppressor.

Gaping wounds of disaffection and rancour were finally healed by the coming together of the staunch Parnellite John Redmond and the anti-Parnellite John Dillon. In Britain, the Conservative Party remained in power until 1906, when they lost the general election to a resurgent Liberal Party under the leadership of Sir Henry Campbell-Bannerman. This sparked hope among Irish nationalists that the long-anticipated change in the political landscape was about to take place. Since the introduction of the First Home Rule Bill in 1886 by then-Liberal leader William Gladstone, Irish nationalists always viewed the Liberal Party as their best allies in the struggle for home rule.

However, nationalist delight at the Liberal Party victory quickly dissipated, as it soon became clear that the Liberals did not have the Irish question at the top of their agenda, which was dominated by proposed social and financial reforms. Nationalists were once again forced to kick their heels in frustration.

By 1906, the nationalist community was well down the road of a cultural revival and had admirably filled the political void left by the death of Parnell and the diminishing influence of the Irish Parliamentary Party. Two very prominent movements had emerged – the Gaelic Athletic Association and the Gaelic League. These organisations were driving forces of nationalism, allowing many hundreds of thousands of Irish men and women to express a cultural identity based on ancient and revered Gaelic customs and traditions.

The Gaelic Athletic Association was founded in Thurles in 1884, by Michael Cusack and Maurice Davin. At this time, British games such as cricket, association football and rugby were popular, contributing to a more Anglicised society across the country. Irish games like hurling were often chaotic, with little in the way of discipline displayed by those who participated in them. They were in real danger of being eclipsed by British games and falling by the wayside forever. That was all to change dramatically. Though the early years of the Association's existence were fraught with political interference, especially by the Irish Republican Brotherhood, it went on, as we now know, to become one of the most influential organisations in the country.

By 1906, the Gaelic Athletic Association numbered many thousands of young men among its ranks, all imbued with the nationalist ideal. They saw participation in Gaelic games as part of a natural progression that would define them as nationalists and eventually republicans. By playing Gaelic games and shunning British games they were, very consciously, shunning a British way of life. The games were deliberately scheduled for Sundays, allowing workmen and farmers to participate and discriminating against Protestants, who were not prepared to indulge in sport on the Sabbath.

It wasn't long before the IRB leadership took an interest in the Gaelic Athletic Association – its thousands of fit young men would make fine revolutionaries when the call to arms came. Many of the statements in the Witness Statements archive were made by men who cut their republican teeth in the Gaelic Athletic Association. Their physical fitness for the tasks entrusted to them during the Easter Rising and the War of Independence was a continuation of the prowess they displayed on the playing fields of the GAA.

The Gaelic League was founded in 1893, to promote the use of the Irish language. It also became a recruiting ground for future republicans who participated in the Easter Rising and the War of Independence. Though it was not intended to be a politically orientated organisation, many men and women cut their republican political teeth in it. It was inevitable that conversations at Irish language classes, social gatherings and outings would often turn to the political situation. Prominent individuals like de Valera, Collins and Pearse found and cultivated common ideals and views through their membership of the organisation. As I researched the archive, I was struck by how many of the men and women who contributed to it had been members of the Gaelic League. Here they formed friendships that continued throughout their involvement in the Easter Rising and the independence conflict.

While the Catholic majority of the population veered politically to nationalism and republicanism, a cohort of the Protestant community also embraced those ideals. They recognised the desire of the majority to move away from Anglicised influences and towards Gaelic culture and traditions. Many Protestants enthusiastically embraced this too, feeling that both traditions could exist in the new

Ireland that might emerge. They accepted that the country had been badly treated under almost 700 years of British subjugation, and that it was now time for all Irish men and women, irrespective of ethnic identity or religion, to strike out and take their place on the world stage.

Though the archive is mainly populated by Catholic nationalists, there are some contributions from individuals from a Protestant and unionist background. One of these is Ernest Blythe, who not only fought in the revolutionary conflict but went on to give the new Irish State very valuable service as a TD and Minister of Finance during the first Free State government under WT Cosgrave. Blythe and others of his tradition and background who contributed to the revolutionary era deserve recognition today. Their view that all Irish people could exist together in a new and independent state, a controversial opinion at that time, turned out to be perfectly correct.

The political situation in Ireland changed dramatically in February 1910, when the British general election saw the Liberals and Conservatives win almost the same number of seats. This meant that the Irish Party under John Redmond held the balance of power – a similar position to Parnell's, some decades earlier. Joy was unconfined among Irish nationalists, who felt sure they could use their newfound political advantage to initiate a new campaign for home rule.

With the support of the Irish Party, the Liberals, under the leadership of Herbert Asquith, formed a government and proceeded to implement their policies, including higher taxes on the wealthy. When the budget was blocked by the Conservative-dominated House of Lords, Asquith felt compelled to go back to the people and called another election in December of that year. Once again, the result was inconclusive. The Irish Party continued to hold the balance of power and backed the Liberal Party in government.

The Asquith-led government then introduced the Parliament Act, which limited the House of Lords veto, preventing legislation passed by the House of Commons being rejected by an unelected higher chamber. This was the opening the Irish Party and all nationalists were waiting for. In return for supporting the government on the Parliament Act, the Irish Party insisted on the introduction of a new Home Rule Bill.

The Parliament Act entered the statute books, and the House of Lords had to accept it could now only delay a bill from the lower house for no longer than two years before being required to pass it. The new Home Rule Bill was passed in the House of Commons in 1912, and Irish nationalists knew it would become law by 1914 at the latest. The political die had been cast, to the delight of Irish nationalists and the chagrin of unionists, especially those in Ulster.

Believing their security, traditions and heritage were about to come under siege, the unionists of Ulster, aided and abetted by their Conservative allies in England and elsewhere, proceeded to arm themselves for the expected conflict with nationalists. They raised the then-enormous sum of £1 million, to purchase arms and ammunition for the Ulster Volunteer Force, founded in January 1913. Unionists of all economic and social classes rallied to the cause of maintaining the Union, and hundreds of thousands of men and women signed the Ulster Solemn League and Covenant, many in their own blood. Throughout 1913, tension mounted across the country as unionists vowed never to surrender the Union and their privileged position within it.

At the same time, nationalists realised they would also have to make preparations to secure their goal of home rule. In November 1913, the Irish Volunteers organisation was formed at a meeting held in the Rotunda in Dublin. The organisation was formed at the instigation of the Irish Republican Brotherhood, and most especially Bulmer Hobson, one of its leaders. The Volunteers were prepared to confront their counterparts in Ulster should the dispute over home rule escalate into a military conflict. With that in mind, the Volunteers imported arms and ammunition into the country through the port of Howth by means of Erskine Childers's yacht *Asgard*, in July 1914. By now, tensions had increased dramatically – not only in Ireland, but also in Europe as the continent moved closer to war. When it was declared, John Redmond and the Irish Parliamentary Party agreed to defer the introduction of home rule until the conflict ended, believing it would be a short, sharp affair and peace would be restored by Christmas at the latest. This assumption, as we now know, was very wide of the mark.

Many of the contributors to the Witness Statements archive enlisted in the Irish Volunteers, determined to play their part in securing home rule. Around

3,000 men joined up at the Rotunda meeting, and many more enthusiastically followed suit as companies were formed in the capital and across the country.

John Redmond addressed the Irish Volunteers at Woodenbridge in September 1914, urging the men to enlist in the British army, 'to account yourselves as men, not only for Ireland itself, but wherever the fighting line extends, in defence of right, of freedom and religion in this war'. The response was, in the main, positive, with the majority of the men supporting Redmond's call to arms. However, a smaller cohort within the Volunteers rejected the call, breaking away to form their own force to pursue the ideal of independence. For them, the promise of home rule, once the war was over, was of no further interest. The age-old adage, 'England's difficulty is Ireland's opportunity', once again came into play. Their sights were set on staging a rebellion and striking out for independence.

The excitement and enthusiasm of those involved in the planning of the rebellion during 1915 is clear to see in many of the statements. There are accounts of Volunteers companies being formed all across the country, with young men enthusiastically drilling and training, working to turn themselves into a fighting force fit and ready to take on the forces of the Crown. They were, it seems, heady days for the Volunteers.

If the nationalist men of Ireland were ready to mobilise for the cause of independence, the archive has more than enough witness statements from republican women to show that they were just as committed to the independence ideal. In fact, many of the women were even more militant than many of the men. When republican women were denied the right to join the Volunteers in 1913, they decided to take matters into their own hands. At a meeting in Dublin in April 1914, they formed their own organisation, Cumann na mBan. The enthusiasm, courage and commitment of the women of the time has been captured to a marvellous extent in the Witness Statements.

The revolutionary journey for the men and women who provided statements to the archive had been a long one for many. The movement had evolved from a more pacifist nationalism and the push for home rule to the more radical ideal of an Irish republic free from British subjugation. The world was changing during the second decade of the twentieth century; people all across Europe were demanding their freedom from the traditional imperial structure that had dominated for centuries, and young Irish men and women added their voices to that demand.

The Irish republican movement of the early twentieth century in Ireland was populated by articulate and confident men and women, determined to secure independence irrespective of the cost to them personally and as a generation. Their determination to succeed was born out of the knowledge that previous generations had failed in their efforts at rebellion – those very painful failures needed to be corrected. The Witness Statements provide a clear roadmap of the revolutionary journey undertaken by so many Irishmen and Irishwomen over the first two decades of the twentieth century.

Chapter 1

The Witness Statements Archive

In 1947, the then-Minister for Defence, Oscar Traynor, did the Irish nation a wonderful service when he initiated the Witness Statement programme in conjunction with the Bureau of Military History. The Bureau's official brief was 'to assemble and co-ordinate material to form the basis for the compilation of the history of the movement for Independence from the formation of the Irish Volunteers on 25 November 1913, to the 11 July 1921'. Between 1947 and 1957, some 1,773 witness statements, 334 sets of contemporary documents, forty-two sets of photographs and thirteen voice recordings were collected. When the work was completed, it was locked away in the Department of the Taoiseach for forty-five years.

In 2001, the archive was transferred to the Military Archives. Here, a team of archivists and support staff under the watchful eyes of Commandant Victor Laing prepared the collection for its public launch in 2003. The staff involved in creating the archive included army officers and civil servants, as well as a number of interviewing officers who travelled across the country to conduct the interviews. The Bureau also had the assistance of some notable historians of the time, including Robert Dudley-Edwards and TW Moody. Interviewing officers were sent to sit down with any individual who volunteered to provide a statement, a huge undertaking in itself.

The result of all of this painstaking work is a comprehensive account of all that took place during Ireland's revolutionary years, an era defined by the determination of so many people to release Ireland from the chains of British subjugation and to make a reality of the long-cherished ideal of independence. This hugely valuable primary source is not only detailed in its content, but enthralling as a stand-alone story of bravery and determination.

Unfortunately from the historian's point of view, many who refused to accept the validity of the Anglo-Irish Treaty of 1921, and the consequent setting up of the Irish Free State, did not cooperate with the programme. Those individuals viewed the Witness Statement project as a 'Free State' exercise and refused to have anything to do with it. This leaves a void that can never be filled, as the archive lacks the contributions of some very prominent individuals, who played integral roles in the Easter Rising and the War of Independence.

It should also be pointed out that there was some reluctance on the part of the State to pursue statements from surviving anti-Treaty people, as the legacy of the Civil War was still casting a dark cloud over the politics of the country.

While we embrace the Witness Statements, we should be aware that the majority of the contributions came from Catholic nationalists who devoted a major part of their lives to the pursuit of an independent Ireland. Of course, Irish society of the time had another important strand to it, namely, the traditional unionist and Protestant community, which, in the main, was not at all anxious to see the status quo disturbed. This community was largely very sceptical of the nationalist ideal and all that it entailed. Many of that persuasion were not convinced that a new, independent Ireland could emerge after the ending of the Great War, full of self-confidence and vibrancy and ready to take its place among the international community of nations.

There was, of course, a range of views within the Protestant community. Individuals such as Constance Markievicz, WB Yeats, Douglas Hyde and Ernest Blythe readily come to mind. They did see a future for a nationalist Ireland, but, importantly, an Ireland that embraced both denominations and traditions. While the archive is predominantly the views of Catholic and nationalist revolutionary Ireland, we must remember that a significant section of the country during that extraordinary time were far from convinced that the outcome of the conflict would be to Ireland's benefit.

Now that we have reached the centenary of the most momentous era in Ireland's history, we can be grateful for Oscar Traynor's great initiative because we have, at our fingertips, a myriad of fascinating and invaluable recollections. What is obvious from reading the statements is the commitment and passion displayed by those involved in the republican movement during that tumultuous time. From the foundation of the Irish Volunteers in 1913, to the calling of the truce in July 1921 that brought an end to the War of Independence, only one thought occupied the minds of so many men and women: that of removing British involvement in Ireland.

While we are all familiar with the major historical events such as the Easter Rising and the War of Independence, the statements provide fascinating and detailed accounts of what went on in the background. Here you will find the stories of many unsung heroes, stories of tragedy and raw courage, incredible inventiveness and resourcefulness, and an unbending commitment to fair play and justice. There are riveting tales of how guns and ammunition were acquired, and how they were transported from place to place; accounts of the establishment of bomb-making factories and intelligence units. The reader will be awestruck at the sheer audacity of the individuals involved. The much-lauded Irish sense of humour can also be detected, from a time when tensions were running high all across the country.

One could spend many hundreds of hours trawling through the Witness Statements archive. The detail of many of the statements is extraordinary, and the archive provides a very vivid and comprehensive picture of what took place during the momentous week of the 1916 Rising, as well as the years before and after. Those who participated in the rebellion were deeply committed to the ideal of an Irish republic and displayed an inordinate amount of courage as they fought against all the odds in an often-chaotic struggle against the power of the British Crown.

The statements come from all areas of the country, both rural and urban, clearly showing that the republican ideal was a national one. These individuals who contributed to the archive all gave their voices freely in making their statements, and this book is intended to share some of those voices, in the hope that future generations will remember the sacrifices made by so many Irish men and woman in the cause of Ireland's independence.

The statements I have chosen to highlight in this book are just a small sample of what is to be found in the archive. I chose them on the basis that those concerned had interesting and important stories to tell and, taken together, they offer up a fine portrait of what took place across the country during the revolutionary era. There are, of course, many hundreds of other statements that could have been included in this book. The statements, which have been locked away for so long, all deserve to be brought into the public domain, and the extraordinary deeds of so many courageous individuals should be celebrated and acknowledged – our modern populace owes its freedom and independence to those who dedicated their lives to the noble cause of a sovereign Ireland.

I owe my thanks to the Bureau of Military History for making it possible to publicise the thousands of pages of the archive. The tremendous work carried out by the interviewing officers and civil servants between 1947 and 1957 has left this country with a wealth of primary source material, which must always be preserved and treasured.

Chapter 2

The Truth About the Rising

Sometime in 1915, I was appointed Dublin Brigade Quartermaster. I obtained rifles from The O'Rahilly, from members of the IRB, revolvers and shotguns, from Henshaws, where I was employed, shotguns and ammunition from Keegan's and Garnett's, gunsmiths. In addition, I obtained rifles from Peadar Breslin and Jack Shaw, who got them from British soldiers by purchase. My brother Humphrey, who was employed on the Liner Baltic used to bring from America about twenty revolvers on each trip to Liverpool. These he passed on to Neil Kerr and P. Cahill who sent them over to me.

(Michael Staines)

One of the more extraordinary statements in the archive is that of Michael Staines, Quartermaster of the Irish Volunteers from 1913 to 1916 and Quartermaster General in the GPO during the Easter Rising. He not only provides a fascinating insight into the Rising, but also into activities and thinking in republican circles in the months leading up to the conflict.

Michael Staines was born in Newport, County Mayo, in 1885, the son of a serving RIC officer. Though a member of the Gaelic League, he was not involved in any militant republican movement until he joined the Irish Volunteers at its first meeting in November 1913. He was almost immediately appointed Quartermaster for three of the organisation's Dublin companies. He was later appointed Quartermaster for the Irish Volunteers Dublin Brigade and set about building up republican firepower in the city. He made contact with The O'Rahilly, who helped him purchase arms, and began collecting money from every Volunteer in order to purchase rifles and revolvers:

I collected one shilling a week from every Volunteer who wanted a Martini rifle and two shillings from every man who wanted a Lee Enfield rifle. Having the money, I was very successful in getting the arms from The O'Rahilly as he wanted the money to purchase more arms. Every man in the three companies had a rifle.

Staines also obtained guns from other sources, such as from IRB men; from Henshaws, where he worked; and from various gunsmiths around the city. He even had guns purchased from serving British soldiers. His brother, Humphrey, worked on a transatlantic liner and brought twenty revolvers with him on every trip into Liverpool, from where they were sent on to Michael in Dublin.

In September 1915, Staines was appointed to Pearse's staff and was instructed by him to resign from the Gaelic League and devote all his time to the Volunteers. At a meeting presided over by Eamon de Valera, he was elected as the first representative of the Dublin Brigade to the General Council of the Volunteers. In his statement, he recalled the thrust of the General Council meetings and the consensus that some protest over British rule in Ireland should be made before the Great War ended, though he does say that not everyone was confident they could defeat the British militarily.

Staines recalled how he and other selected Volunteer officers attended lectures given by James Connolly on how to carry out street-to-street fighting. In early March 1916, he was instructed by Éamonn Ceannt to give up his employment at Henshaws and take up full-time duty as Quartermaster General. He would replace The O'Rahilly, who by that stage was opposed to a Rising. According to Staines, 'The O'Rahilly readily handed over the reins without protest.' Staines's duties included distributing munitions to Volunteers units across the country from various locations in Dublin. He recalled how he also had to buy picks, shovels and crowbars for the Rising:

I bought one hundred and twenty of each of these implements, and, in order to divert attention, I told Henshaws, from whom I purchased them, that they were being used by Mr Batt O'Connor, a builder, for the purpose of a large building estate. I also purchased wire cutters and sandbags and incandescent paraffin lamps in case the ordinary lights should fail.

While each Battalion had to make its own arrangements about food, Staines also purchased items such as cheese, tinned meat and Oxo cubes to hold in reserve, while de Valera purchased medical supplies. He mentioned that he purchased two ship's lamps, which he handed over to two ladies from Tralee, to be used at Fenit Harbour during the planned landing of guns and ammunition from the Aud. He also hired a large marquee, on the instructions of Seán MacDermott, to provide shelter for the men in Fenit, and he sent arms to Liam Mellows in Galway and Terence MacSwiney in Cork.

Near the end of 1915, Staines recalled Seán MacDermott making an arrangement with John Devoy in America to purchase arms and ammunition. He was also aware of Robert Monteith's trip to Germany and his efforts there, together with Roger Casement and Joseph Plunkett, to procure arms and ammunition and to raise an Irish Brigade made up of Irishmen held in the country as prisoners of war.

Staines was responsible for arranging transport for Easter Sunday. He recalled that he engaged the services of twenty cars for that day, but that they were not available on the Monday, because they were occupied transporting racegoers to Fairyhouse. He had also arranged for some trucks from the haulage company, Thompsons, to turn up if needed.

Shortly before the Rising, he was personally introduced to James Connolly for the first time by Thomas MacDonagh.

It was late on Spy Wednesday or early Holy Thursday morning when Staines got confirmation of the impending Rising. On Good Friday, he learned from Seán MacDermott that the arms from the *Aud* had been lost. He broke the news to Sean Heuston, who was incandescent with rage.

On Easter Sunday, after attending mass and having breakfast, he went to Liberty Hall, where he saw Connolly, Pearse and MacDonagh in conversation, and recalled the mobilisation being called off just before noon. He was instructed by MacDonagh to bring the news to de Valera, and was accompanied on the journey by Sean Heuston. A sceptical de Valera threatened to take Staines as a prisoner and refused to confirm that he would not take his men out.

On Easter Sunday evening, Pearse ordered Staines to report to Liberty Hall at 8am the following morning. On arrival, he met James Connolly and was given the job of transferring arms and ammunition by cab from the Hall to the GPO. He amusingly remembered that he paid the cabby some years later, after forgetting to pay him on that Easter Monday.

He also mentioned that The O'Rahilly turned up unexpectedly. Despite the pleadings of his sister Áine, The O'Rahilly offered the use of his motor car, which was readily filled with more arms and ammunition. The men set out for the GPO at noon:

At the head of the procession, I noticed James Connolly, Padraig and Willie Pearse and Sean McGarry. The O Rahilly and I took the rear with the car and the cab. We proceeded up Abbey St and wheeled into O'Connell St towards the pillar. I was seated in the cab surrounded by homemade bombs and ammunition of all sorts. It was a mercy the whole thing did not explode.

Once in the GPO, Staines took the munitions into a sorting office, using the pigeon holes for sorting it all out. The O'Rahilly kept his car in the yard of the GPO during Easter week and it was used a number of times to bring in ammunition. On the Monday, they also commandeered a judge's car, and his chauffeur stayed in the GPO all week.

Staines wasn't long in the GPO when The O'Rahilly mentioned the top floor had not been taken over – some people were still up there working. Staines recalled:

I got six men and made a rush for the stairs – the staff were coming down, most of them appeared hostile, but one girl named O'Callaghan said to me 'That's the stuff to give them Michael'. When the stairs were free we ran up them. I heard the shout 'Halt' and saw six soldiers above us pointing their rifles at us. We rushed up and I shouted to my men fire, which they did. We were armed with revolvers. One man, a sergeant, fell, I ran up with my men and seized the rifles. I demanded the ammunition but found they had none.

Staines arranged for the slightly wounded sergeant to be taken to Jervis Street Hospital for treatment. He later returned to the GPO and he and his fellow Rangers asked for their rifles back because they wanted to fight on the side of the rebels. Instead, they were put to work in the kitchen as cooks, where they were assisted by members of Cumann na mBan.

Staines discovered almost immediately that a lady in the telegram room was still sending out messages by telegraph, including death notices. He advised her to leave the building, promising to send out the most urgent messages. That job was given to JJ Walsh, a trained operator, and it seems Walsh began to contact offices in Cork, Galway, Athlone and Wexford to announce the beginning of the Rising. Walsh also told many of his colleagues in the GPO that neither Cork nor Kerry had come out. Staines reprimanded him for this and reported the matter to Pearse, who ordered that Walsh desist or face being shot.

Staines then hoisted the tricolour on the roof of the GPO:

When on the roof I had a look around generally and I saw Pearse reading the proclamation. He stood on the edge of the footpath at a point in front of the window where there is now a door, on the Prince's St side of the portico. There was a large number of people around when this was happening, there was no demonstration.

He also saw a troop of Lancers on horseback gallop down Sackville Street towards the GPO, coming under fire from the Volunteers.

During those first hours, news filtered through that Sean Connolly and his Irish Citizen Army comrades had failed to take Dublin Castle. This greatly disappointed Pearse, as he had intended to set up his headquarters there.

Francis Sheehy Skeffington arrived at the GPO and asked for permission to organise a Citizen's Committee to prevent looting. Father O'Flanagan, the Pro-Cathedral curate, also arrived to hear the men's confessions, and he stayed for the whole week.

Sometime later, Staines found the badly wounded Connolly in Williams Lane after his ankle was shattered by a bullet and, with the aid of four other Volunteers, brought him into the GPO, where he was tended to by future Fianna Fáil government minister Jim Ryan, who was, at the time, training to be a medical doctor.

Staines recalled that bombs were made in a back office almost as soon as the GPO was taken over by the rebels. The consumption of alcohol was prohibited; however, when a public house opposite the GPO was looted, some local women handed bottles of stout in through the windows to members of the Citizen Army, but by then military discipline had kicked in and the bottles remained unopened.

The initial couple of days were so hectic Staines hardly managed to sleep, but he does mention that on the Wednesday night he shared a room with Tom Clarke and both men slept on mattresses placed on the floor. When Staines awoke on Thursday morning, Clarke seemed to be very cold. Staines recalled how he 'remonstrated with him for not taking one of my blankets and he replied that as I was sleeping so soundly, he did not wish to disturb me. I gave him some of my blankets and he went to sleep.'

Thursday morning saw an escalation in the fighting, as British troops arrived in Brunswick Street, College Green and Findlater Place. Continuous fire rained down on the GPO and Staines was put to the pin of his collar making sure there was sufficient ammunition available for his comrades. Such was the valour and determination of the rebels, the British were unable to manage an assault on the GPO.

Incendiary shells struck in North Earl Street and Abbey Street, causing the rebels there to seek refuge in the GPO. The intensity of the fires soon threatened the building. The Volunteers were covered in soot and some were burned by steam as they worked to prevent it from going up in flames. An attempt was made during Thursday to burrow under Henry Street in case it became necessary to evacuate the GPO, but the plan was quickly abandoned. However, openings were made through the walls of adjoining buildings as far as the Coliseum Picture Theatre.

The shelling became ever more intense around the GPO. The first shell to strike the building landed around noon, causing a fire to break out, but this was quickly brought under control by the rebels. The first shell to cause real damage to the building struck at 3pm, starting a fire in the lift shaft, which spread to the cellar. Staines suggested in his statement that the British had finally got their range, and now shells poured down on the building. He was forced to move bombs and ammunition to the courtyard.

By dusk, the building was totally alight and Pearse ordered a complete evacuation. At that point, Connolly decided he would attempt to reach the Williams and Woods Factory in Parnell Street and sent The O'Rahilly out in charge of what would be an ill-fated advance guard. Staines, on Pearse's orders, checked to see that all the rebels had been evacuated. Then himself, the Pearse brothers and the judge's chauffeur, who was still in the GPO, carried the stricken Connolly out of the building on a stretcher and, despite coming under fire, managed to get him to number 10 Moore Street. Staines's statement provides a vivid account of Joseph Plunkett and Sean McLoughlin heroically directing some of the rebels to safety at the end of Moore Lane in the face of British machine gun fire:

We found some of the men in a panic as Henry Place at the end of Moore Lane was under machine gun fire from the Rotunda hospital. Sean McLoughlin lined the men up and steadied them as Joe Plunkett drew his sword and stood exposed in the middle of the machine gun fire and allowed two men to rush across each time he dipped his sword. All got over safely including Connolly on the stretcher.

Connolly was placed in a bed in the Moore Street house, and the bedroom became his headquarters. Connolly complimented McLoughlin on his bravery and promoted him to Commandant. Staines recalled:

I placed a green flag with the harp on it, which I had taken from the GPO with me, over his bed. We then cut through the walls along Moore St until we reached Sackville Lane. It was there reported to us that O'Rahilly's body was lying in the lane.

On the Saturday, there were rumours a truce was being sought. Pearse, Clarke, MacDermott, Plunkett and Connolly were engaged in deep conversation. Elizabeth O'Farrell, who had been on duty in the GPO since the beginning of the conflict, had joined them in Moore Street. According to Staines, Pearse and MacDermott were preparing at that stage to go to the Castle to discuss terms with the British, but that wasn't to be, as the military authorities demanded an unconditional surrender.

It was also planned that James Connolly would be brought to the Castle to witness the discussing of terms. With that in mind, Staines was asked to select six stretcher bearers to transport the stricken Citizen Army leader. He recalled:

We carried Connolly through the houses until we reached Gore's Chemist's shop, no 17, and then brought him down the stairs to the street. We were to be met by British military at the top of Great Britain St. They were to guide us to the Castle. A Major Walsh came down to us, but he knew nothing of the arrangement. Diarmuid Lynch, who had followed us, explained that we were going to the Castle and that it had been arranged.

Walsh then made contact with his headquarters and was told that Connolly should be brought directly to the Castle by the stretcher bearers. Staines recalled:

All down Great Britain St to Capel St we were booed by the crowd and would have been attacked in some places, only the Notts and Derby's, who lined the street, kept them back. The only place we got a cheer was passing Gt. Strand St. where there was quite a crowd of people.

I recognised one man in the crowd. When I met him about twelve months afterwards I asked why they cheered while the others jeered. His answer was 'We were prisoners'.

The rebel party went through the Upper Castle Gate. They were met by an officer, who gave instructions for Connolly to be taken into the Castle and the other men to be escorted to the guard room. Staines objected to this, pointing out that they had come under a flag of truce to witness the terms of the surrender. He then demanded to be returned to his unit, but this was ignored. Connolly was taken into the Castle and Staines and his comrades were marched to Ship Street Barracks and held in the guard room there. An officer eventually arrived and took a statement from Staines, who again made it clear he had come under a flag of truce. As Staines was wearing a private's uniform, the British failed to ascertain that he was, in fact, a captain.

The following day, Sunday, Staines and his comrades were transferred to Kilmainham Gaol. He was allocated a cell with two looters, who kindly gave him the one available bed. Before dusk, he was transferred with the other Volunteers to the hospital wing. They were held here, fourteen men to a room, overseen by a British Army sergeant from Wexford by the name of Doyle, who Staines described as a decent man.

Staines heard three volleys on 3 May and instantly knew that three of the leaders had been executed. That evening, he saw Joseph Plunkett exercising in the yard and saluted him, which raised the ire of a British Army sergeant by the name of Smith, who claimed Staines had breached regulations. Staines recalled:

Sergeant Doyle came over and asked what it was all about. Smith said I spoke to his prisoner. Doyle then asked me if I wanted a chat with my pal and I replied that I did. Doyle told me to go and talk to him. I went over and walked round with Plunkett.

The conversation was just every day. Joe Plunkett said to me 'you are extraordinary; you can smile under all conceivable circumstances'. He said it was a glorious week and we had our protest. He did not criticise anybody.

That night, Sergeant Doyle brought Staines the evening paper, which confirmed the names of the leaders executed that morning. He heard four volleys the next morning and knew four more leaders had died.

The following Saturday, 6 May, he and other Volunteers were transferred to Wakefield Prison in England. During their first week of incarceration, they were confined twenty-four hours a day and Staines recalled how the food was poor and they were always hungry. During the second week, the men were allowed ten minutes' exercise every day and this was extended to an hour the following week, when visitors were also allowed into the prison.

The first visitor was a priest from Derry, who arranged for a local priest to come in and say mass and hear confessions. At first, he was rather reluctant to do so, claiming the prisoners were 'a pack of murderers', but It seems he later changed his opinion of them

Staines ended his statement by recalling how a number of Irish girls living in Leeds came to visit the men. One particular girl took his uniform and posted it to his mother, replacing it with a suit of clothes.

Three weeks later, near the end of May, Staines and most of the other prisoners were transferred to Frongoch Prison in Wales. Here he was elected Commandant of the prisoners and, in the words of one prisoner, he became 'a highly efficient officer, who earned the love and respect of every individual there'. The prisoners remained here until Christmas 1916.

Michael Staines survived the Easter Rising and the tumultuous years that followed, and went on to give valuable and extensive service to the new Irish State, both as a teachta dála and as a senator. He was also closely involved in the setting up of the Garda Síochána and was the organisation's first commissioner.

Chapter 3

Cork Awaits the Call to Arms

As we neared Macroom, rain began to fall, lightly at first. We entered a restaurant to have a meal. We were not long there when others of our Cork men arrived. The rain had come down heavily and some of them were drenched. Many were discontented, dissatisfied, loud complaining; a few angry and loudly critical. These felt they had been fooled, in some way or other, they had expected a different ending to the Easter 'manoeuvres'. I rather sympathised with them.

(Liam de Róiste)

Outside of the capital, republicans all across the country were also preparing for the Easter Rising, more than willing to get involved in the fight for Ireland's independence. One of the more strongly republican-minded counties was Cork, where the level of activity in the months leading up to the Rising was so significant that it attracted the attention of both local and national authorities.

Many hundreds of Volunteers were on standby, awaiting the call from Dublin to fight for Ireland's independence. However, with the failure of the *Aud* to deliver her shipment of arms and ammunition at Fenit, their plans were scuppered. The brave republicans of Cork never got the chance to participate in a Rising they fervently believed would change the course of their country's history.

The Irish Volunteers were formed in Cork, at a meeting held in the City Hall on 23 December 1913, attended by Roger Casement, Eoin MacNeill and JJ Walsh. Initially, the organisation was basically ignored in Cork, just as it was all over the country. But as the numbers multiplied and the strength of the movement increased, it came under the scrutiny of John Redmond, leader of the politically dominant Irish Parliamentary Party, and his home rule colleagues.

Eventually, Redmond insisted on his nominees being given places on the Irish Volunteers Executive Committee, so that he could maintain control over the movement. The question of control of the Volunteers was put before the men at a parade in the Cornmarket Exchange in Cork. The home rule-supporting majority sided with Redmond and joined the National Volunteers, while the independence-supporting minority opted to remain with the Irish Volunteers.

By early 1916, the Irish Volunteers in Cork were reputed to be some of the best-organised groups in the country. A number of dedicated men left Cork city every weekend and cycled some fifty or sixty miles out into the countryside at their own expense in order to organise local battalions. Initially, these battalions had little in the way of arms, mainly seizing what they could from local British Army personnel – it was said that prior to the Rising, not one live shot was fired in Cork. By the time of the Rising, it had been decided by the leaders in Dublin that the men in Cork should have ten rounds per rifle when it was time to come out against the enemy.

The leaders in Dublin decided that the main objective of the Cork Volunteers for the Easter Rising should be to obstruct and delay British forces at Millstreet and Rathmore. This was to be done by cutting off the railway line until the arms and ammunition from the *Aud* arrived. When that plan fell through, there was no alternative plan and confusion reigned across the 'rebel' county.

In a witness statement made by Cork City Battalion Volunteers Sean Murphy, Thomas Barry, Patrick Canton and James Wickham, the four men recalled their leaders, Terence MacSwiney and Tomás MacCurtain, being very unhappy with the orders issued to them from Dublin. Seán MacDermott's orders had been delivered by a Miss Foley of Cumann na mBan about a week before the due date for the Rising. The Cork leaders sent MacSwiney's sister Eithne to Dublin to ask for a meeting. She was promptly sent back to Cork by Tom Clarke, with the instruction that 'under no circumstances whatever were either of them to leave Cork but were to carry out the orders which had previously being issued to them'.

The suggestion here is that the Cork Volunteers leadership did not have full confidence in the plans laid out for them by the Rising's leaders in Dublin, that there were logistics and problems particular to Cork city and county. The statement also recalls that Miss Foley arrived back in Cork on the Wednesday before the Rising with further conflicting instructions from MacDermott.

On Good Friday, JJ O'Connell arrived from Dublin with an order from Eoin MacNeill cancelling all previous orders received in Cork and giving him control of all Volunteers south of a line from Wexford to Kerry. Later that day, Jim Ryan arrived from Dublin with another despatch from MacDermott, claiming that all differences at Headquarters between MacNeill and the Military Council had been resolved and the original instructions for Easter Sunday were to be carried out. That harmony was further emphasised later on Good Friday night, when O'Connell, Ryan, MacSwiney and MacCurtain met to finalise arrangements. However, before that meeting concluded, all plans were thrown into disarray when Lieutenant Fred Murray of 'A' Company in Cork arrived with the disastrous news of the *Aud*'s capture and Casement's arrest. O'Connell and Ryan left for Dublin on the 7am train on Easter Saturday, and O'Connell was not seen in Cork again for the duration of the Rising.

Despite the undercurrent of confusion, witnesses recalled the Cork City Battalion parading at the Volunteers Hall in Shears Street on Easter Sunday morning, under the command of Sean O'Sullivan. They then marched to Capwell Station, where they boarded a train to Crookstown. From there the men marched to Béal na mBláth, where they were joined by the West Cork Battalion. They then proceeded on foot to Macroom, arriving in the mid-afternoon.

They intended to march the six miles or so to Carriganima that evening, where they were to be joined by other battalions from rural Cork. The intention was for all battalions to remain in Carriganima overnight before occupying the positions planned for them in Macroom and Rathmore on Easter Monday. They would then destroy the railway line, thereby delaying British troop movements.

As the Cork City Battalion were en route to Crookstown, another despatch arrived at their headquarters in Shears Street. It was from Eoin MacNeill, cancelling all previous orders and directing all commands to carry out the field manoeuvres planned for that day. At the end of the manoeuvres, all units were to be disbanded and the men were to return home.

The orders were received by senior officers who had delayed their departure to Crookstown. Two of them left the hall and travelled by road to Crookstown to inform the departed battalion. There they met Communications Officer Pat Higgins, and gave him a message for Sean O'Sullivan, instructing him to proceed to Macroom with his men and disband all units there that evening.

The *Sunday Independent* had reached most country districts by early to mid-morning, carrying MacNeill's famous cancellation order, which heightened the chaos even further and left the men puzzled and confused. The Cork leadership had been repeatedly told by the Rising's leaders in Dublin that Roger Casement's Irish Brigade would help them and that ample arms from the *Aud* would be provided. When those plans failed to materialise in the days prior to Easter Sunday, and no other plan had been put forward, it compounded an already confused situation. The Volunteers from the city set out that morning full of anticipation, but the day ended in anti-climax and their months of dedicated preparation for the Rising seemed in vain. They had no option but to return home.

Nine different despatches reached Cork city from Dublin in the days prior to and during Easter Sunday and Monday, contributing to a state of confusion in the city and across the county. When Eoin MacNeill's cancellation order was received at the Volunteers headquarters in Shears Street late on Easter Sunday morning, the plan of action for the city and county was thrown into disarray. Up to 1,200 men had been mobilised all across the county. The two Brigade leaders, Tomás MacCurtain and Terence MacSwiney, realised the men in the rural regions of the county would have to be stood down. They decided to undertake a tour of the regions where the battalions were concentrated to deliver the devastating news from Dublin.

Unfortunately, MacCurtain and MacSwiney's car broke down at Carrigadrohid, about four miles east of Macroom, late on Easter Sunday night. It was not possible to carry out repairs there and then, and so they were forced to stay overnight in Carrigadrohid. The following morning, they made their way to Ballingeary via Inchigeela.

Meanwhile, a Ms Perloze, a Cumann na mBan member, had arrived at Volunteer headquarters in Cork city between 12.15 and 12.45pm on Easter Monday. She was carrying a message from PH Pearse, written on the fly-leaf of a small pocket diary:

'We go into action today at noon. P.H.P.'

Though it appeared not to be a military order – it was only initialled, while other despatches from Dublin had been signed in full – it was agreed that it should be forwarded to the in-transit MacSwiney and MacCurtain. As motor cars could only be used at that time by special permit from the RIC, a cyclist was sent by the 1pm train to Macroom to try to get in touch with the two Brigade commanders.

Unfortunately, MacSwiney and MacCurtain had set out for Cork city before the cyclist reached Ballingeary. Pearse's order was therefore not acted upon and the Volunteers of Cork returned to their homes that evening from Carriganima rather than coming out in support of their Dublin counterparts. The excitement and anticipation that was palpable during the previous days had come to nothing.

The failure of the Cork city and county Volunteers to rise up during Easter 1916 was catastrophic for the prosecution of the rebellion outside of Dublin, but blame for this can only be laid at the feet of the Rising's leaders in Dublin, who sent many contradictory and confusing despatches to the Volunteers leadership in Cork. A number of witness statements clearly show that the Cork Volunteers were more than willing to fight, even if they were not exactly equipped to do so.

* * *

One such statement was made by Patrick Coakley, who was attached to the Ballinagree Company of Volunteers. The company was formed on the first Sunday of December 1915, when a local man, Bill Cotter, put up a notice on the church gate announcing a meeting to form a company of Volunteers would be held directly after mass. Guest speakers from nearby Macroom attended, and sixteen men joined that morning. This was typical of how Volunteers companies were formed across the county, at a time when the majority of people supported home rule and the war effort. About two weeks after their initial meeting, the Ballinagree men elected their officers, with Denis O'Neill taking on the role of Captain.

The Ballinagree Company paraded one night a week, marching halfway out the seven-mile road to Carriganima, where they met the Volunteers from that village. On Sundays, Volunteers leaders such as Jack Lynch or Mick Murphy came out from Macroom to Ballinagree to put the men through their paces. The Volunteers of Ballinagree paid 2d a week into a fund for the purchase of equipment and, by March 1916, all the men had haversacks, belts and bandoliers. On St Patrick's Day, twenty-two men from Ballinagree marched in the parade in the city. Fourteen were armed with shotguns – a visible signal that they were prepared to fight for independence.

A British recruiting meeting was held in Ballinagree village one Sunday in February 1916 and Coakley recalled: 'we made a collection and drilled opposite the other meeting, but the whole thing passed off peacefully enough'.

The fact that both meetings were held at the same time shows that the community in Ballinagree, like similar communities around the county, was politically divided between those who supported John Redmond's call to go to the Western Front and those who rejected it.

Coakley also recalled:

Mick Murphy of Macroom brought us the orders for Easter Sunday 1916. He came from Macroom on Good Friday night. The orders were to the effect that we were to go to Carriganima immediately after first mass on Easter Sunday with all arms and equipment and rations for three days.

That morning, twenty-two men gathered in Ballinagree under the command of Denis O'Neill and marched four and a half miles across country to Carriganima rather than the seven miles by road. Coakley recalled:

We were armed with twenty-two shotguns, some of single barrel and some of double barrel. Twelve of these were the property of members of the company, the remainder were borrowed from local farmers. We had four boxes (about 100 rounds) of shot gun ammunition, none of which had been slug loaded. We had two or three .22 revolvers and some ammunition for them. We had no pikes or explosives.

This was hardly a well-armed company, but one has to admire the bravery of the men, who were willing to take on the might of the British army. When the Balli-nagree men arrived in Carriganima, Coakley recalled:

> *The Macroom unit had just arrived and Jack Lynch took charge of us. Some exercises were carried out and we were there all day until a message came in the evening that the parade had been cancelled and we were to return home. Before we left Carriganima, Jack Lynch took our four boxes of ammunition. It was dark and very wet when we started. We marched the seven miles back by road. There was only one overcoat amongst the twenty-two of us that night and everyone got soaked.*

The disappointment among the men was great as they disbanded. The Ballinagree Company, like all the other companies across the county, awaited further orders during the rest of the week, but they never came. The chance to play their part in the fight for Ireland's independence was denied to all of them. The bravery of the twenty-two men who made up the Ballinagree Volunteers Company has not been forgotten and today in the village a plaque proudly remembers their exploits. The Volunteers in Cork city and across the county did not have an opportunity to fire a shot during the Easter Rising, much to their disappointment, but the fact they were ready and willing to fight for Irish independence marks them out to this day as true heroes and patriots.

Chapter 4

An Influential Monsignor

Between half-past eleven and noon on Easter Monday, I have noted in my
diary that, while I was talking to Mr Quinn down in the garage, a telephone
message was brought to me that Sean T O'Kelly wanted to see me in Rutland
Square. I sent word by messenger that I would be there in half an hour. At that
time, I had not known that the Rising was going to take
place or that it was so desperately close.
(Monsignor Michael Curran)

One of the most comprehensive recollections in the archive was provided by Monsignor Michael Curran, Secretary to the Archbishop of Dublin, Dr Walsh, from 1906 to 1919. Monsignor Curran kept a personal diary in which he recorded many fascinating insights into the political scene in Ireland during that era. He had, in his capacity as secretary to the Archbishop, unrestricted access to many of the major political and Church leaders across Ireland, and this allowed him to draw his own conclusions about the pressing issues of the day.

Michael Curran received a call from Sean T O'Kelly around noon on Easter Monday 1916, asking to meet him in Rutland Square in Dublin. Soon after, Count George Plunkett arrived at the Archbishop's residence to inform him the rebellion was about to start. Almost immediately, news came through that the General Post Office had been seized by the rebels. Within minutes, Curran was cycling into town from Drumcondra, meeting many Volunteers in uniform on the way.

The first person he came in contact with at the General Post Office was James Connolly, who was brandishing a revolver and issuing orders. When he saw the priest, he shouted, 'All priests may pass,' and allowed him into the building. Curran made his way in, to see a flushed but calm and authoritative Patrick Pearse, who he knew well. Asking him if there was anything he could do, Pearse suggested:

> Some of the boys would like to go to confession and I would be delighted if you would send over word to the Cathedral. I promised I would do that, left the GPO and went over to the Pro-Cathedral.

Around mid-afternoon, he attended to the first fatality of the Rising, anointing a British soldier who had been shot in the throat near Nelson's Pillar. Curran also witnessed wholesale looting that afternoon and when he returned to the Archbishop's house in Drumcondra, he asked his superior to write an open letter to the people of inner-city Dublin, urging them to refrain from looting and to behave sensibly by staying away from Sackville Street.

Throughout the week of fighting, Michael Curran was a constant presence around the city centre, offering his help to the rebels and the people of the city wherever he could as well as maintaining contact with the military and political authorities.

In the months following the Easter Rising, Curran encountered many individuals who had either been involved in the conflict or had views on it. During the second half of 1916, he recorded a number of observations on what was happening in the country in the wake of the rebellion. On 10 September, he recorded in his diary the visit of George Gavan Duffy to the Archbishop's residence:

> Mr Gavan Duffy called at one o'clock with copies of the correspondence with Cardinal Bourne over his action in refusing faculties for the reconciliation of Casement to the church unless he signed a statement expressing regret for any scandals he caused either by his private or public life.

Curran claimed Casement declined the request 'in all humility' and the prison chaplain, Father Carey, wrote to the Cardinal in an effort to persuade him to change his mind. However, no reply was ever received, and Casement was reconciled to the Catholic Church, into which he had been baptised as an infant, 'in articulo mortis' (at the moment of death), though he was never confirmed. Curran noted there was no formal condemnation by the Vatican of Bourne's decision, but he was of the view that the general opinion among officials of the Roman Curia was that the Cardinal had acted incorrectly.

In the early days of November, a Requiem Mass was held in Dublin for those who died in the Easter Rising. It was given great prominence in the national press, signalling a distinct change in the general public's attitude to the conflict. In mid-December, the new Commander of British forces in Ireland, General Sir Bryan Mahon, decided to ban Volunteer units from practising military drill, a move that had the support of John Redmond, who was anxious to reduce the influence of the organisation.

Later that month, the Chief Secretary for Ireland announced in the House of Commons that he had advised the Prime Minister that the danger of releasing the interned republican prisoners from Frongoch, Reading and Aylesbury Jails was less than the danger of their detention. His advice resulted in an initial release of 146 prisoners, who arrived in Dublin on 23 December, with the remaining 300 or so arriving the following day.

Monsignor Curran was as prolific as ever in recording observations during 1917. His first diary entry concerned the screening of a film called *Ireland A Nation* at the Rotunda cinema. The film had initially been passed by the censor and attracted huge crowds, but the military authorities withdrew it, feeling it was contributing to an increasing national fervour.

Around this time, Arthur Griffith called a conference of the different sections of nationalist opinion, with a view to planning a cohesive republican strategy for the future. Opinion at the meeting was divided, with many younger delegates favouring the physical force approach rather than the constitutional one. At the conference, Count Plunkett was proposed as Sinn Féin candidate for the forthcoming North Roscommon by-election, a proposal he officially accepted one week later.

On the other side of the political divide, John Dillon made a speech in Swinford on 17 January claiming he and his party had made strenuous efforts to stop the executions of 1916 and had worked very hard to alleviate the suffering of the interned prisoners. Many, including Curran, were not convinced by Dillon's claims.

Count Plunkett was in the news again the following day, when he was asked by the Royal Dublin Society to resign his membership, though no reason was given. Curran noted that Eoin MacNeill was also asked to resign from the Society around the same time. The result of the North Roscommon by-election was announced on 5 February 1917, with a stunning victory for Count Plunkett. Curran claimed that:

> ... rarely has there been so much excitement over an election result. Count Plunkett started at the eleventh hour with little local backing. His chief support came from Father O'Flanagan and Larry Ginnell. Though his supporters had hopes of his success, they never for a moment dreamed of such a resounding victory. The news of the success astounded and delighted 'the man in the street'. The Archbishop remarked that there was nothing like it since Butt's victory in Limerick during the previous century.

Curran put Plunkett's win down to the memory and execution of his son Joseph, his banishment from the RDS and the imprisonment of his other two sons.

In early February 1917, the authorities attempted to bolster the ranks of the British army with young Irishmen. The band of the Irish Guards was sent from London to Ireland as part of the recruitment drive.

On 21 February, Ash Wednesday, some prominent republicans across the country were arrested, including Sean T O'Kelly, Terence MacSwiney and Tomás MacCurtain. Curran recalled O'Kelly being apprehended by two policemen, one of whom had been shadowing him for some time. O'Kelly was allowed to pick up clothes and belongings from his home and then brought to Arbour Hill.

The following morning, he and some other prisoners were given the choice of where to go from a number of places. They chose Oxford, where they all boarded in a house owned and offered to them by Count Plunkett. They had to fend for themselves on arrival in Oxford, and were required to remain within the bounds of the city.

However, O'Kelly went to London on St Patricks Day and then simply returned to Ireland to campaign for the Sinn Féin candidate in the Longford by-election. The Sinn Féin revolution was underway at home, and not even imposed exile in the sleepy academic city of Oxford was going to keep the determined and committed republican, and future President of Ireland, from making a contribution to the new political force sweeping across his country.

On 5 March 1917, Andrew Bonnar Law, the unionist Chancellor of the Exchequer, confirmed to the House of Commons that the proceedings of the Easter Rising's courts martial would not be published, despite earlier promises by the government they would be made public.

Some days later, the Irish Parliamentary Party published a new manifesto, which Curran, like many others, found to be insincere and unconvincing. The manifesto, he believed, promulgated no real policy. The party's appeal to the United States and the colonies was merely a response to Sinn Féin's determination to appeal to both the United States and the Peace Conference. The manifesto also contained a reference to the Irish pro-German Revolutionary Party (meaning Sinn Féin), which upset many people. Curran's own ire was further heightened by John Dillon's tribute to Lloyd George when he said: 'I recognise that he has been a faithful friend of Home Rule during all the years in Parliament.' This was a view clearly not shared by the more republican elements in Irish society.

There was an increase in British military activity around Dublin and across the country during March. Curran put it down to the government's fear of a new attempt at rebellion or the possibility of a German invasion. Military units were stationed throughout the country in places where soldiers had never been seen before, leading many to speculate that the government was about to introduce conscription in Ireland. Curran wrote in his diary that:

> ... *two armoured cars, with guns protruding behind, have been ostentatiously parading through the streets. To-day they came down Dorset Street as far as the North Circular road and went back. Sand bags and iron sheeting have been placed on the roofs of the Bank of Ireland, Four Courts and Custom House. It is said that machine guns have also been placed there.*

Curran recalled around 200 soldiers marching down Dorset Street one day. The general view was that the government and military authorities were very nervous and feared another uprising around St Patrick's Day. This never materialised, but British nerves continued to jangle, and they looked for other means to suppress republican fervour.

On 7 April, the *Nation* newspaper was no longer allowed to be sent abroad and, two weeks later, the Under-Secretary for Ireland confirmed in the House of Commons that ten newspapers in Ireland were to be prohibited from circulating abroad. A proclamation was issued by the Commander in Chief of the British Forces in Ireland prohibiting the holding of processions within Dublin's city limits, with the exception of the Lord Mayor's procession. Near the end of the month, Lloyd George made a speech in London's Guildhall revealing his anxiety to see a solution to the Irish question:

... to have a well-knit and powerful Empire, we must convert Ireland from a suspicious, surly and dangerous neighbour to a secure and friendly Ireland, and because I know from facts brought home to me every hour, an Irish settlement is one of the essentials of victory.

Curran believed the speech was for the benefit of listening colonial representatives. It would cut very little ice with Sinn Féin members, but would probably please their counterparts in the Irish Parliamentary Party.

April also saw a Convention held in Dublin's Mansion House, seeking to determine how a cohesive voice could be given to a very fragmented republican movement. Curran reported the Convention as an enthusiastic gathering, attended, by his reckoning, by some 600 delegates, though there were likely many more than that in the hall. He was struck by the attendance of many young priests, who were obviously politically active. Other delegates represented seventy public corporations and councils, as well as trade unions and labour movements.

By the end of the day, a consensus emerged, with Count Plunkett anointing himself as the movement's figurehead. It was, in essence, the start of a new era in Irish politics – for the first time, there was a serious political alternative to the Irish Parliamentary Party.

On the anniversary of the Rising, numerous requiem masses were held in Dublin and across the country, all attracting huge crowds. Republican flags were hoisted at locations throughout the country, later to be torn down by the British military. In one case, Curran recalled, the flag was actually fired on.

On 30 April, a letter from the Bishop of Limerick was made public, despite it being suppressed by the censor. In it, the Bishop complained about the treatment of Irish prisoners by British authorities.

Early in May, newspapers published an important manifesto against partition, permanent or temporary, signed by eighteen Catholic bishops, three Protestant bishops and five chairmen of county councils. The manifesto stated that no real organised effort was being made to elicit the views of the country as a whole on the issue, and declared that no decision on the dismemberment of the country should be taken without at first gauging the will of all of the people of Ireland.

The South Longford by-election took place 9 May, and Curran, rightly, equated its importance with the by-election held later that year in East Clare. The Irish Parliamentary Party decided to spend whatever was necessary to get its candidate, Mr McKenna, elected. Leaders like John Dillon and Joe Devlin turned up in the constituency to canvass on his behalf, and they were confident of victory, as was the *Freeman's Journal*, the party's organ. They were to be bitterly disappointed, however, as the Sinn Féin candidate, Joseph McGuinness, won by thirty-seven votes. Curran recalled that the IPP directed much of its ire against the Archbishop and the younger, more republican-minded clergy of Longford.

The following week, the government published proposals for the settlement of the 'Irish question', including the exclusion of the six counties, to be reviewed by parliament after five years unless terminated by the action of an all- Ireland consultative body. The proposal was not universally accepted and even the *Freeman's Journal* rejected the plan for permanent exclusion. It was obvious, even then, that any attempt to divide the island of Ireland was going to be a controversial and emotive issue.

While nationalists complained about censorship of publications sympathetic to their point of view, those of a unionist viewpoint were also in a complaining frame of mind. For example, an article in the *Church of Ireland Gazette* strongly attacked nationalists' penchant for magnifying the influence and deeds of Irish rebels like Lord Edward Fitzgerald, Wolfe Tone, Robert Emmet and the Fenians in books like the Christian Brothers, *Irish History Reader*. The writer complained about the Protestant Commissioners allowing such books to remain in their schools, and demanded they be removed without delay.

Curran recalled Lloyd George's announcement of 21 May 1917 concerning setting up an Irish Convention to allow Irishmen from all facets of society to put forward proposals for the governance of their country. The Convention convened in Trinity College the following July and continued through various phases until April of the following year, ending with a report that was never acted upon. Curran noted that practically all nationalists regarded the Convention as 'a dishonest device of Lloyd George', with both Sinn Féin and the Irish National League refusing to have any association with it. He also noted that the Gaelic League distanced itself from the Convention despite its founder, Douglas Hyde, having agreed to attend.

On 15 June 1917, Andrew Bonar Law announced in the House of Commons a general release of Sinn Féin prisoners, who began arriving home into Dublin three days later. They arrived around eight o'clock in the morning, and Curran recalled:

> They were met by thousands who had been there since 6am, many had been waiting all night. They received a tremendous ovation. It was noticed that de Valera was apparently the recognised leader. Many showed signs of their late hardship.

Within a month, de Valera was cementing his leadership of Irish republicanism with a famous by-election victory in East Clare. The Sinn Féin bandwagon that had started rolling some months earlier was showing little sign of slowing down. On Sunday, 1 July, there was an enthusiastic demonstration at Mount Argus Church in Dublin on the occasion of a mass celebrating the release of the Irish prisoners from British jails. That same day, a public meeting was held in the Phoenix Park:

> A public meeting was held to-day (Sunday, 1 July, 1917) in the Phoenix Park to protest against the partition of Ireland and a nominated Convention. Twenty-four speakers spoke against the partition proposals of the Convention to a gathering of over thirty thousand people. Four platforms were arranged for the speakers, representative of the Four Provinces, each with its chairman. The resolutions from all four platforms were put simultaneously, on the signal of a trumpet blast, and carried amid prolonged cheers.

Later that month, Eamon de Valera took the seat for Sinn Féin in East Clare with a resounding and somewhat surprising majority of 2,975 votes. In Curran's view, this result sounded the death knell for the Irish Parliamentary Party – its candidate in the election, viewed as a very strong one, was soundly defeated. The result prompted victory demonstrations around the country and set the IPP into a panic. Sinn Féin flags were flying everywhere and Sinn Féin clubs were cropping up in every town and village. Curran noted in his diary the absence of any major public disorder during the election campaign. Both candidates insisted on respect and manners, and Sinn Féin further ensured civility by enlisting the help of Volunteers armed with hurleys.

Sinn Féin's popularity increased with 'enormous rapidity and enthusiasm', as for many people the country's future rested with that movement. Even some British-based newspapers came to the same conclusion, with the *Daily Mail* correspondent in Dublin writing:

> *The wave of Sinn Féin enthusiasm which swept over East Clare is now submerging familiar political landmarks in every part of the country. From Cork to Derry and from Dublin to Galway comes the same story of the constantly growing strength of the new Party. It is important to remember that Ireland now possesses what she has not had for a century – a generation of young men. The ban on emigration left the country probably seventy–eighty thousand young fellows, and from the spirit and enterprise, which would have sent them overseas, is now derived the great impetus of the Sinn Féin movement.*

The writer continued that the authorities should not underestimate the significance of the Volunteers drilling and marching. By the end of the month, they seemed to have taken that advice on board and on 30 July, a proclamation was issued by Sir Bryan Mahon, Commander of the British Forces in Ireland, prohibiting the wearing of military uniforms and the carrying of hurleys in public. The order was clearly targeted at the Volunteers. There was also a general suspicion that Mahon's order had the backing of a dysfunctional and panic-stricken Irish Parliamentary Party, which could see its long-held political domination disintegrating rapidly.

The *Irish Times* of 10 September 1917 reported that meetings planned for Mitchelstown and Omagh were proscribed by the authorities because it was felt they would give rise to disorder and cause undue demands to be made on the police and military. The *Irish Independent* of that day reported:

Two hundred police were drafted into one town backed up by a large military force and armoured cars paraded in the streets. Machine guns were placed at various vantage points with snipers posted on several trees.

However, a large political meeting was held in Cork on Sunday, 23 September, addressed by Eoin MacNeill, Arthur Griffith and Count Plunkett. Smaller protest meetings were held at Smithfield and outside Mountjoy Prison, where some republican prisoners had begun a hunger strike on 20 September. On 25 September, one of the prisoners, Thomas Ashe, died. His death and funeral, according to Curran, created thousands of new supporters for Sinn Féin.

On 23 October, in the course of an Irish debate in the House of Commons, the Chief Secretary for Ireland, Henry Duke, presented what Curran described as a 'blood-curdling picture of Irish rebellion and conspiracy'. Lloyd George expressed the 'intention of his government to suppress all attempts at incitement as well as any efforts to stage a rebellion', and further declared that 'the sovereign independence of Ireland could not be countenanced by England'.

Two days later, a Sinn Féin Convention began, chaired by Arthur Griffith and described by Curran as an 'epoch-making one' in Irish political life. A resolution was passed authorising the party leadership to secure international recognition of Ireland as an independent republic. The Irish people would then be free to determine their own form of government. The Convention denied the right of the British Parliament and British Crown, or any other foreign government, to legislate for Ireland, and it suggested that every means possible should be used to prevent Ireland being held prisoner by a military force. Interestingly, the Convention also called for the equality of men and women in the Sinn Féin organisation, a principle that was to be emphasised in all speeches and leaflets.

Curran claimed the event staggered the non-nationalist press, with one reporter recounting the following day that 'among the seventeen hundred delegates almost every interest in Ireland was represented … There were priests, by the score', for the most part 'the younger clergy with the dust of Maynooth still on their boots'.

He also mentioned there were 'a great many grey-haired clergymen who wield a tremendous influence in the country parishes whose destinies they rule', and that 'well-groomed professional men rubbed shoulders with untrimmed Goliaths, fresh from the fields of the West'. The delegates were, in the main, young and energetic, but conducted themselves in an orderly manner, which impressed the writer greatly.

The Convention elected a new executive, tasked with coordinating the future direction of the republican movement. Eamon de Valera was elected President, with Griffith and Father O'Flanagan as vice-presidents. Liam Cosgrave and Larry Ginnell were elected as treasurers and the secretaries were to be Austin Stack and Darrell Figgis. Curran recalled de Valera giving a strong anti-English speech, asserting Ireland's right to independence.

The *Irish Independent* was not enamoured with the Sinn Féin phenomenon. Its issue of 3 November contained a solemn appeal to the public not to attend the planned Sinn Féin meeting in Newbridge fixed for the following day, a meeting which had already been proscribed by the authorities.

Tensions increased across the country around the beginning of November, as Curran's diary entry for the fourth of the month confirmed:

The situation in Ireland has been ominous of late. The provocative speeches of the government during the Irish debate on 23 October, the numerous daily arrests for drilling and marching, the resentment over the Ashe tragedy with its inquest and verdict, the frequent Sinn Féin meetings and suppression of their processions all have roused public feeling.

The British sent General Hutchinson to Ireland in an attempt to calm the situation down. Hutchinson had protested against many acts carried out by the military during the Easter Rising, and had been promoted to the position of General of Supplies in order to remove him from Ireland. His return to Ireland seemed like an act of desperation by the British.

On 25 November, a letter from Cardinal Logue condemning the unrest in Ireland was read at all masses in the Diocese of Armagh:

An agitation had sprung up and is spreading among our people, which ill-considered and Utopian, cannot fail, if persevered in, to entail present suffering, disorganisation and danger, and is sure, to end in future disaster, defeat and collapse. And all this in pursuit of a dream which no man in his sober senses can hope to see realised;

the establishment of an Irish Republic, either by an appeal to the potentates seated at a peace conference, or an appeal to force by hurling an unarmed people against an Empire which has five-millions of men under arms, furnished with the most terrible engines of destruction which human ingenuity could devise.

Such a view emanating from a hugely influential member of the Catholic hierarchy must have been very disconcerting to people who longed for the day when an Irish republic would be a reality. It serves to underline the division that existed at the time.

Throughout 1918, this division only grew. The republican agenda of Sinn Féin had caught the imagination of many and became a source of concern for a visibly crumbling Irish Parliamentary Party. The picture was further complicated by differing views within the Catholic Church. Older clerics were, in the main, supporters of the political status quo, while the younger generation was increasingly drawn to the ideals of republicanism and Sinn Féin. Set against all this was the intransigence of a government in London and a unionist community in Ulster who were determined to maintain the union of Ireland and Britain. This potent mixture of opinions would inevitably lead to further conflict.

The general election of December 1918 was a resounding success for Sinn Féin, and the first meeting of Dáil Éireann took place on 21 January 1919. Curran recalled that there was much anxiety over whether the meeting could be held in public at all – the fear was that the British military and the Dublin Castle authorities might combine to suppress it. He noted that some sixty-nine pressmen were present in the Mansion House on the day, including many from abroad.

All of the proceedings in the chamber were undertaken in the Irish language and no applause was allowed. Curran was impressed both by the manner in which the business of the house was conducted and the decorum adhered to by all involved.

There was no sign of the once powerful Irish Parliamentary Party, because its six elected members chose, together with the Unionists, to attend at Westminster. Curran commented that it had been so long since IPP members had appeared in public in Ireland that the people had actually forgotten who they were. The meeting signified the eclipse of the old political order in the country.

The twenty-seven members who did attend that day were the successful Sinn Féin candidates who happened not to be in jail, while Michael Collins and Harry Boland were in England, planning de Valera's escape from Lincoln Jail.

Political momentum was up and running, but there were many republicans who could not participate in it, because they were incarcerated in Ireland and in Britain. Arthur Griffith, who was in Gloucester Jail, wrote to Curran on behalf of his fellow prisoners, expressing his thanks to the Archbishop for securing Mass for them on Christmas Day.

An inquiry opened in Belfast on 28 January, to look into the treatment of Sinn Féin prisoners in the city, but the prisoners refused to take any part in it. They were represented by the newly elected TD Eamon Duggan, who stated that their refusal to engage in the proceedings was because the prison authorities and the Government had refused to guarantee that the facts given in evidence would not be censored for publication. The Government had also refused to produce all the necessary documents for the Inquiry.

Eamon de Valera, Sean Milroy and John McGarry escaped from Lincoln Jail in February, and Curran took part in an elaborate scheme to hide de Valera from the authorities. On Tuesday, 18 February, he received a telephone call from a Mr Keohane of Gill's informing him that Harry Boland wished to see him at their premises on the following morning. Curran met Boland as arranged, and again two days later, when they were joined by Michael Collins.

Boland and Collins proposed that Curran should conceal de Valera in the Archbishop's house, as it was the last place the authorities would expect him to take refuge in. Curran admitted to being 'astonished by the suggestion', but he agreed to get involved in the scheme. Boland pointed out that all the usual places of refuge were either known to the authorities or under observation. There was also the bonus of de Valera being able to engage in physical exercise within the grounds of the property. De Valera had not yet arrived back in Dublin after his escape from jail.

On Friday, 21 February, Boland and Collins turned up unannounced at the Archbishop's house to inspect a place that Curran proposed should be used to hide de Valera. The first condition Curran laid down was that 'every possible precaution should be taken to safeguard the position of the Archbishop. Accordingly, the first step was that he was not to be informed or know of it.'

With that in mind, Curran ruled out the Archbishop's house itself, but suggested de Valera could be accommodated in one of the property's two lodges – a house located towards the Tolka River end of the estate or the gate lodge on the Drumcondra Road. The Tolka lodge was ruled out because it was too much under observation from a neighbouring cottage, and so they opted for the lodge on the Drumcondra Road, occupied by the Archbishop's valet William Kelly and his family. Curran and his co-conspirators were somewhat concerned that Kelly's two young boys might give the game away, though they would be unaware of who the visitor actually was. Boland and Collins were happy enough with the arrangement, and they expected de Valera to arrive within the week.

No one knew of de Valera's imminent arrival apart from the Kelly family and the Archbishop's housekeeper, Ms Julia Corless. Indeed, the house welcomed many other visitors at that time, with meetings being held there regarding the beatification of some Irish martyrs, but Curran recalled that not one of the visitors realised the great Irish leader was so close by.

Curran received a note from Boland on the afternoon of Monday, 24 February, advising that he should expect his guest, who was alluded to as 'the parcel', that evening about ten o'clock, which was later changed to eight o'clock. It seems de Valera was coming from Dr Farnan's house in Merrion Square, which had been declared unsafe. He went from there to the sports buildings in Croke Park, where he remained until the route to the Archbishop's house was scouted and deemed safe to travel through.

De Valera arrived with Boland, as Curran recalled:

A few minutes before eight o'clock, I left the dinner table and made my way to an unused gate which gave access to the eastern side of the estate. Soon, de Valera and Boland arrived and had a conversation with me during which they made arrangements for their next meeting. De Valera also asked Boland to procure a large size fountain pen for him which he could use on board the ship during his planned trip to America.

Curran escorted de Valera through the deserted grounds of the estate, passing the brilliantly lit windows of Clonliffe College. During the walk, de Valera recalled his own personal associations with the College.

De Valera occupied a room to the right of the entrance of the lodge which was fitted up as a bed-sitting room. He spent most of his time revising a paper he called 'Ireland's Claim to Independence', which he intended to be presented to the Peace Conference in Paris.

Each evening after dinner Curran joined him for a walk in the grounds of the Archbishop's house. He also arranged for Father Tim Corcoran, who would later have a strong influence on WT Cosgrave's Free State government, to visit de Valera on the evening of 28 February, when they discussed the pending appeal to the Conference. Curran also recalled a meeting of the Provisional Government in the adjacent Dublin Whisky Distillers, chaired by de Valera while he was staying in the lodge.

De Valera left rather abruptly around 3 March, surprising Curran who believed he would remain somewhat longer. His stay was not detected by the authorities and he managed to carry out his business with relative ease. The Archbishop himself never knew that the leader of Irish republicanism and the future leader of a free and independent Ireland had taken advantage of his hospitality.

Though he claimed no credit for his part in keeping de Valera safe from the authorities, Monsignor Michael Curran's willingness to participate in the subterfuge clearly marked him out as a man who wholeheartedly supported the republican ideal.

Curran was transferred to Rome later in 1919, taking up the position of Vice-Rector of the Irish College. He eventually succeeded as Rector in 1930, serving until 1939. His time as Secretary to the Archbishop was an eventful one, especially during the Easter Rising of 1916 and the years immediately following it. His statement clearly defines him as a man who, despite his important and very public position, went out of his way to facilitate, in any way he could, the ushering in of an independent Ireland.

Chapter 5

The Curious Tale of 198 Parnell Street

Small boys are natural radicals, and the boys, given a uniform and some semblance of a military organisation, needed no encouragement to declare themselves openly as revolutionaries who looked forward to the day when they might strike a blow in another fight for freedom. Of course, adults smiled tolerantly at this, not realising that the boy will soon be a man, and that the sentiments imbibed in his formative years are likely to remain with him in after life, to fructify as deeds when opportunity offers.

(Joseph V Lawless)

T he statement of Colonel Joseph V Lawless, an officer of the National Army and member of the Investigating Staff of the Bureau, who had been an officer in the Volunteers, is fascinating. It includes a very interesting account of the establishment of the first republican bomb-making factory.

The story begins with the evolving friendship of two men, Joseph Lawless and Archie Heron. Lawless had been involved in the republican struggle from a young age, together with his father and brother. He had participated in the Howth gun-running operation in 1914, and the Battle of Ashbourne in 1916, which claimed the lives of twelve people. He spent the months after the Easter Rising incarcerated in Frongoch prison camp, being released just before Christmas 1916. He fondly recalled the moment he and his fellow prisoners were informed of their release from the camp on 23 December. They were all assembled in the dining room when the Camp Adjutant announced that:

... an order had been received from the Home Office for our immediate release. There was not a sound following the announcement, and I think the Adjutant thought we had not understood the purport of his words. Collins, acting spontaneously as spokesman for the rest of us, pushed forward towards the Adjutant's table and replied in his usual forthright manner, 'It's no use, you'll get no names or addresses from us.' The Adjutant replied, 'I don't give a damn about your names or addresses, all I am concerned about is to get you all to hell out of here.'

Lawless returned home to work on the family farm, despite having served eighteen months of an engineering apprenticeship beginning in 1913. It seems somewhat inevitable that he should remain deeply involved in the campaign for his country's independence.

Archie Heron was a Belfast man and an active Volunteer even before the Rising. He was also a friend of James Connolly. He left home for Dublin to take part in the rebellion and never returned. After the Rising, he found a job as a shop assistant in the hardware store of Gleeson O'Dea and Company of Christchurch Place. He was staying with friends of Lawless when both men met for the first time in 1917. Heron was, at that time, active in the Volunteers and a respected member of the IRB.

Lawless recalled that in late 1917, Heron:

... suggested to me, that I should consider setting up a small business to capitalise on my mechanical skills. He told me that in O'Dea's shop lots of household items were left in to be repaired but the firm found great difficulty in finding anyone to carry out the repairs satisfactorily. He then brought some items home for me to repair and make an assessment of the viability of setting up a business venture based on a partnership of both men.

They both agreed the venture had potential and quickly set about finding a suitable building to trade from. Though it was not intended at first, the business in due course became a front for the first republican bomb factory.

Initially, Lawless carried out his few jobs at home. He then acquired a backyard premises at 132 Drumcondra Road belonging to brothers by the name of Fleming, who refused to take any rent. Money was tight at the beginning of the venture and only a few basic tools and light equipment could be afforded.

Heron kept the accounts and touted for work, which was acquired mainly from O'Dea's and another hardware establishment called Henshaw's. To both men's surprise, the business quickly began to flourish, showing enough profit to warrant expansion. A larger business premises was required and, in the spring of 1918, they came across a vacant building at 198 Parnell Street in Dublin city centre.

Having agreed a deal to rent the premises, the partners put up a sign, 'Heron and Lawless', and commenced trading from here. They also expanded the enterprise to include the repair and sale of bicycles. As Lawless recollected in later years, the premises became primarily a bicycle shop, though other repair work continued to be taken on.

With the business doing well, Heron left his job at O'Dea's to work full-time in Parnell Street, concentrating on sales, accounting and commercial contacts. An assistant was employed to help Lawless and a young boy called Christy Reilly was taken on to run errands and keep the premises tidy. Reilly would later become a member of the Volunteers munitions staff, serving in that capacity until the truce in 1921.

As it transpired, the premises had been used in previous years as a small brass foundry, manufacturing plumbing fittings. The foundry itself was in the basement under the shop. Since there was no back door to the premises, the foundry could only be entered through the shop and down a stairway.

Lawless rigged up the forge in the basement with the help of a part-time smith. He also tried his hand at manufacturing simple items, like door and gate bolts and cycle carriers. He recalled:

> Owing to the war conditions existing at the time, all kinds of manufactured items of this type were in short supply and so we were well on the way to building up a good business though our total capital in the beginning was only £100 overdraft which my father and Batt O'Connor guaranteed to the bank.

There were two old furnaces at the back of the basement and, though Lawless knew it would cost money to refurbish them, he said he always had it in his mind to put them to use. He recalled that the Volunteers were, at that time, having great difficulty in procuring arms. The days, he said, 'of sending men out armed with pikes or obsolete weapons to fight a force with modern firearms were gone'.

The amount of weaponry being obtained by subterfuge was patently insufficient for the number of men to be armed and so the Volunteers leaders turned their thoughts to the possibility of manufacturing bombs on a large scale.

Around July 1918, Heron engaged Lawless in a discussion about converting part of their premises into a bomb-making factory. He had been approached by Mick Lynch, the Fingal Brigade Commander, with a proposal to manufacture bombs. It had already been decided to employ a man full-time to carry out the work. The difficulty, as the Volunteers leadership saw it, was locating a suitable workshop where regular supplies of material could be delivered without arousing suspicion. Lawless discussed the matter with Lynch who, he said,

> ... *told me he had been appointed Director of Munitions on the GHQ Staff and that he was anxious to get going at once in turning out a type of bomb that would need no expensive plant or highly skilled staff to produce, and he wanted these in large quantities.*

If the project was to be successful, it would be necessary to engage the right personnel, and so the search began to find someone with experience in the area of bomb-making. It did not take very long to find that person. His name was Matthew Gahan and Lawless recalled how he:

> ... *quickly began work sawing off four-inch lengths of one and a half-inch steel piping, notching them longitudinally and circumferentially with a hacksaw and enclosing each end with a screwed plug and drilling one of the plugs to take a fuse.*

The bombs were very crude, and Lawless believed something better could be made. He maintained that the old foundry in the basement could be restored to working order with just a small part of the money being spent by Gahan. The Volunteers' Director of Munitions, Mick Lynch, believed the proposal was neither worthwhile or practical. However, he mentioned Lawless's idea to the Commanding Officer of the Volunteers Dublin Brigade, Dick McKee. He was very interested in the proposal, as was Count George Plunkett, who heard about it during one of his frequent visits to the shop.

George and Jack Plunkett were of mechanical and scientific minds, and they were convinced that the proposal was viable and should be proceeded with at once. George Plunkett accompanied McKee and Peadar Clancy to the shop in Parnell Street to discuss the idea with Lawless and Heron. Lawless recalled it was the first time he met Clancy, who said very little during the conversation. By that time, Clancy was Quartermaster of the Dublin Brigade and was brought along to familiarise himself with any commitments made during the meeting.

Lawless enthusiastically elaborated on his idea and was supported by Plunkett, who urged McKee to find the money to commence the work. Lawless provided an estimate of the cost to refurbish the foundry, which he later admitted was a rough guess, and McKee undertook to locate and secure the best and most reliable staff to help out with the work. He also promised to send Rory O'Connor, the Assistant Dublin City Engineer, to the shop to give his technical opinion on the proposed project. O'Connor also held the position of Director of Engineering on the Volunteers General Staff.

Rory O'Connor duly turned up to inspect the premises. He was concerned about the chimney flue, which was originally designed for domestic use – the worry was that it might not be capable of carrying off the gases from an iron melting furnace. This was the first time Lawless had met O'Connor, who he remembered as:

> ... *particularly solemn and unsmiling, one might say lugubrious, and did not appear to listen to what I said when I began to explain the details of what I considered as my plan for a bomb factory. Taking him down to the basement, he cut short whatever I was telling him by asking where the furnace was and said he wanted to examine it.*

Despite being warned that the foot grate covering the draught pit in front of the furnace was missing, O'Connor walked towards the furnace in the dark and promptly fell head-first into the pit. Thankfully, his pride was hurt more than anything else, though Lawless did admit he and Heron shared a snigger behind his back.

O'Connor's report was a favourable one and arrangements were made to go ahead with the work. Within a week, Matt Furlong from Wexford arrived to get the place ready. Furlong, a reserved man, was introduced to Lawless by Mick Lynch, and he had clearly been well briefed on the nature of the work he was expected to do. At first, Lawless recalled, Furlong was:

... resentful of me and that he was not inclined to accept any help or suggestions. However, over the following few weeks relations between us gradually improved as the fitting out of the factory gathered pace.

Two other men, Tom Young and Sean O'Sullivan, arrived to help get the foundry up and running. Young's father, who was at that time in charge of the foundry in the engineering branch of the Dublin College of Science, provided valuable technical advice. Lawless accompanied Tom Young to the College of Science, where his father explained in detail the advantages of the steel-cased furnaces in use there. They took the dimensions of the furnaces in the College and produced exact replicas in 198 Parnell Street.

Before long, a new and important piece of machinery was acquired:

A five inch, German made, screw cutting lathe with an attached motor was secured through the efforts of George Plunkett from Ganters, the watchmakers of George's Street. This tool had been purchased or hired by the British authorities for war munition in the Shell factory in Parkgate Street, and its return was at this time offered to Ganters. Matt Furlong had worked at one time as a turner in the munition factory and knew this lathe which was a beautiful tool.

As work got underway at the factory, word came down from the Volunteers leadership that Lawless, Heron and the other men involved in the operation were not to:

... attend any Volunteers parades or identify themselves publicly in any way with Volunteers or other national activities for fear of attracting any unwanted attention from the authorities.

The design of the bomb was worked out by the General Headquarters engineering staff in accordance with the limitations of the plant and the only available high explosive, which was gelignite. It was based on the famous 'Mills' bomb used by the British in the Great War. The quality of the bombs manufactured in the factory was surprisingly high, though initially it seems there was a flaw in them – there was no bend in the fuse, such as was in the 'Mills' version, which meant there was a risk of an accidental flash. The flaw was soon corrected.

The assembled bombs without the explosives were removed initially from Parnell Street every evening or alternative evenings by members of the staff, who, according to Lawless, 'hung them about their persons on a type of harness covered by greatcoats'. However, as production increased, a new way had to be found to spirit the bombs out of the factory. A man called Chris Healy was hired to undertake the task with his horse and cart. Healy carted the bombs away from Parnell Street and also brought the raw materials and the foundry coke to the premises.

While all those involved in the factory were confident about the secrecy of the enterprise, there was always a fear that the premises could be raided by the authorities. Michael Collins was a frequent visitor to the shop and was well aware of the activities being carried out in the basement. He was anxious that all measures should be taken to maintain the secrecy of the operation. Consideration was given to boring an emergency exit into a neighbouring premises, but this was not done, for fear it would arouse suspicion.

Lawless fixed up a signal light in the foundry, connected to a switch upstairs in his workshop, designed to warn those working in the basement of an impending raid. He also fitted a Yale lock on the door leading downstairs from the shop, which was always kept locked while the staff worked below. The men also took the precaution of excavating a cavern in the earthen floor under the forge bellows, capable of containing six or seven dozen bombs and other incriminating materials. The cavern was covered with a steel plate, on top of which about a foot deep of the loose dry earth of the floor rested.

While there was no real confrontation with the British during 1918, the republican leadership insisted on continuing preparations for a resumption of hostilities. Luckily, there were no sudden police or military raids on the premises during the year and by the end of it, the first bomb casings had been manufactured. With amazing determination and ingenuity, Joseph Lawless and his republican colleagues not only managed, against all the odds, to set up a bomb-making factory in the centre of Dublin city, but also concealed it from the British authorities. The bomb-making operation was never discovered, and contributed significantly to the cause of Ireland's independence.

Chapter 6

Procuring Arms and Gathering Intelligence

About June 1916, Liam Archer summoned me to attend a meeting of the officers of the Dublin Brigade who had escaped arrest at the surrender and who were on the run at the time. The meeting was held in Cathal Brugha's house in Fitzwilliam Terrace, Upper Rathmines. Cathal Brugha was very ill at the time, having received fourteen bullets from a machine-gun during the Rising. During the course of the discussions, he made a statement the gist of which was: 'we were not to think that the fight was over, it was only the beginning, and we were to get in touch immediately with any members of our Companies and Battalions who were free. We were to organise them into units and keep them together until all our comrades had been released from prison which, he hoped, would be soon.'

(Nicholas Laffan)

I f 1917 was a year of great political change, with the emergence of Sinn Féin as a credible alternative to the Irish Parliamentary Party, the following year was given over by many republicans to preparing for what they saw as an inevitable resumption of hostilities against the British. The many Irish Volunteers units across the country were conscious that if there was to be a conflict, it would be necessary to thoroughly prepare for it. As well as amassing as much as possible in the way of arms and ammunition, intelligence would have to be gathered, to monitor the forces of the Crown.

One very detailed and interesting statement was made by Nicholas Laffan, from Cork Street in Dublin. He had been a Captain in the Dublin Brigade's 'G' Company and was very involved in nationalist activities in the capital city. He recalled that a great deal of attention was paid to the procuring of arms during 1918, and in April of that year his company succeeded in getting four rifles and about 150 rounds of ammunition from Islandbridge military barracks. The rifles were hidden in a military car, coming out one at a time, for which the driver was paid three pounds.

Laffan was inducted into the intelligence sphere of Irish republicanism in June 1918:

Brigadier Dick McKee and Vice-Brigadier Peadar Clancy instructed me not to appear on public parade with my Company as they were going to give me other important work to do. Owing to my position in the Dublin Alliance Gas Company as a District Inspector, I could always get into any house, institution, barracks or prison for the purpose of inspecting gas installations.

His superior officers decided to take advantage of his privileged position, ordering him to take coded messages into Mountjoy prison. These were placed under or near a gas meter, where they could be picked up by their intended recipient, most likely a man called Thomas Walsh.

On one occasion, Laffan took Peadar Clancy through a number of houses in the city, including three houses in the Mount Street area that were later raided by republicans searching for Secret Service agents from Scotland Yard. Clancy also asked to visit Arbour Hill Barracks and Laffan, together with Robert Oran, a fellow 'G' Company comrade and a fitter in the Gas Company, arranged to test the meter in the barracks. With Clancy posing as a gas company employee, the three men managed to enter the barracks. While they were testing the meter, Laffan recalled:

... a military policeman who was sent with us on the job called me aside and asked me who was in charge. I told him I was. He then advised me to get Clancy out of Arbour Hill as quickly as possible before someone else recognised him. We took his friendly tip and left, Peadar commenting it was a narrow shave.

Clancy called on Laffan one evening around five o'clock and asked him to bring an urgent message to Tom Walsh in Mountjoy prison. Laffan told him he had no reasonable excuse to visit the prison at such an hour, but Clancy was adamant that he should try to gain entry. Laffan agreed, and took an elderly fitter called Hynes with him:

> I went to the prison gate and was met with the remark, 'What the hell do you want at this hour?' I said I wanted to see Mr Faulkner, the Governor. Before being admitted, the gateman phoned the Governor who ordered that I and the fitter be brought to his office. Here I was severely cross-examined over the lateness of the hour and in the end the Governor phoned Dublin Castle requesting permission for us to enter. He gave our names and the reason for our visit which I said was to test the gas supply for pressure.

Before allowing Laffan and Hynes into the republican prisoners' wings, the Governor insisted on both men being searched. They had to leave their pipes, tobacco and cigarettes in his office until their return. They were then escorted by military police to A and B wings, where all the republican prisoners deliberately gathered around them. Laffan recalled how he:

> ... bided his time until he managed to slip the message to Walsh together with a number of cigarettes which he had managed to conceal in his pocket and had not been detected when he was searched.

On another occasion, Laffan received a note from Clancy asking that he meet him at Kingsbridge railway station. Laffan claimed Clancy told him to:

> ... bring 'a sandwich' which, in effect, meant I was to bring my gun with me. On arrival at the station I met Peadar who had an old Ford car with him. We went into the railway station and met a British army captain who had two large suitcases which he put in the car. He accompanied us to Islandbridge Barracks where we were stopped at the gate. The Captain produced some papers and we were admitted.

They proceeded to one of the barracks stores, which the Captain entered while Clancy and Laffan remained in the car. He returned with a soldier, who carried the two cases to the car. As they left the barracks, a military policeman stopped the car, took a cursory glance at the occupants and waved them on. After parting with the Captain at Westland Row, Clancy and Laffan brought the cases, which contained revolvers and ammunition, to the relative safety of their arms dump in Rutland Place, where they were kept in readiness for the resumption of hostilities against the British.

Laffan recalled a deserter from the British army known as 'Mouse', who indicated to him that soldiers in Portobello Barracks were willing to sell rifles through the railings of the barracks at night time. Over time, Laffan and a number of his comrades procured fifteen Lee Enfield rifles, six revolvers and about 1,000 rounds of ammunition this way.

I had a bicycle with two six-foot lengths of timber tied on to it and I put the rifle between the timber so that it could not be seen. We also wore our overcoats with slit pockets, so that we could get a grip on the rifle as we carried it away. We paid 'Mouse' £3 each for the rifles and revolvers.

Unfortunately, not all attempts to procure arms were successful, and one particular failure really irked him. In November 1918, he and his company took part in a raid on the College of Surgeons in Dublin, where the rifles for the College's Officer Training Corps were kept. Laffan went to the trouble of having a key made for the side door, but then it was discovered that the rifles had been removed by the British Army to the Shop Street Barracks.

* * *

Failed attempts to procure arms also befell companies outside the capital. One such incident in County Cork was recalled in the statement of Patrick Ahern of the Fermoy Company. A plan was made in May 1918 to hold up a train at Castletownroche. Ahern recalled Liam Lynch, later the de facto leader of the 'irregular' forces during the Civil War, receiving information from a contact in the army stores in Cobh that a large consignment of rifles and ammunition was due to be despatched to Fermoy on a date in early May. Lynch decided to hold up the train in order to seize the arms.

Together with other members of the Fermoy Company, Ahern proceeded to a pre-arranged meeting spot at a place known locally as Renny boreen, about six miles outside Fermoy on the road to Castletownroche. There, they met other Volunteers as well as Lynch and Liam Tobin of the General Headquarters Staff. Also in attendance were three railway workers and selected members of local companies, who were put on scouting and outpost duties. The captured arms were to be transferred to a number of cars, hired on the pretence of taking mourners to a funeral.

Four Volunteers drove on to Castletownroche railway station to await the train. As Ahern recalled, two of them were to:

> … *board the footplate as the engine was about to pull out and to compel the driver to halt the train at Renny boreen where the main party were. The others in the vicinity of the station were to board the train also while the railwaymen were to be prepared to take over the train in an emergency.*

The plan went awry when the Volunteer delegated to cut the telephone wires as the train was about to leave the station instead cut the wires when it entered the station. Because of the absence of telephone communication with Ballyhooley, the next station down the line, the train did not leave the station. The raid was reluctantly aborted.

Patrick Joseph McElligott, a battalion commanding officer of the Irish Volunteers in Listowel, recalled his role in a raid for arms in his home town in 1918. The raid focussed on all the hardware shops in the town, aiming to procure shotguns, dynamite and ammunition. They succeeded in obtaining approximately nineteen shotguns with some ammunition, as well as a number of revolvers and a quantity of dynamite.

One of the shopkeepers, Jack McKenna, who owned about ten or twelve of the seized shotguns as well as the dynamite, refused to give the RIC an account of the guns that were taken. He was arrested, tried and sentenced to twelve months' imprisonment in Belfast jail.

McElligott also received a Lee Enfield rifle and 100 rounds of ammunition from an ex-soldier not long after McKenna's arrest. That rifle, together with the rest of the cache, was hidden by a local officer in the forge where he worked, and remained there until it was needed.

An unsuccessful arms raid was recounted by Patrick Whelan, a Volunteer in Ring, County Waterford. In 1918, he and his comrades raided farmhouses in their local area for shotguns and ammunition as well as revolvers, one of which, he said, he kept for himself. Over time, his company amassed about a dozen shotguns and three revolvers.

Whelan was told by a girl who worked in the house of the Sheriff at Helvick that her employer:

> ... had a few guns and ammunition in his house and any night her employer's yacht was out in the harbour he was sure not to be at home and the Volunteers could freely walk into the house and she would show them where the guns were kept.

One evening, Whelan spotted the yacht in the harbour and contacted another Volunteer, Dan Terry, with a view to raiding the house. Whelan recalled:

> As the time was early evening, we donned masks. I took my revolver. He had one also. We were turning into the door of the Sherriff's house when the son and mother came out. I gave them 'hands up' and told them to go inside. I asked who was in the house and the son said his father, a bank manager named Going and a military officer were there. When the son went in with his hands up, the others laughed when they saw him – thinking he was joking.

As it happened, the guns had recently been transferred to Dublin Castle for safety. All that was available to Whelan was a quantity of ammunition and a number of empty cartridge cases. Leaving the house with their meagre haul, they were pursued by the occupants and Whelan had to fire a shot over their heads in order to effect a getaway.

They did, in fact, make use of the empty cartridges by getting a local man, Patrick Lenane, to fill them with homemade buckshot and gunpowder.

Every opportunity was taken to bring arms into areas where it was believed they would be needed in the event of a major conflict with the British. This was never more evident than in a statement made by George Fitzgerald, a member of the Volunteers Dublin Brigade. An order came from Michael Staines, the Brigade's

Quartermaster General, requiring Volunteers to clear a big supply of ammunition that had reached the grain merchants Dodd's in Dublin's Smithfield. Fitzgerald and a party from his company made their way to Smithfield and retrieved small sacks of ammunition hidden in larger sacks of oats. He recalled:

> Though we worked late into the night we weren't able to empty all the sacks and only a portion of the ammunition was cleared. As the ammunition came from the sacks it was laid to one side, then taken by some of the Volunteers to a nearby yard.

The following day, the grain store was raided by the police and military and the remaining arms and ammunition were confiscated. A few days later, Fitzgerald and his comrades returned and prepared the stowed guns and ammunition for distribution by Michael Staines.

✳ ✳ ✳

Volunteers also manufactured their own weapons and, as they had access to a good supply of gelignite left over from the Easter Rising, they used it to make hand grenades. They displayed a good deal of ingenuity and no small amount of nerve in carrying out this very dangerous work.

In a statement made by James O'Conner, a Captain in the 3rd Battalion of the Dublin Brigade, he recalled how gun barrel was scooped and capped at both ends and a fuse and detonator attached. These crude grenades made a fine bang and were a forerunner of the more sophisticated hand grenades produced later by the Dublin Brigade at 198 Parnell Street. O'Conner also recalled some of the more scientific-minded Volunteers producing a highly effective explosive that they called 'war flour'.

Homemade mines were also manufactured, according to the statement of Martin Fahy, a member of the University Company of Volunteers in Galway who later went on to be the Brigade Engineer in southwest Galway. Fahy recalled learning how to fill the mines and make them ready for use by attaching detonators and fuses. The mine was made from the box of a horse-cart – the roughly twelve-inch metal portion of a wheel hub. It had a diameter ranging from three inches at the wider end to two inches at the smaller end. A blacksmith fitted a cap over each end, held in place by a bolt running along the outside of the cylinder. More often than not, the explosive used was gelignite, packed as tightly as possible into the mine.

The work was done in the College Club, under the pretence of holding a GAA meeting. The mines were then taken out of the College for distribution around the Galway area.

Michael Healy, a Captain in the Bullaun Company in Galway, recalled how he and his comrades collected guns in their local area during 1918. By July, they had amassed ten shotguns and a quantity of cartridges. The owners of the guns had handed them over to the Volunteers willingly.

In October 1918, Healy and a comrade, Lieutenant Timothy Nevin, took part in a raid on four houses in the neighbouring townland of Kilrickle. They were met by four Volunteers from the Kilrickle Company, and it soon transpired that Healy and Nevin had been asked to carry out the raid because they would not be recognised in the raided houses. Healy and Nevin entered the houses while the Kilrickle men waited outside. Healy recalled:

> *We had no trouble in three of the houses where the friendly occupants willingly handed over three shot guns and cartridges in total. In the fourth house the owner, a man named Hardy, was very hostile and he and his son claimed they had already handed over guns to the Volunteers, which was untrue.*

After a prolonged period of not-so-gentle persuasion and argument, the occupants eventually handed over a double-barrelled shotgun, but not, as Healy confirmed, with any great deal of grace.

The Volunteers adopted a more professional approach over time and an impressive command structure was put in place. Across the country, selected men were directed to monitor the movements of Crown forces and engage in intelligence gathering. The leadership in Dublin believed it was also essential to keep an eye on individuals across the country suspected of spying on the organisation.

Joseph Kinsella, a member of Dublin's Inchicore Company, recalled how he was ordered to concentrate on intelligence work. Near the end of 1918, a meeting was held to set up a fully functioning intelligence unit. Kinsella was instructed to visit various companies and select a section of eight men and a sergeant from each for the Intelligence Unit. A very important factor was the nature of their daily work and places of employment. Kinsella recalled:

Men were selected from Guinness Brewery, from the various banks across the city, from the post offices and from the railway. We had men who were employed on boats at the Quays, and we had shopkeepers. We had quite a number of men from the water-works and various other places in the Corporation. We had one man who was employed in the Kildare Street Club, and we had tram conductors and drivers. We had men who were employed as civilian clerks in different barracks around the city. Our agents who were employed in the banks were very useful to us in the matter of giving us gold for notes. Dáil Éireann at the time was very anxious to procure all the gold that could possibly be collected.

Kinsella claimed that they often exchanged up to £20 for gold in one week, handing it over to the Brigade's Intelligence Officer. He also used his agents in the Post Office system to get hold of letters sent by members of the public to the authorities in which they offered up information about the Volunteers. Those people were, he claimed, dealt with accordingly and often very severely.

Chapter 7

Tipperary Republicans
Lead the Way

*In the period after July 1917, when the prisoners arrested after the Easter
Rising in 1916 were all finally released from jails in England, and public
drilling and open recruitment for the Irish Volunteers started, there was a huge
increase in the strength of the organisation in the next three or four months. As
a result, it became necessary to form several new companies in mid-Tipperary
and, by the end of the year, I think we had a company in every parish.*

(James Leahy)

When the first shots of the War of Independence rang out at Soloheadbeg on 21 January 1919, little did people realise that a major and bloody
conflict had just been set in train. On that fateful day, two members of the Royal
Irish Constabulary lost their lives at the hands of prominent Tipperary republicans. The consequences of the ambush in the 'Premier County' would eventually
reverberate across the whole country.

Since the Easter Rising of 1916, the intensity of republican activity in
Tipperary had increased year on year in anticipation of a national conflict.
The level of commitment across the county to the cause of independence was
personified by the likes of Dan Breen, Sean Treacy, Seumas Robinson and
Sean Hogan, all of whom went on to become household names across the
country, but of course many others in Tipperary were just as committed to
the republican ideal.

One Volunteer with a fascinating tale to tell was Patrick O'Dwyer, Captain of 'C' Company, 3rd Battalion, 3rd Tipperary Brigade. O'Dwyer was born and raised in Hollyford in County Tipperary, the son of an old Fenian, and joined the Irish Volunteers in 1915. He played a pivotal role in many IRA operations.

Early in his statement, O'Dwyer recollected how, in August 1918, he had been instructed by Sean Treacy to cycle to Tipperary Town to take part in a proposed attack on the local courthouse. The IRA had reason to believe rifles belonging the National Volunteers were being stored in the building and they planned to break in and seize the arms. The men assembled at midnight and waited for Dan Breen to arrive with a jemmy to break the locks. Instead, a Volunteer called James Moloney arrived on the scene with an order from Breen that the 'raid was to be cancelled and the men should immediately disperse'. O'Dwyer recalled:

> As Breen cycled into town, he was set upon by a number of RIC men who were guarding some shops and business houses where a strike was in progress. He had the jemmy in his hand, which he used to good effect on the R.I.C. men. Then, drawing his revolver, he kept the policemen at bay as he backed away from them. He succeeded in contacting Moloney, who was at a céilí, and instructed him to get word to us to disperse.

O'Dwyer recalled how Sean Treacy and Dan Breen constantly moved from one place to another in order to escape the attention of the authorities and that they set up a headquarters of sorts with Sean Hogan in a County Council cottage in Greenane. While there, they often experimented with explosives, and O'Dwyer recalled an accidental explosion blowing the roof from the cottage one day. To avoid publicity and embarrassment, the cottage was quickly repaired by trusted men of the local Volunteers unit and the headquarters was moved to another cottage at Ardivalane.

O'Dwyer was heavily involved in the ambush at Soloheadbeg on 21 January 1919, from the planning of it to the moment of the fateful shots and their aftermath. He recalled reporting to the cottage at Ardivalane one day around the middle of January. Breen, Treacy and Hogan were there and they apprised him of their plans. A consignment of gelignite for the County Council was due to arrive any day at the Soloheadbeg quarry from the military barracks in Tipperary Town.

The plan, they said, 'was to hold up the convoy and seize the gelignite before it reached the quarry'.

The usual procedure in the transfer of explosives was for the Council foreman to call to the barracks with a hired driver and horse and cart. The consignment would then be escorted back to the quarry by an armed party of police, who might number anything from two to six men. O'Dwyer recalled:

> There were two roads, the Donohill road or the Boherkine road, by which the gelignite could be brought to Soloheadbeg, and my task for the next few days was to cycle to Tipperary each morning to watch out for the gelignite and its escort leaving the military barracks and then report back to the others who generally waited in a disused quarry in Soloheadbeg.

That ritual continued, according to O'Dwyer, for about four or five days. His watch on Tipperary town ended on 21 January, when he saw a horse and cart leave the military barracks, driven by James Godfrey accompanied by a Council ganger named Patrick Flynn and escorted by two RIC men. O'Dwyer quickly cycled via the Donohill road back to Soloheadbeg and reported the activity to Treacy, Breen and Hogan. They had been joined by four other men – Seumas Robinson, Michael Ryan, Patrick McCormack and Tadhg Crowe.

O'Dwyer recalled that they all went to their pre-arranged positions, around 250 yards from the entrance to the quarry, on a bank overlooking the by-road leading from the Tipperary to Dundrum road to the village of Soloheadbeg. A screen of whitethorn bushes provided some amount of cover from the view of anyone passing along the road.

The plan was for O'Dwyer and Robinson to get out on the road when they heard the others call on the men with the cart and the escort to halt and put their hands up. O'Dwyer confirmed in his statement that at least seven of the ambush party were armed with revolvers, the exception being Treacy who, O'Dwyer believed, was carrying a small automatic rifle that he was very fond of.

> It was around 12.30pm when the cart and its escort arrived and it was then I heard Dan Breen and Sean Treacy shout, 'Halt, put your hands up.' Robinson and I immediately started to get out on to the road, and almost simultaneously either one or two shots rang out. I distinctly remember one of the RIC men bringing his carbine

to the aiming position and working the bolt, and the impression I got was that he was aiming at either Robinson or myself. Then a volley rang out and the constable fell dead at the roadside.

Everything happened very quickly, perhaps in about half a minute, O'Dwyer estimated. He was at pains to point out in his statement that the intention of the ambush was to hold up the escort, disarm them and seize the gelignite without bloodshed if possible. Interestingly, O'Dwyer does not mention the death of the second constable, so we cannot be sure if he witnessed his shooting or not. The two constables, James McDonnell and Patrick O'Connell, both family men, had been stationed in Tipperary town. Their deaths caused outrage not only in Tipperary, but also across the country.

O'Dwyer recalled that the driver of the cart and the ganger were terrified, but Dan Breen spoke to them and assured them that 'nothing was going to happen to them'. The cart man, Godfrey, actually knew both Breen and Treacy, and Flynn, the ganger, probably did as well.

O'Dwyer collected the carbines belonging to the constables as Breen, Treacy and Hogan drove the horse and cart away with the gelignite. Robinson, Ryan and McCormack remained on the road with Godfrey and Flynn until their comrades had made their escape. O'Dwyer and Crowe hid the carbines at a spot on the railway line about a half a mile away from the ambush site. O'Dwyer then made his way home to Hollyford on foot.

O'Dwyer's bicycle was eventually found by the RIC at the home of Dan Breen's mother in Donohill. He had, he said, no idea how it got there, but the police failed to identify it as his property.

The decision to carry out the Soloheadbeg ambush was essentially a local one, and the operation was not sanctioned by the Volunteers leadership in Dublin. Ironically, that very same day, the constitutional element of Irish republicanism was also making its presence felt, as twenty-seven Sinn Féin TDs met in Dublin's Mansion House for the very first sitting of Dáil Éireann.

In a postscript to his recollection of the ambush, O'Dwyer recalled being in a local shop the following morning when two RIC men came to the door and stood for a while. They were, he said,

... taking a keen interest in me and so I opened the newspaper and read aloud, with a feigned amazement, the report of the ambush at Soloheadbeg. The policemen remained at the door listening and, in order to give the impression that I wasn't the least bit perturbed by their presence, I condemned in no uncertain terms the shooting of the constables.

Luckily enough, O'Dwyer was then hailed by a friend from outside the shop and he made his way home without encountering any trouble. From that day on, O'Dwyer maintained, Dan Breen and Sean Treacy were 'very anxious for [his] safety'. They constantly urged him to join them 'on the run', but he refused to do so, believing the RIC in Hollyford did not suspect him of involvement in the ambush.

O'Dwyer recalled a Sunday morning near the end of 1919, when two Volunteers called to his home and told him that three men staying at Scanlon's of Riska wished to see him. Arriving at the house, he found Seumas Robinson, Sean Treacy and Sean Hogan waiting for him. They had come from Dublin some nights earlier to attend a Brigade convention and when leaving the train at Goolds Cross, they were fired on by a group of RIC men. This meant that the police knew the three men were in the area. It was imperative for them to get out of the locality without being detected, and they asked O'Dwyer to find a car to take them back to Dublin.

He went to Tipperary town to look for a car while another man, Paddy Keogh, went to Doon on a similar mission. O'Dwyer had no luck in Tipperary and so he made his way to Doon in the company of James Linnane, a mechanic and driver, who willingly undertook to drive the three men to Dublin once a car had been commandeered. O'Dwyer recalled:

At Packy Ryan's in Doon I learned that a car could be commandeered at 'The Glebe', the residence of O'Kelly-Lynch the manager of the local branch of the Munster and Leinster Bank. Yank Carty, Bill Duggan, Dan Allis and some others, including a boy named O'Dea who worked for O'Kelly-Lynch, came with me to get the car. The latter was not a Volunteer, but we required him to handle a troublesome bulldog which was at 'The Glebe'.

As they took possession of the car, a mixed party of RIC and military in three lorries passed by. O'Dwyer and Linnane eventually met the convoy at a junction further up the road and thought the best course of action was to fall in behind it when it passed by. They travelled about a mile and a half behind it, eventually parting ways at another junction.

They proceeded to pick up Treacy, Robinson and Hogan, who had moved from Riska to Burke's at Templederry with the help of another Volunteer, Paddy Murphy. There they obtained petrol from the creamery manager to get them to Borrisoleigh, where they had to knock up the owner of another car who lived beside the RIC barracks to get some more petrol. O'Dwyer and Murphy then left the party and O'Dwyer recalled making his way home on foot before 'going on to a dance at Hollyford'.

Linnane drove Robinson, Treacy and Hogan on to Kildare, where the car was abandoned. He then took the train home, but was arrested by the RIC at Limerick Junction. He was sentenced to a year's hard labour in Waterford prison and, despite being offered his freedom and a large amount of money during his incarceration, he didn't reveal the names of the men he drove that night.

Sean Fitzpatrick was adjutant to the 3rd (South) Tipperary Brigade and Divisional Liason Officer. His statement provides a fascinating insight into the activities of republicans in Tipperary and again shows the commitment of all those involved in the independence struggle. Fitzpatrick, from Tipperary town and from a family steeped in the Fenian tradition, recalled that the Brigade in his native county was well organised in 1918, but was 'poorly equipped'. The Brigade consisted of six battalions, made up of fifty-seven companies, and comprised around 1,000 men. Seumas Robinson was, at that time, the Brigade Commanding Officer.

Fitzpatrick recalled the Volunteers were very much aware of the many shotguns, revolvers and rifles in private houses around the county, and they often had little or no difficulty in taking possession of them. He also recalled how, in Tipperary town, John Redmond's National Volunteers were dispossessed of a quantity of serviceable rifles. There were other sources of supply, but they were known only to certain members of the Brigade staff with well-established contacts in Dublin and elsewhere.

Fitzpatrick stated that a very efficient intelligence service was developed, with Volunteers reconnoitring enemy posts as well as intercepting military despatches. This was all done despite the 3,000 British troops in the county at that time. He also recollected how the Volunteers movement in Tipperary swelled to enormous numbers during the conscription crisis:

Young men and old, who feared being forced into the British army to fight on the Western Front, joined up but when the threat of the press gang faded away, so too did our newly fledged recruits, but those who remained steadfast were of the right calibre.

Martial law was proclaimed in the county after the Soloheadbeg ambush and it remained in place right up to the truce because, Fitzpatrick said, 'the authorities recognised the extent of republican activity in the county'.

Fitzpatrick recalled the Knocklong rescue of Sean Hogan in May 1919, involving four Brigade officers, actively supported by members of the Galtee Battalion. Hogan, who had taken part in the Soloheadbeg ambush, had been captured in Annfield. Taken as a prisoner to Thurles, he was being transferred to Cork when the rescue took place at Knocklong station. Two of the police escort were killed in a shootout, while Dan Breen and Sean Treacy were badly wounded.

When the firing stopped, Hogan was taken to a nearby butcher's shop, where his handcuffs were smashed open with a meat cleaver. Breen and Hogan had their wounds tended to by local doctors in safe houses. Though an extensive search was carried out by the authorities, they narrowly evaded capture and made their escape from the area.

Fitzpatrick was a marked man. While serving his time in the printing works of the *Tipperary People*, owned by the nationalist-supporting McCormack family, he was served with an expulsion order by the RIC, ordering him to reside outside the province of Munster. Fitzpatrick, in his own words, did not 'feel like obliging them'. He went 'on the run' to the districts of Kilross and Lackelly, five miles outside Tipperary town. He stayed mostly with friends, who gladly protected him, especially the Moloneys of Lackelly, who accommodated Robinson, Breen and Treacy the night prior to their rescue of Hogan.

* * *

A statement made in 1956 by Colonel Liam Hoolan who was Commandant of the Tipperary No 1 (North Tipperary Brigade) is equally enlightening and offers up further confirmation of republican activities in the county. A Nenagh native, Hoolan joined the Irish Volunteers in 1914, and was also involved in the National Aid and Prisoner's Dependant's Fund which brought him into contact with Michael Collins. Hoolan recalled the parades and drills in an old building in Pound Street in Nenagh and the number of recruits increasing through 1917, which led to the formation of a company.

Hoolan was also involved in organising Sinn Féin clubs around the county and eventually became Secretary for the Sinn Féin Party in North Tipperary. He also recalled that private houses, mainly owned by members of the Protestant community or people who still maintained an allegiance to the Irish Parliamentary Party, were raided for any guns and ammunition they might have.

In April 1918, Hoolan escaped capture with the help of Denis Hogan, the local Petty Sessions Clerk. Hogan received word from a friendly RIC man that Hoolan's office at Nenagh Courthouse was about to be raided, and he was on the list of individuals to be detained. This necessitated Hoolan going 'on the run' for three months, but he continued his organisational work, going to Offaly and to Waterford city to assist Sinn Féin candidates in by-elections. He was eventually arrested in June 1918 and sentenced to six months in Belfast jail.

Hoolan recounted a couple of amusing incidents during his time in the prison. The first concerned a prisoner called Dan Hogan, who later became a Major General in the Irish Army. He was refused admission to the prison when he returned off parole at 10pm one night. He duly booked in to a local hotel and the following day presented his bill to the prison authorities, which they obligingly settled. Another incident involved Hoolan himself: On the day he was to be released, he feigned illness in order to remain in the prison. He recalled: 'This was due to the fact that I had received information that the British authorities intended to re-arrest me outside the jail gates and to deport me.'

Hoolan abandoned the sham sickness after four days, when he heard the practice of re-arresting and deporting prisoners had been stopped. However, his prison days were not over – he was arrested again in December 1919, and spent the following six months in Limerick prison.

In his statement, he paid special tribute to the work of Cumann na mBan in the county. The first branch of the republican women's organisation was set up in Nenagh by a Miss O'Rahilly, a Cumann na mBan organiser from Dublin, after which other branches were established across the county. According to Hoolan, the women did excellent work, such as caring for the needs of prisoners and their dependants. They also carried out intelligence work and delivered despatches right up to the truce in 1921.

* * *

James Leahy was Commandant of the No 2 (Mid-Tipperary) Brigade. From his statement, it is clear that his republican views originated from time he spent in the employ of a man called Michael 'Mixey' O'Connell, a businessman and a prominent Sinn Féin and Irish Volunteers member in Thurles. O'Connell's house, in which Leahy resided, became the headquarters of the Mid-Tipperary Brigade.

In an extensive statement submitted in 1956, Leahy detailed his activities during the revolutionary era, showing that life for him and other active republicans in Tipperary in 1918 and 1919 was fraught with all kinds of danger. Leahy joined the re-established Volunteers in Thurles in 1915, and was inducted into the IRB in February 1916 by a man called Jimmie Kennedy, the Thurles Town Clerk.

Leahy recalled the funeral of Thomas Ashe in September 1917, which he attended as a member of the graveside honour guard. The following day, he participated in a parade in Thurles and again wore his Volunteers uniform. A week later, he was arrested and put on trial, charged with illegal drilling and wearing a military uniform. He was given a six-month sentence, to be served in Mountjoy Jail. In prison he went on hunger strike with other prisoners. He was eventually released under the 'Cat and Mouse Act', meaning he could be called upon at any time to serve the remainder of his sentence.

That call came in March 1918, just prior to the conscription crisis, when the local Head Constable arrived in the shop where Leahy was working and informed him that he was being re-arrested under the Cat and Mouse Act. Leahy asked permission to go upstairs and inform his employer, Michael O'Connell:

My boss was in bed at the time the policemen called and I requested permission to be allowed to go upstairs to tell him that I was being sent back to jail. The Head Constable agreed to this, but sent one of the police upstairs with me. As we were coming back into the shop I opened the door at the foot of the stairs and held it open to enable my guard go into the shop in front of me. He did so and I banged the door after him and dashed out the back door which I slammed after me. I ran as fast as I could towards the bridge which crosses the River Suir in the town, pursued by the police. On reaching the bridge I ran down the Mall and from there I jumped into the river to get across to the college grounds. The police in the meantime had divided their forces, the Head Constable kept on my tracks, two others got into the college grounds, while the fourth man was dispatched to the barracks for reinforcements. As I was halfway across the river I saw the two policemen waiting to receive me on the college side and I then turned back again towards the Mall. By this time, news of the chase had spread through the town and a crowd of about 30 had gathered on the Mall side of the river. They were mostly Volunteers among them being Jack Feehan, one of the captains of the Thurles companies. The crowd held up the Head Constable and Feehan handed me a bike which he had. I quickly mounted the machine and rode off into the country.

He took refuge in Tuohy's of Cabra, where, he said, 'I got a change of clothes and sat down to a good meal which I was able to enjoy as I watched the police on bikes setting out for my home in Tubberdorra.'

Leahy recalled a shooting that took place early in the summer of 1918. Tom Meagher of Annfield was sent with a despatch to Liam Manahan, the then-Commanding Officer of the Galtee Battalion. When he approached the village of Drumbane on his bicycle, he ran into a mixed party of RIC men and soldiers, under the command of District Inspector Hunt. Meagher was called upon to stop, but he failed to do so and was fired on and hit in the arm.

Managing to keep control of his bicycle, he made his way around a bend and up a laneway to the farmhouse belonging to Michael Dwyer.

He discarded the bicycle and ran into the house, where a number of people had gathered to hear a special Mass being celebrated by Father O'Donoghue, the local priest. He noticed Meagher was in an agitated state and stopped the ceremony in order to help him out a window to the back of the house, from where he made his way across the fields to the home of Michael Flynn, four miles away. He remained there for five days, having his wounds treated by Dr Barry from Thurles, before returning home.

The latter months of 1918 saw the Brigade in need of arms and ammunition, which necessitated raids on big houses in the area and the seizure of guns, whether the occupiers cooperated or not. Leahy and his comrades also raided the two hardware shops in Thurles, taking possession of their shotguns and ammunition. Many of the staff working in those businesses were Volunteers, so it wasn't difficult to gain entry to them on a designated Sunday night. Twenty-two guns and a vast amount of ammunition were taken, and transported to a safe hiding place by horse and cart.

Soon after the general election in December 1918, Leahy was again arrested after a raid on the Meagher family homestead in Annfield, where he was staying, and brought to Belfast jail. He remained there until his release in the first week of June 1919.

Not long after Leahy returned to Thurles, his employer and mentor, Michael O'Connell, was arrested, implicated in the rescue of Sean Hogan at Knocklong. The following day, Leahy stated that a number of his Brigade comrades approached him with a plan to assassinate District Inspector Hunt of the RIC in Thurles. Leahy recalled that Hunt 'had for some time previously been very hostile towards the Volunteers and Sinn Féin supporters and led numerous raids and baton charges in the town'.

Leahy agreed to the plan, which was to be carried out the next day when Hunt was due to attend the Thurles races, and recalled:

It was not found possible to get a suitable chance while he was on the racecourse, but the three men who had been trailing him kept on his tracks on the way back to town.

Hunt was walking along the road in company with a couple of other policemen and, just as he reached the entrance to the Square he was fired at and shot dead. The other policemen took to their heels towards the barracks.

That evening, the police, fuelled by alcohol, ran amok in the town, beating up anyone they could find. Leahy, working behind the bar in O'Connell's, remembered the evening clearly. He served the Head Constable, an elderly and decent man who had no truck with the mayhem his colleagues were causing around the town. Martial law was declared in the town, and fairs, markets and sports events were banned. Police numbers were increased in Thurles, leading to heightened tension in the community.

O'Connell's business became an even greater place of suspicion for the police and, in early November 1919, a number of active republicans were arrested. O'Connell's premises were surrounded by the police and Leahy, who had been out of the shop, saw the commotion as he returned to it. Not wishing to go back to jail, he slipped away and once again went 'on the run', though he secretly returned to his place of work and residence on numerous occasions during that time.

Like his comrades in the republican movement, James Leahy's experiences in 1918 and 1919 served only to galvanise his determination to secure his country's independence. Life for Volunteers on active service in Tipperary had, by that time, become fraught with danger and tension. As every day passed, they were forced to look over their shoulders and take precautions to preserve their liberty and often their lives.

Chapter 8

Ambushes and Attacks in the Rebel County

When, with the other prisoners from Macroom who had been arrested after Easter Week, I was released from Frongoch Internment Camp, we arranged with other Cork prisoners, who were released at the same time, to hold a meeting in Macroom on the date of the annual sports meeting there, about mid-August 1916. The meeting, which was held in Regan's licenced premises, was attended by representatives from practically every Volunteer unit in Cork city and county. This was, I think, the first reorganisation meeting held anywhere following Easter Week. At this meeting it was decided to set about reorganising the Volunteers immediately.

(Daniel Corkery)

There has long been a tradition of defiance in the 'Rebel County', and it was no surprise that it should take the lead in Ireland's War of Independence. Across the county, the activities of the IRA from the early months of 1919 to the calling of the truce in July 1921 became legendary in their own right.

Quite a number of statements were provided to the Bureau of Military History by men and women from all over County Cork. Their recollections provide us with a wonderful tapestry of stories and anecdotes from a tumultuous time which brought out the best in so many people in terms of their bravery as well as their commitment to the cause of Ireland's independence. It is clear from these statements that the fighting men were aided by thousands of civilians –

those who, for whatever reason, were unable to participate in the fighting, but were eager to play their part in the struggle.

Daniel Corkery was Commanding Officer of the Macroom Battalion and later a member of Dáil Éireann and the Seanad. He was initially elected to Dáil Éireann as a Sinn Féin candidate, before sitting as an anti-treaty deputy and eventually as a member of Fianna Fáil. It is evident from his recollections that the IRA was very active in the town and its hinterland. After the first reorganisation meeting in Macroom, those present returned to their own areas and began to establish Volunteer units. Corkery recalled that in the Macroom area, he and his comrades 'organised units in Clondrohid, Ballinagree, Kilnamartyra, Kilmurry and Macroom'. All of these units, he said, 'had been organised before the end of 1916. All sections drilled in secret and recruiting was intensified as the year 1917 advanced.'

In a detailed statement, Corkery said that he and his men were watching for every opportunity to strike at the enemy. On numerous occasions, for one reason or another, the best-laid plans failed to come to fruition, but they also experienced good days when they successfully struck at the heart of the Crown forces.

During 1917, the Macroom company carried out arms raids in the area, seizing several shotguns. Other guns were willingly handed over by people who sympathised with the republican cause.

Eamon de Valera visited Macroom in December 1917 as part of a country-wide tour, and Corkery recalled how he and his men organised:

> … a big parade of all units in the district. The strength of the Volunteers organisation in the area was revealed by this parade and attracted a great deal of attention. As a result the interest of young men in other districts was aroused, and units varying in strength from 20–50 were organised in Kilmichael, Inchigeela, Ballyvourney, and Coolea within weeks.

As in other areas across the country, the conscription crisis in early 1918 brought an influx of men into the Volunteers in the Macroom district, and Corkery recalled how he had to find arms and ammunition for them. Every available weapon in the area, he said:

... was taken over by the Volunteers; pikes were fashioned, in the local forges, cannister bombs of various kinds were improvised, gunpowder and buckshot were manufactured. In addition, all units were involved in organising the general public for the coming fight.

In July 1918, an aeríocht (feis) was held in Ballyvourney, and a number of RIC men from Ballingeary attended. Corkery recalled that:

The RIC men were attacked on their way back to the barracks by some men from Ballyvourney, Reinaree and Ballingeary companies. Their arms were seized. As a result of this attack, Martial Law was proclaimed in the Macroom district. This was the first time that Martial Law was proclaimed in Ireland.

By the middle of 1919, Corkery was travelling full-time around the county, attending to the organisation and training of his men. He was also closely involved in the work of the Brigade and Battalion Councils, and stated that all units in the county were engaged in the collection of the National Loan on behalf of Dáil Éireann.

On 7 September 1919, the Ballyvourney Battalion attacked a military patrol at a place known locally as the Slippery Rock, and they captured some arms and bicycles. Expecting a reprisal attack from the garrison stationed in nearby Macroom, Corkery assembled about sixty men, armed with shotguns, rifles and home-made bombs and took up strategic positions at various points around the town. They remained in position until dawn the following day, but there was no enemy activity and the IRA men returned to their homes.

Their next major engagement was an attack on Kilmurry RIC barracks, a somewhat isolated barracks about a quarter of a mile from Kilmurry, on the night of 3 January 1920. This involved about sixty men, all under Corkery's command. Corkery recalled:

About sixty men drawn from various companies took part in the attack which was unsuccessful. They were armed with shotguns, three or four rifles and cannister bombs. All men were in position around 11pm, when fire was opened on the building and several bombs were thrown at the door. The garrison returned fire and the shooting continued intermittently for two hours.

With little prospect of taking the building, Corkery decided to withdraw his men.

IRA activities intensified throughout 1920, and all company commanding officers were instructed to take every opportunity to launch attacks and ambushes on the RIC and the military. The Macroom men attacked a military transport squad at Mount Massey on 15 March, capturing a number of rifles. Also around Easter, three local RIC barracks were destroyed in an operation carried out by around 100 men.

On 1 June, Blarney RIC barracks was attacked, and on 9 June, an attack was carried out on Carrigadrohid RIC barracks. A large force was mobilised from various companies in the battalion area to participate in this attack. All roads in the area were blocked to prevent the arrival of any military assistance from the nearby garrison towns of Ballincollig and Macroom.

The main attacking party managed to get on to the roof of the barracks through the Post Office next door. They then smashed their way in through the roof and poured paraffin around in order to set the building on fire, in the hope it would force the RIC men to evacuate. Corkery recalled:

We had now been attacking the barrack for about two hours, and the fire which we had succeeded in starting in the upper floor did not appear to be making much progress. We now collected some blankets and other bed clothes in the post office, and having soaked them in the remainder of the paraffin, we pushed them through the hole in the roof of the barrack. We then set them on fire, and in a few minutes the upper floor of the building appeared to be burning fiercely.

The garrison was called on to surrender, but no reply was forthcoming, though the shooting did subside. The Volunteers withdrew at daylight, fearful that military reinforcements might arrive. Corkery and a handful of his men remained for a while, hoping the RIC men inside would surrender as the building continued to burn. With no sign of a surrender, he called off the engagement. He later learned that the garrison did eventually evacuate the building and made their way to Macroom.

On 21 August 1920, the Kilmurry Company, in co-operation with men from Macroom, took up ambush positions early in the morning at Lissarda, about six miles from Macroom on the main road to Cork. They planned to attack a military convoy that had been passing the road regularly for some time. However, the convoy failed to appear and the men withdrew that evening. The next day, a lorry carrying RIC and Black and Tans did pass through the area on the way to Macroom. News of the convoy was relayed to Corkery and he ordered 'all available men from the Kilmurry and Crookstown areas to mobilise immediately and report to the ambush position which they had occupied the previous day'.

Corkery recalled:

Only some of the men had taken up positions – mainly south of the road – when the enemy lorry drove into the ambush from the west (Macroom). It was halted by a cart which had been pushed across the road by William Powell. Fire was opened on the occupants, who immediately jumped from the lorry and took cover behind a roadside fence north of the road. The exchange of fire continued for an hour after which the IRA party south of the road were forced to withdraw. They had sustained one fatal casualty (Mick Galvin) and one wounded (Dan O'Leary). The enemy casualties were never definitely established, but it was said that two RIC men had been killed and a number wounded.

Galvin, a married man with children, was a company quartermaster and a fine representation of the men of the IRA during that era. Many such volunteers who gave their lives in the War of Independence would not be recognised nationally, but are still remembered in their own locality, often by a commemorative headstone or monument.

Corkery noted that the presence of men from his flying column in various company areas helped to boost the morale of the people. The men regularly mobilised into small parties and took up ambush positions in the hope of engaging small enemy convoys that might happen to enter the district. Great patience was required by the men of the column.

Corkery gave an example of that virtue, describing how a small party of his men together with half a dozen local fighting men took up a position at Caum, about three miles from Macroom, on 16 March 1921. They were deployed to ambush an RIC patrol but, despite waiting in position from midday to darkness, no patrol appeared. However, some weeks later, near the end of the first week in April, the same party occupied the same position and ambushed an RIC patrol, which was accompanied by some Black and Tans. In the firefight, one Tan was killed and his revolver was captured with some ammunition.

About three weeks later, on 20 April 1921, three members of the column and three locals from the Macroom company, all armed with revolvers, ambushed a party of Auxiliaries at Glen Gate, Macroom. One Auxiliary was shot dead and his revolver and ammunition was taken. On the same day, a lorry carrying a number of military personnel was attacked at Coolcower on the Macroom to Bandon road, but the enemy managed to escape.

Denis Lordan was Quartermaster of the 3rd West Cork Brigade from 1919 to 1921. One of the more interesting incidents recounted in Lordan's statement revolved around an agrarian dispute that not only divided a community, but also spilled over into the struggle for independence.

Kilbrittain Castle and its grounds were bought in 1918, by a company trading as Doyle and Riordan, operating out of Cork city. The grounds were well-wooded and the new owners began to extract the timber, employing a number of local men to carry out the work. Previous to the purchase of the estate, a number of families in Kilbrittain village had rented parcels of the land on a yearly basis for tilling and grazing and, as Lordan pointed out, for those people this was their sole source of income. When the lease renewal date arrived in 1919, a local man, John O'Brien, offered a higher rent for the whole parcel of land and the traditional renters lost out.

There was much resentment in the local area, as the unsavoury incident reminded Lordan and others of the old-style land grabbing of previous decades and centuries. Most of the smallholders concerned were supporters of Sinn Féin, and many of the leasing families had members in the Volunteers. Attempts to broker an agreement to protect the traditional leaseholders were unsuccessful, and it was decided that action needed to be taken.

A boycott was declared – all those working on the estate in connection with the tree felling were to cease work. A number of men continued working on the estate, however, and one day, a steam tractor used to transport timber to Bandon was fired on and one of the workers was wounded.

Doyle and Riordan now applied to the British authorities for police protection. This, of course, changed the dynamics of the situation. With the British armed forces now involved, the local IRA unit decided to step into the controversy.

One night, all the horses belonging to Doyle and Riordan on the estate, as well as a number of cattle belonging to John O'Brien, were driven off, and several tonnes of timber ready for loading on to a ship at Burrin Pier were thrown into the sea. A detachment of British soldiers was sent to occupy Kilbrittain Castle after the incident, with orders to protect the men still working for Doyle and Riordan.

Doyle and Riordan and John O'Brien received heavy compensation from the British authorities for the loss of the timber and cattle. Lordan recalled the compensation amount was levied on the people of the district.

In the weeks after this incident, it was noticed that a convoy of soldiers, accompanied by an RIC man as a guide, went each night to Burrin Pier from Kilbrittain Castle. Lordan and his local IRA unit made plans to attack them. He recalled:

> ... that after careful scouting a British patrol was attacked on the night of 28 June 1919 and, without the use of firearms, we successfully disarmed the soldiers and left them bound together at the side of the road.

A Brigade officer meeting was held in the Kilbrittain Castle area on 17 January 1921, during which a series of operations were planned. The following night, Brigade Commanding Officer Charlie Hurley, Brigade Adjutant Liam Deasy and Column Commanding Officer Tom Barry reconnoitred the locality to select the best position for ambushing a military patrol. Lordan recalled the situation his comrades were drawn into that night, saying that they:

> ... carried rifles, bandoliers and revolvers and wore the usual column trench coats. At a point on the Dunmanway–Bandon road near Pallas-Ann the above mentioned officers came across an individual who apparently was waiting on the roadside for someone. On seeing them this man approached and on being questioned by the Officer Commanding the Column it became evident that he mistook the party for British Auxiliaries for whom he apparently had been waiting. He started to give information in connection with the movement of certain IRA Officers and of the times and places where they could be most easily captured, and promised further information and assistance in return for money.

At that stage the Brigade Adjutant who was known to the individual was brought over as if he was a prisoner and as soon as the spy recognised him, he suggested that he, the Brigade Adjutant should be shot at once. The spy was probably prompted to this suggestion by fear of the Brigade Adjutant escaping from what he thought were his captors and of his [the spy] being recognised by the Adjutant again. At this stage the spy was informed that he was under arrest.

The spy in question was Michael (or Denis) Dwyer, an ex-British soldier, and the following day he was court-martialled and sentenced to death. A priest was summoned to administer spiritual aid before Dwyer was shot. Lordan recalled that 'his body was left on the roadside at Farranalough near Bandon with a label pinned to his clothes bearing the words "convicted spy"'.

After the execution, the area, which had continuously been subjected to intensive raids whenever IRA officers were in the vicinity, was rarely if ever visited again. Spies were dealt with in an unforgiving and ruthless manner in Cork throughout the independence conflict. A research study of some years ago headed by Dr Andy Bielenberg, a senior lecturer in University College Cork, suggests that around eighty spies or informers were executed by the IRA during 1920 and 1921.

* * *

The statement of William Regan, Vice-Brigadier of the 2nd Cork Brigade and Commanding Officer of the Doneraile Company, highlights the bravery and determination of the witness and his comrades in the Doneraile area. Regan recalled the formation of the Brigade column in September 1920. Its first operation was to be an attack on an enemy convoy travelling along the Cork–Mallow road. However, plans were hastily changed when, on the basis of intelligence received, it was decided instead to attempt a capture of the Mallow military barracks.

Just before dawn on the morning of 28 September, the column, with the help of some men from the Mallow Battalion, entered the town. They took up positions in the Town Hall, waiting until it was time to move out and start the attack on the barracks at 9am. Regan was aide-de-camp to Liam Lynch, Commanding Officer of the 2nd Cork Brigade, for the duration of the operation. Two of their comrades, Dick Willis and Jackie Bolster, were already in the barracks, being conveniently employed there. Another comrade, Paddy McCarthy, was also in the barracks, posing as the representative of a building contractor supposedly measuring for an upcoming job.

Ernie O'Malley approached the gate with a letter he wished to have delivered and, while it was being examined by the officer in charge, he rushed the gate, aided by Paddy O'Brien and John O'Brien. They were then followed by Liam Lynch and Regan and the rest of the raiding party. Quickly capturing the barracks, the stores were raided. A cache of lances, saddlery, bandoliers, twenty-seven rifles, two Hotch-kiss guns, a revolver and thousands of ammunition rounds were spirited away in three cars. An attempt was made to set the barracks on fire, but it failed and the whole column departed for the relative safety of Burnfort. The raiding party suffered no casualties in the attack, but one member of the garrison, a Sergeant Gibbs, was killed.

* * *

Patrick O'Brien of Ballineen in Cork was an Adjutant in the 10th (Dunmanway) Battalion of the Cork Brigade, and a member of Tom Barry's flying column, which carried out the famous ambush at Kilmichael in November 1920. His statement recalled in great detail that infamous event, which rocked the British establishment and became an integral part of the folklore that now surrounds the independence conflict. O'Brien recalled:

> We had Father O'Connell that Saturday night from Enniskeane to give us General Absolution. We left about 5 in the morning and we were North at the ambush site about 8. The Column was divided up then into two parts, one each at the two positions selected to deal with the two lorries. Michael McCarthy in charge of one, and Tom Barry in charge of the other.

Every man was placed in his position and they settled down to wait for the enemy. *The Auxiliaries in two tenders came along about four o'clock. The driver of the leading one was shot and this tender stopped immediately. Firing had started when*

Barry threw a Mills bomb and it landed definitely into the tender. Barry's section jumped out on the road and immediately rushed the tender. As well as the driver, two Auxiliaries in the back were killed, four others had taken cover underneath, two more were lying wounded on the road. Barry rushed on to the second tender where firing was going on, and where three of our men had been shot, one killed outright and two seriously wounded.

The aftermath of the ambush was a grim scene, with dead and dying scattered across the area. Sixteen Auxiliaries died in the ambush, while only two of their number survived the fight. One, HF Forde, was badly injured and left for dead, with a bullet to his head among other injuries. He was found the following day by British forces and brought to hospital in Cork. He survived his injuries, but continued to live with brain damage, and it was reported that he received monetary compensation. The other surviving Auxiliary, Cecil Guthrie, though badly wounded, managed to escape. Reports suggest Guthrie asked for help at a local house, which, unbeknownst to him, was occupied by two IRA Volunteers. They promptly shot him dead with his own gun.

Three of O'Brien's comrades – Tim Sullivan, Michael McCarthy and Pat Deasy, who was only sixteen years old – lost their lives in the encounter and were temporarily buried by members of the local IRA company. Deasy was not part of the original column, but he followed it to Kilmichael, hoping to be allowed to participate in any action. Because he refused to leave before the ambush began, Barry relented and allowed him to stay on.

After the ambush, the column moved off, laden down with captured arms and ammunition as well as their own gear. They eventually settled down at a camp at Granure. There they slept on beds of straw and requisitioned bed clothing. They were fed hot meals by the women of Cumann na mBan before moving on.

Tom Barry took ill in a safe house near Ahiohill a week later and O'Brien sent for a local doctor called Fehily, who gave him two injections. O'Brien stayed with Barry for two days before moving him on the night of 7 December. He was helped by Cumann na mBan member Mary O'Neill, a trained nurse, and they took him to her house in Shanaway.

Two days later, he was moved again by O'Brien and O'Neill. With the road well scouted in advance, they took him in a pony and trap to Reardon's of Granure. At Granure, Bebe Lordan took over nursing duties. She and her brother took Barry to a house at Newcestown, from where he was spirited to hospital in Cork city, where he made his recovery.

* * *

Patrick O'Brien recalled how anyone who openly sided with the Crown forces ran the risk of bringing trouble on themselves. He recounted that, in May 1920, eighty military arrived in Ballineen village, and took over the house of the local doctor. They were there as a result of a boycott in place against a local baker named Cotter. The baker, according to O'Brien, 'had made himself unpopular in the area by openly siding with the police against the local populace even to the point of accompanying them on their patrols and raids'.

Cotter's business was boycotted, but he persisted in making his deliveries. His van was stopped one day and his horse was shot, while on other occasions, the roads were deliberately blocked to prevent his bread being delivered.

O'Brien also recalled the constant targeting of IRA men by Crown forces. They were frequently arrested and interrogated. In July 1920, two of his comrades, Tom Hales and Pat Harte, were arrested and brought to Bandon barracks for interrogation. They were firstly struck with rifles and Harte was knocked unconscious. O'Brien maintained Harte never recovered from the blow and his brain was permanently damaged. The military also 'used pincers on them and brutally extracted their fingernails in their attempts to get both men to give up information'.

They were taken to a military hospital in Cork, where they were kept for eight weeks. While there, they were charged with possession of a revolver, ten rounds of ammunition and a copy of the IRB Constitution. This was a fabrication, as neither of the men had any of those items in their possession when they were arrested. Harte, who was the Brigade Quartermaster, did have £100 in his possession, which was confiscated. After the trial, they were moved to Pentonville Prison in England.

Pat Harte never recovered his health and, according to O'Brien, died some years later in a mental hospital. Tom Hales went on to oppose the Anglo-Irish Treaty and fought with the 'Irregulars' in the Civil War. His brother Sean supported the treaty and was elected to Dáil Éireann. He was assassinated in Dublin on 7 December 1922, by a member of the anti-Treaty IRA.

Patrick O'Brien recalled an incident in October 1920 when Timothy Warren, Commanding Officer of the Ballineen Company, and Jack Hennessy, also of Ballineen, were arrested around four o'clock one morning by members of the Essex Regiment. They were taken to the Ballineen Bridge and severely beaten. When they were completely unconscious, they were both hung over the bridge by their legs, before eventually being released. Both men had no option then but to join Tom Barry's flying column and go 'on the run'.

There was a constant need to find arms, and to supplement those acquired through raids and ambushes, an Arms Fund was set up. This took the form of a levy on all householders in an area. The amount to be paid was based on a valuation of property, and if the householders refused to pay the amount due, cattle were seized and sold at fairs, with the proceeds going into the fund. O'Brien recalled in October 1920, the fund amounted to £2,400, not including money received for the sale of any cattle.

O'Brien recalled a raid on a house in Manch, where he and some of his comrades acquired British officers' uniforms and equipment for making buckshot. They also raided a house owned by a family called Cox in Carrigmore, where two of the sons in the house, British officers, were staying while on leave. Their father was an ex-RIC Sergeant. O'Brien and his comrades had to fire through a window to get in, and they eventually managed to take two revolvers.

O'Brien also recalled a raid on Kilcaskin Castle where they seized two trunks containing property belonging to a Colonel Kirkwood and a Captain Wilmer, the son-in-law of the owner. Both men were staying in the Castle at the time while on leave. The haul included one revolver and a .38 automatic, as well as a Volunteers officer's uniform, complete with a belt and revolver holster. Though it was never discovered why a British officer would have such a uniform among his belongings, this was subsequently worn by Tom Barry during the whole west Cork campaign.

There is little question that the fighting men of Cork led the way in the independence struggle and their actions inspired many others across the country to take up the fight against the forces of the Crown. The incidents recounted here are but a small sample of the many recorded in the archive, but they are a fine testament to everyone in the 'rebel county' who participated in the struggle for Ireland's independence.

Chapter 9

The Brave Republican Women

Easter Sunday, April 23rd, 1916. We mobilised to parade at Mount Street. Waited there for further orders. We were dismissed to attend at 6 Harcourt Street. We waited there for some time and there were all sorts of rumours about. Finally, our Commandant dismissed us with orders to be ready for a further mobilisation and not to leave the city during the weekend.

(Rose McNamara)

While women like Constance Markievicz and Elizabeth O'Farrell are often celebrated as the public female faces of the Rising, there were many others whose bravery and determination has largely gone unsung. We are now in a position to recognise the contributions made by many women to the Rising because of statements they made under Oscar Traynor's initiative. It is clear from their statements that they contributed in no small way to a rebellion which profoundly impacted on the lives of all Irish women.

Kitty O'Doherty was Quartermaster for Cumann na mBan in Dublin during 1916, as well as acting as a courier whenever called upon by the Rising's leaders. According to her testimony, O'Doherty was given some indication that the Rising was imminent three weeks before the event by Thomas MacDonagh. She stated that he told her: 'Within three weeks we will have a stir'. Kitty O'Doherty's house was a welcoming place for many prominent republicans, such as MacDonagh, Seán MacDermott and PH Pearse. She was very fond of Pearse, whom she labelled a 'dreamer' but who lacked the finance to see his dreams come true.

During the early months of 1916, Kitty O'Doherty housed and looked after men who arrived from Glasgow and Liverpool to fight in the Rising. She recalled:

> *Instructions were given by Seán MacDermott to get groceries for these men in the flat, from Farrell's in Dorset Street. Bulmer Hobson came on Friday evenings to check the accounts. I met him there and showed him the dockets for the different things I got. He paid the bills.*

O'Doherty recounted how she witnessed a large cheque arriving from Joe McGarrity, a leading Irish-American activist in Philadelphia, into the Irish Volunteers headquarters for the purchase of arms. She also recalled how Clan na Gael in America arranged for gold sovereigns in small tin canisters to be brought into the country by men working on the transatlantic ships. The issue of finance was always a live one and O'Doherty regularly collected donations from a list of supporters provided to her by Seán MacDermott.

Cumann na mBan put on concerts to raise funds, and on one occasion, MacDermott gave O'Doherty the takings and said: 'I want you to go to the Junior Army and Navy Stores in D'Olier Street, and buy all the Army blankets you can – also, basins and soaps. If you are caught, you don't belong to me.'

O'Doherty was asked on a number of occasions to retrieve guns and ammunition from safe houses that were about to be raided by the authorities. At one point, she and her husband were hiding 110 guns in their home at 32 Connaught Avenue.

Seán MacDermott introduced her to Michael Collins on the Wednesday before the Rising. He had been staying in a house on Rathdown Road since his return from England and, in order to maintain his cover, he was allowed by Donal O'Connor, a Chartered Accountant, to use his office on Westmoreland Street as a decoy to evade Castle personnel.

On Good Friday morning, Michael O'Hanrahan called to O'Doherty's house with a message from Eoin MacNeill, requiring her to report to the Volunteers headquarters in Dawson Street. On her way there, she stopped at Tom Clarke's shop, and Clarke told her to 'report back to him what MacNeill wanted her for'.

When she arrived at the Volunteers headquarters, MacNeill asked her to take charge of all of his personal papers and keep them safe until they were called for in the future.

That afternoon, O'Doherty went to Liberty Hall, where an excited Constance Markievicz showed off her new military uniform. Markievicz brought O'Doherty in to see James Connolly, who was printing copies of the proclamation. On Holy Saturday, O'Doherty made a number of trips to Lawler's of Fownes Street to purchase webbing and water bottles. At that stage, she believed plans for the Rising were going well, because 'during the day various people came looking for arms, ammunition and equipment'.

Late on Holy Saturday night, O'Doherty's husband was asked by Seán Mac-Dermott to collect Padraig Pearse from Sean T O'Kelly's house and take him to a meeting in Hardwicke Street, which went on for some time.

O'Doherty recalled the confusion which prevailed on Easter Sunday and how it impacted on her home, as men came and went all day. Michael O'Hanrahan, who was destined to be executed, turned up, as did Michael Staines, and O'Doherty spent her day cooking meals for the men. On the Monday, other Volunteers arrived, either bringing foodstuffs or picking up tools.

Claire Gregan arrived to pick up MacNeill's private papers, which O'Doherty had hidden. Gregan, who was engaged to Bulmer Hobson, a prominent member of the Irish Republican Brotherhood, was in tears because she could not locate him. It seems that on Monday, 17 April 1916, a meeting of the Military Council convened to put the finishing touches to plans for the Rising. They also discussed Hobson, who, for some years, had been close to Tom Clarke and Seán MacDermott, and the possibility that he might hinder their plans. The previous evening, Hobson had given an impromptu speech at a Cumann na mBan concert. He had warned the audience of the real danger of being drawn into a rebellion, saying that no man had the right to put at risk the future of a country just so that he could carve out for himself a place in that country's history.

Hobson discovered the plans for a rising on Holy Thursday and he and MacNeill confronted Pearse over the famous Castle Document, which claimed the leaders of the Volunteers were about to be arrested. The document, almost certainly forged by Pearse and MacDermott, was designed to bring the Volunteers on board for the Rising, but the ruse was discovered by Hobson. When he and MacNeill confronted Pearse over the matter, he readily confirmed that plans for the Rising on Easter Sunday were well in hand. Knowing that Hobson had knowledge of the Rising, the Military Council decided to act against him to prevent him from attempting to stop it.

In his book *Easter 1916*, Charles Townshend claims that on the orders of MacDermott and the Military Council, Hobson was abducted by some of his colleagues on the Leinster Executive of the IRB. He was brought from Volunteer Headquarters in Dawson Street in Dublin to the home of Martin Conlon, another IRB man. At the house in Cabra Park, Phibsboro, he was met by four or five men, who produced guns and told him he was under arrest. Hobson later recalled in a 1961 *Irish Times* interview that he 'laughed and said, "You are a lot of damn fools." There was nothing I could do, so I sat back and accepted the situation. I felt I had done my best to stop the rising.'

Famously, Hobson was released by Sean T O'Kelly, having been held in captivity for a number of days on the orders of the Military Council. When invited by O'Kelly to join the Rising, he refused and went home.

The rest of the week was uneventful around the O'Doherty residence, but she did recall how her neighbours opened their doors to British soldiers and offered them tea and food. On Thursday, she left with her children to stay with her brother, a priest, in Kinnegad. However, her involvement in the republican movement continued after the Rising, as she played a leading role in looking after the financial welfare of the prisoners' dependents as well as the dependents of those killed in the conflict.

* * *

Another remarkable woman involved in the Rising was Dr Kathleen Lynn, who was posted to the Dublin Castle Garrison of the Citizen Army under the command of Sean Connolly. Lynn, the daughter of a clergyman, came from a family with no tradition of republicanism, so it was surprising that she should take an active role in the Easter Rising.

Kathleen Lynn trained as a medical student at the Royal University and later at the College of Surgeons, where she eventually took a fellowship. She converted to the republican ideal around 1912, mainly as a result of her friendship with Helena Moloney, Madeleine ffrench-Mullen – her closest friend – and Constance Markievicz, who she described as 'a grand soul and a fanatic but of sound sense and practical'.

Lynn was an avid supporter of the Women's Suffrage Movement. When the Irish Citizen Army was founded in 1913, she agreed to give First Aid lectures in Liberty Hall, as well as to members of Cumann na mBan at their headquarters in Harcourt Street. All of the women, according to Lynn, were aware in the weeks leading up to the Rising that something very important was about to happen, but they were unaware of the exact date on which it was to take place.

On occasion during the weeks prior to the Rising, Lynn took James Connolly and some other Citizen Army men out in her car on reconnaissance trips around Dublin. She recalled:

One night during Holy Week I went out with the car to St Enda's and there they loaded it up with ammunition and put some theatrical stuff on top of it, hoping to get through. Willie Pearse and I brought it in and landed it safely in Liberty Hall where there were many hands willing to unload it.

She also recalled arms being brought from Belfast and hidden behind her house. Volunteers arrived on Easter Saturday night to collect them, and she commented that none of her neighbours had any idea about the activities going on in their neighbourhood.

Lynn recalled being presented with a brooch by James Connolly and members of the Citizen Army on Holy Thursday in recognition of her work with the organisation and she also received a presentation from Cumann na mBan.

By Easter Saturday, tension was high in Dublin and Lynn and her Citizen Army colleagues were sure that something was about to happen, but they all felt it was their duty to maintain secrecy. She was told by James Connolly to report early to Liberty Hall on Easter Sunday, and she duly arrived there around 10am. Lynn recalled how she and other Citizen Army people 'tried to busy themselves as they waited for orders from their leaders all of whom looked stressed as they scurried about'.

With plans suspended until the following day, Connolly sent Lynn to stay with Jenny Wyse-Power in the hope that she 'would get a good night's sleep'. Sleep did not come, as she wondered what might unfold the following day.

On Easter Monday, Captain Kathleen Lynn received her orders, signed by Michael Mallin. She was to accompany the garrison ordered to take over City Hall, with a view to eventually storming Dublin Castle. A very enthusiastic and excited Constance Markievicz joined Lynn on the journey to City Hall in Lynn's car, carrying medical supplies and equipment. Markievicz was ordered to keep the car so that she could make inspection tours of rebel positions across the city. However, when she reached St Stephen's Green, she abandoned Lynn's car and stayed with Mallin's garrison, ending up in the College of Surgeons. It would be some months before Kathleen was reunited with her car.

City Hall was taken easily by the rebels. On arriving there, Lynn saw the body of a policeman, later identified as Constable James O'Brien, lying beside the nearby Dublin Castle gate. Once in City Hall, she was ordered up to the roof by Sean Connolly, where she was joined by Helena Moloney together with five or six men. She recalled:

> It was a beautiful day the sun was hot and we were not long there when we noticed Sean Connolly coming towards us, walking upright, although he had been advised to crouch and take cover as much as possible. We suddenly saw him mortally wounded by a sniper's bullet from the Castle. First aid was useless. He died almost immediately.

A young boy was later wounded in the shoulder, which necessitated treatment by Dr Lynn. The British Army arrived in the afternoon and managed to enter the Castle without any opposition. They opened fire on the rebels occupying City Hall, which continued until after dark. There was no way for the rebels to escape, especially after the electricity in the building failed.

Eventually, the British entered City Hall. Seeing Dr Lynn tending to the wounded, they assumed she had just arrived, only to be quickly informed by the brave doctor that she was part of the Citizen Army garrison.

Dr Kathleen Lynn and her Citizen Army comrades were marched through the Castle Yard to Ship Street Barracks. She was later transferred, along with other republican women, to Kilmainham gaol and on to Mountjoy jail, before being eventually deported to England.

Once back in Ireland, some months later, Kathleen Lynn continued to play a role in politics. She was elected to Dáil Éireann in 1923, though like her Sinn Féin colleagues, she refused to take her seat. She is probably best known in her later years for her work in St Ultan's Children's Hospital, which she founded with other female activists in 1919. This was the only hospital in the country run entirely by females.

* * *

Rose McNamara was a member of Inghinidhe na hÉireann, a radical Irish nationalist women's organisation founded by Maud Gonne, since 1906, and Vice-Commandant of Cumann na mBan in 1916. Prior to the Easter Rising, McNamara was very much involved in helping the poor of Dublin, sewing clothes for them and arranging meals for schoolchildren. She took part in an organised demonstration against the visit of King George and Queen Mary, distributing handbills denouncing English rule in Ireland. She recalled how her republican colleague Helena Moloney 'drew a stone from her pocket and aimed it so well she smashed one of the pictures. She was arrested shortly after, but we had all scattered by then.'

In 1914, Cumann na mBan was formed and subsumed Inghinidhe na hEireann, and McNamara recalled how they immediately began parading in public. One of their first public roles was participating in the funeral of O'Donovan Rossa in August 1915. In the months leading up to the Rising, she and her comrades made field dressings and organised collections to purchase arms and ammunition. They also learned and practised First Aid, and attended rifle practice under the stewardship of Constance Markievicz.

In her lengthy and very enlightening statement, McNamara recalled buying material for field dressings, which she and other Cumann na mBan women made at number 2 Dawson Street on Good Friday. They were anticipating some sort of news that day as tension mounted within republican circles. The following day,

Easter Saturday, McNamara said that she hadn't much to do, but in the evening she was given her instructions for Easter Sunday. She and her comrades were to mobilise at Mount Street during the morning and await further instructions, which never came. The women were dismissed and told to wait at number 6 Harcourt Street until further orders were issued. As the day progressed, it became obvious that nothing was going to happen. Eventually, they were told to return home, but not to leave the city and to prepare for a new mobilisation at 10am the next day.

That mobilisation took place at the Weavers' Hall in Cork Street. Twenty-five women turned up and marched to Emerald Square. Here they were given orders by Éamonn Ceannt to follow a group of Volunteers who had also mobilised in the Square. At noon, both groups marched to the Distillery in Marrowbone Lane, being used at the time as a fodder store by the British.

When they reached the Distillery, a Captain Murphy of the Volunteers knocked at the door and demanded that it be opened 'in the name of the Republic'. Some prisoners were taken, including the lodge keeper and a soldier. Four women taken as prisoners were later released, blindfolded, when darkness fell.

The Cumann na mBan women remained in the cellar all day, waiting for further orders. They heard the sounds of heavy fighting, which lasted until dark. McNamara recalled they only had one slight injury during the day, which was easily dealt with. A reinforcement detachment of sixty Volunteers arrived during the day, as well as two women who brought food. The Cumann na mBan women were divided into squads and posted close to the firing lines, where they lay on sacks of grain.

The following morning, McNamara and another woman got up early to prepare some sort of breakfast for the Volunteers. Some of the Volunteers in the Distillery held up Quinn's Bakery cart and took very welcome loaves of bread, and also commandeered two cans of milk from a passing cart. Two British army snipers were shot by Volunteers and some light firing continued until dark. Around 11pm, two clergymen arrived from Mount Argus to hear confessions, and McNamara recalled that 'all the women and some of the men availed of the opportunity to make their peace with God'.

The following day, Wednesday, the Volunteers took nineteen chickens from a passing messenger boy, which were cooked by the women for dinner. As they lacked kitchen utensils, the cooked chickens were extracted from the pots with bayonets, and a good meal was enjoyed by all. McNamara recalled Captain Murphy's wife joining the group that day. Again, there was light gunfire in the vicinity during the day. The women attempted to make the beds more comfortable and warmer, as it had become very cold.

Thursday saw one Volunteer, Mick Liston, suffer a graze on the forehead, and the wound was dressed by some of the women. Three live calves were captured that day and one was killed by a Volunteer, a butcher by trade, who prepared the meat for consumption. It became obvious to everyone on Thursday that the enemy was ratcheting up the assault on the rebels around the city, as the sound of machine gun fire increased dramatically.

McNamara recalled: 'I rose early on Friday morning with some other women and we fried veal cutlets for the men's breakfast.' Dinner that day consisted of meat and potatoes and, with more chickens procured, everyone was well fed. In the evening, Captain Murphy informed the company that the sounds they were hearing came from a British attack on the Four Courts. McNamara recalled she went up to the firing line and witnessed two British soldiers 'lying dead close by', and that their rifles had been taken by the Volunteers.

On Saturday, 29 April, a female spy was captured near the Canal around mid-afternoon and McNamara and some other girls were detailed to search her. Nothing was found and eventually the girl was released with a warning. During the evening, the company noticed fierce fires burning in the city centre. Captain Murphy sent out word for a priest to come in the following day to say Mass.

There was a general mobilisation at 2am on Sunday morning, but nothing serious happened and everyone went back to bed. The women were up early to cook breakfast, and McNamara recalled that 'everyone readied themselves to attend Mass but the priest did not show up'. Captain Murphy delivered a rousing speech during the morning and the men planned a singsong for that evening, to which the 'brave cailíní' were invited.

The singsong never happened, because at 4pm, the garrison received the devastating news of the surrender, which caused much consternation and anguish in the camp. McNamara recalled seeing a 'distraught McDonagh crying bitterly and refusing to accept the fight was over'. Con Colbert then appeared and ordered the women to go home, which they refused to do.

The Volunteers formed up and marched out the gate to St Patrick's Park and the Cumann na mBan women followed suit, singing heartily. They were encouraged to sing by McDonagh and Major John McBride, who told McNamara to 'sing away', reassuring her that 'you'll be alright' and 'you'll be out tomorrow'. She replied, 'and what about you?', meaning all the men. McBride sadly replied, 'Ah no. We won't be out. We'll be shot.'

During the march, the men gave their small arms to the women to conceal from the British. From the Park, they were marched under military escort to Richmond Barracks, where a Sergeant advised them to hand over their arms as they would be searched at their final destination, Kilmainham Gaol. On their way to Kilmainham, McNamara recalled that they were 'verbally abused by the British soldiers and the people of Dublin'. In the Gaol, they were searched and placed four to a cell and given soup, meat and dog biscuits.

On the following Tuesday, the women were woken by shots outside their windows as the executions got under way. McNamara recalled the women arranging a sixteen–hand reel during the day to raise their spirits. On Wednesday morning, she recalled: 'We were awoken by more shots and later that day we were questioned by British officers who were given no information by determined and loyal prisoners.'

On Saturday, the women were still in custody and were told to write home to request fresh clothes. That day, they had a visit from Father Albert of the Capuchin Friary and they also heard loud cheering coming from outside the prison gates. On Sunday, Mass was celebrated by Father McCarthy from James's Street Church, attended by Éamonn Ceannt and Michael Mallin.

The following day, 8 May, the women were again awoken early by the sound of shooting. They heard a terrible moan and a shot, followed by silence. Four leaders of the Rising – Ceannt, Colbert, Mallin and Heuston – were shot that day, and the mood among the women was of despair. However, that night, the cell doors were opened and they were told of their impending release. Before they were allowed to leave, they were given a lecture by British officers and the prison Governor and told to behave themselves in the future. Most of the women remained in the Gaol until after breakfast for fear of leaving in the dark while martial law was still in force.

When Rose McNamara was released from prison, her commitment to the republican cause did not diminish. By December 1916, she was active in the republican movement again and came out to welcome home the prisoners released from Frongoch and elsewhere. In 1917, she actively participated in the reorganisation of Cumann na mBan and oversaw drilling and First Aid classes. She helped with the distribution of National Aid funds and took part in the anti-conscription campaign. When the War of Independence broke out in 1919, she and her Cumann na mBan comrades were on hand to help the IRA in any way they could in the conflict. During the Civil War, she took the side of the anti-treaty forces when fighting broke out in Dublin and offered her services in tending to the wounded.

Chapter 10

Father Aloysius: Chaplain to the Republican Heroes

As a priest, I am the minister, that is the servant of all classes – or perhaps rather I should say, I know no class, for every soul is equally precious. But my ministry has been chiefly cast amongst the working class of Dublin, and I am proud to think that I may call them my friends. I have always felt at home with them.

(Father Aloysius)

William Patrick Travers, otherwise known as Father Aloysius, was initially somewhat reticent about providing a statement, but in the end felt he had a duty to do so, in recognition of the bravery of the revolutionaries he had ministered to. Travers was born in Cork on 20 March 1870, into a devout Catholic family. He entered the Capuchin order in 1887, taking the name of Aloysius, and was ordained in 1894. His elder brother, John, was also a Capuchin and took the name of Anthony, while his sister became an Ursuline nun.

Father Aloysius promoted temperance and was President of the famous Father Matthew Hall between 1903 and 1913. In 1909, he inaugurated the Father Mathew Feis, designed to promote Gaelic culture. He spent his life championing the poor and the working class and was a firm advocate of buying Irish rather than imported goods. He was a friend of both James Connolly and the trade union leader Jim Larkin, and attended on them both prior to their deaths.

Father Aloysius began his statement with an account of a concert held in the Father Matthew Hall on Easter Sunday night. A large crowd attended and heard, among others, Ms Joan Burke, singing a spirited version of 'The Minstrel Boy'. He recalled that 'there was tension in the hall that evening as there had been rumours around the city during the day that something big was about to happen'.

It was well known that a planned Volunteers parade had been cancelled and Father Aloysius was of the opinion that some in the audience, as well as a few of the artists, had an inkling that a rebellion was about to break out. The following morning, Easter Monday, he was making his way over to Gloucester Street to say mass at the convent when he noticed some Fianna scouts on bicycles. He later saw Padraig Pearse and another young man cycling by. They did not recognise him, he said, 'but they seemed intent on reaching their destination'. He later realised Pearse's companion was his younger brother, Willie, and recalled having the feeling there was 'something in the air' and the day was set to be one of real consequence.

Around midday, Father Aloysius and his brethren in the Friary realised a rebellion had started. They had just sat down to lunch when news came that a little boy had been shot dead near the Father Matthew Hall. A wounded man was brought to the Friary, and about 1.30pm, barricades went up in Church Street, manned by the Volunteers.

The Father Matthew Feis was due to take place that very afternoon in the Hall and some competing children, who had arrived early, had to be sheltered under the stage until it was safe to let them home. Father Aloysius met an Australian man outside the Friary who happened to be visiting Dublin. He was a medical doctor and offered to tend to the wounded men who began arriving at the Friary.

In the evening, the gunfire became much more intense. Father Aloysius recalled that 'towards night volleys of firing became more frequent – and at midnight it became so violent it seemed to be at our very gates'.

The following morning, Tuesday, the sound of gunfire reached an even higher intensity. The Richmond Hospital requested that some of Father Aloysius's brother friars go to the wards and minister to the wounded. They did so, remaining at the hospital for the duration of the Rising.

The Volunteers took over the Father Matthew Hall and set up a temporary hospital, run by members of Cumann na mBan, who despatched the more obvious emergency cases to the Richmond Hospital. Rumours swirled around the city that the GPO and Dublin Castle had been taken over by the rebels. News also came through of the very sad death of Sean Connolly, the prominent Irish Citizen Army leader, shot by a British army sniper while he was on the roof of City Hall.

Father Aloysius recalled the Volunteers taking possession of newly built Corporation houses in Church Street on Wednesday and proceeding to protect the windows with sandbags. Wild rumours again circulated across the city that day, but Father Aloysius remembered it as one of the quieter days of the week, though the rifle and machine gun fire was continuous.

On Thursday, extensive fires were to be seen in the city and Father Aloysius and his fellow friars correctly speculated that they were in O'Connell Street, principally in the GPO. That day, the Volunteers took prisoners, mainly soldiers stationed in the Linenhall barracks, as well as a Dublin Metropolitan policeman, and put them to work filling sandbags in Father Matthew Hall.

Friday saw continuous gunfire, and large explosions were heard coming from the direction of the Bay. By then the friars, like many others, were having difficulties in obtaining provisions. The Volunteers were working very hard to source food to deliver to the Friary, while some fearless Fianna boys also attempted to source food supplies. That same day the friars were told about two young boys who had climbed to the top of the clock tower in the North Dublin Union, only to be shot dead by British Army snipers.

The gunfire continued through Friday night and into Saturday afternoon. Father Aloysius recalled the sounds of many explosions and he and those with him in the Friary saw many buildings on fire. The number of wounded men was increasing all the time and many were brought to the Father Matthew Hall. By four o'clock on Saturday afternoon, the British Army had reached the junction of King Street and Church Street and were firing on the Church Street barricades. Father Aloysius recalled the Cumann na mBan women in the Father Matthew Hall becoming very concerned for the wounded men in their care.

Desperation was setting in by this stage, and Father Aloysius recalled Father Augustine sending out Colonel Miceal O'Folghludha of the Volunteers with a white flag, in an effort secure the services of a doctor. Colonel O'Folghludha was detained by the military. A second man was then sent out under a white flag and a red cross flag with a note addressed to the military commander. This confirmed that he was a priest and asked for a face-to-face conversation at the barrier to explain that the Hall was in fact being used as a hospital and some very seriously injured men were in there.

The response was a negative one and it was made very clear that the wounded rebels would be treated as outlaws. At that point, the friars decided to look for a meeting with the commanding officer. Father Aloysius recalled that:

... we set out to do so accompanied by a Volunteer by the name of Doyle who carried the white flag. We passed the barrier and between two soldiers with fixed bayonets, we went to North King St until we reached opposite the new houses near Lurgan St where we were told we should wait the arrival of Colonel Taylor who was in charge.

While waiting, they noticed a large number of troops arriving in the area. An armoured car and ambulance were standing by. When the Colonel arrived, Father Aloysius recalled that 'he listened to what we had to say, he made no answer but unceremoniously turned and walked off'.

The friars were left standing there for what seemed an inordinate amount of time. Eventually they managed to speak to the Colonel again, and Father Aloysius remembered how 'he informed us that a truce had been called but just as he was speaking some shots rang out from a house between North King Street and North Brunswick Street'.

There was consternation among the troops and Colonel Taylor ordered Miceal O'Folghludha, still being held by the military, to prevail upon the Volunteers to stop the shooting. Father Augustine bravely stepped out to assist O'Folghludha and shouted out the news that 'Padraig Pearse had ordered the Volunteers to surrender and that a truce had been arranged'.

The Volunteers agreed to cease fire, but insisted on seeing Pearse at the earliest opportunity in order to satisfy themselves of the truce arrangement. With that agreed, Father Aloysius and Father Augustine returned to the

Father Matthew Hall with the news that the wounded men could be transferred to the Richmond Hospital.

Father Aloysius and his brethren in the Friary had been in the thick of the action during the week of the hostilities. Once the fighting ceased, they believed their involvement with the Volunteers was over, but in fact, it was only beginning. The friars were soon called upon to minister to many of the Volunteers who were arrested and detained by the military. Little did Father Aloysius realise just how important he would become during the final days of the men who were about to face death by firing squad.

On Sunday, 30 April, the day after Pearse issued his surrender order, Father Aloysius and Father Augustine celebrated Mass at seven o'clock in the morning and followed that with a light breakfast of tea and bread. They then proceeded to Dublin Castle in the hope of obtaining a permit to see Pearse, who was being held in Arbour Hill. Upon arrival at the Castle, they were given an interview with General Lowe, commander of the British forces. Lowe received both men very courteously and granted them a permit to visit Pearse. He also suggested they visit Connolly. Father Aloysius recalled:

He took us to the room in the Castle where Connolly was a patient. In our presence he asked Connolly if his signature attached to Pearse's letter ordering the surrender was genuine. Connolly immediately replied: 'yes, to prevent needless slaughter' and added that he: 'spoke only for his men'.

General Lowe then placed his car and driver at the disposal of the friars and suggested they make their way to Jacob's factory after seeing Pearse. Lowe hoped the friars could assure the Volunteers in the factory that Pearse's surrender order was genuine, as he thought that the men holding the building were unaware of the cessation of the fighting. If Father Aloysius and Father Augustine succeeded in convincing the men in Jacob's to surrender, it would be, according to Lowe, 'a great charity otherwise he would be forced to attack and demolish the factory with a great loss of life'.

Father Aloysius recalled that they travelled by car to Arbour Hill and had a meeting with Pearse and were assured by him that he had indeed signed the surrender order. The text of the notice read:

In order to prevent the further slaughter of Dublin citizens, and in the hope of saving our followers, now surrounded and hopelessly outnumbered, the members of the Provisional Government present at Headquarters have agreed to an uncon- ditional surrender, and the commandants of the various districts in the city and country will order their commands to lay down arms'.

Father Aloysius recalled one of his brethren, Father Columbus, obtaining a copy of the surrender notice. He informed the Volunteers in many districts of its exis- tence, leading them to lay down their arms.

Father Aloysius and Father Augustine made their way to Jacob's factory and were admitted through the Peter Street entrance and brought to Thomas MacDonagh, the Commanding Officer of the Volunteers garrison. Elizabeth O'Farrell also arrived, with a copy of Pearse's surrender document.

Major John McBride, the second-in-command in Jacob's, made it very clear that 'he was opposed to the surrender and would do all in his power to prevent it'. Father Aloysius recalled MacDonagh saying:

Pearse and Connolly were no longer free men and their authority could have no weight among the men still holding out. He was next in command and felt he could not, in all conscience, enter into negotiations with anyone except the General Officer commanding the British Military.

MacDonagh claimed he was prepared to meet General Lowe anywhere in the city in order to talk. He also maintained he and his men had ample provisions to hold out for several weeks and were prepared to do so if necessary. The two friars agreed to convey that message to General Lowe and promised to return with his response.

When the friars eventually met Lowe, he brought them to meet with General Maxwell, the Supreme Commander of British forces in Ireland. Maxwell agreed that Lowe should meet with MacDonagh. The decision was to be conveyed to him in a typed letter, proposing the men should meet at the northeast corner of St Patrick's Park at noon. There was also a guarantee that MacDonagh would have safe passage back to his men in the factory after the meeting.

Father Aloysius and Father Augustine accompanied MacDonagh and another Volunteer to St Patrick's Park. Lowe and MacDonagh 'talked for some minutes on the footpath before withdrawing to Lowe's car to continue their conversation'.

Once finished, MacDonagh returned to the two friars. He confirmed he had decided to advise his men it was time to surrender, and a truce was in place until three o'clock that afternoon. He planned to consult with his own men at Jacob's as well as the Volunteers at the South Dublin Union and Marrowbone Lane, and would give a final decision to General Lowe at three o'clock.

Father Aloysius and Father Augustine had decided to return to the Friary in Church Street, believing their work was done. But General Lowe requested that they 'stay on and see the whole process through'. They agreed to the request and Lowe again placed his car at their disposal. The friars returned to Jacob's with MacDonagh, where a meeting of all officers took place. As soon as that meeting ended, the friars accompanied MacDonagh to the South Dublin Union. He recalled they left the car at the military barrier at Basin Lane and continued the journey on foot.

They were met by Éamonn Ceannt on their arrival. Another meeting of officers took place, during which it was agreed the garrison should surrender.

Father Aloysius recalled that he and Father Augustine then accompanied MacDonagh back to the Basin Lane barrier, where they unexpectedly came under fire from a British soldier. Thankfully, he missed, and it later transpired that the soldier 'missed not because he was a poor shot, but was the worse for wear as a result of having had an amount of drink taken'.

One of the officers apologised profusely and confirmed the soldier in question had been put under arrest.

At three o'clock that afternoon, Father Aloysius and Father Augustine found themselves at St Patrick's Park, where Thomas MacDonagh took off his belt and handed his revolver to General Lowe. Both men agreed MacDonagh should return and oversee the surrender at Jacob's as well as at the South Dublin Union and Marrowbone Lane. Father Aloysius and Father Augustine, together with MacDonagh and two British Army officers, one of whom was General Lowe's son, made their way to Marrowbone Lane. Here there was a delay, because the Volunteers were reluctant to surrender. They were confident of holding out for a considerable length of time, and believed they had ample provisions to do so. Eventually, after some discussion, the men agreed to lay down their arms and surrender.

At the South Dublin Union, Éamonn Ceannt agreed to the surrender. Accord-ing to Father Aloysius, the two British officers were very surprised at the small number of Volunteers who were holding that vast, sprawling complex. It seems the British believed the garrison there was in excess of 500 men, and they had drawn up elaborate plans to win back control of it.

Back at Jacob's, the friars observed the Volunteers lining up in the basement and preparing to leave. Father Augustine took messages from the men to be passed on to their families, and another priest, Father Monahan, arrived to offer his services. Suddenly, there was a tremendous crash, which sounded like an explosion but was in fact looters smashing windows of the factory. One Volunteer reported that 'looters had smashed the window and were breaking in to the office at the Bishop Street side'.

Father Aloysius and Father Monahan confronted the looters with the stolen goods and Father Aloysius addressed them from a window with, as he described it, 'words of fire'. He made it known to the looters that he believed their conduct to be 'wretched and despicable', compared to the 'manly and straightforward con-duct' of the men who had borne the brunt of the past trying week. He recalled the crowd relenting and promising to leave immediately and return to their homes. A good number of the looters actually left their stolen goods back and sheepishly left the building.

Father Aloysius and Father Augustine bade their farewells to the Volunteers in Jacob's and made their way back to St Patrick's Park. Here they witnessed Éamonn Ceannt and his garrison arriving from the South Dublin Union and surrendering. Soon after, Eamon de Valera arrived with his men and surrendered. Father Aloy-sius recalled that, to his surprise, some women were among the Volunteers and were armed. By seven o'clock that evening, he and Father Augustine were back in the Friary, very hungry and tired after the most trying day of their lives.

The following days saw prisoners removed from Richmond Barracks and transferred by cattle boats from the North Wall across the Irish Sea to British jails. Father Aloysius recalled the men 'proudly marching through the streets of Dublin and enduring the ignominy of being booed and jeered by the gathering crowds. It was a sad spectacle.'

However, he stated that the mood of the people changed dramatically a day or two later, when the executions began. Many of Dublin's citizens now went out of their way to express their admiration for the executed leaders and their contempt for the British authorities in Ireland. The decision to execute the leaders of the Rising had a profound impact on Father Aloysius, who might well have felt by then that his work with the Volunteers was done. That notion was quickly dispelled and the most harrowing phase of his work was about to begin.

On Monday, 1 May, he was requested to attend at Dublin Castle by Father Murphy, the Military Chaplain, as James Connolly had asked to see him. On arrival, he was met by Father Murphy, who had made all the necessary arrangements for the visit. Father Aloysius recalled:

With a Captain Stanley I went to the ward or room in which Connolly was a patient. At the door the sentry challenged Captain Stanley, saying that his instructions were to allow no one to see the prisoner unless with a special permit.

Captain Stanley went off to obtain one, returning with it sometime later. Once in the room, Father Aloysius recalled being surprised to see 'two soldiers guarding the stricken Connolly with rifles and fixed bayonets'. He protested that he should be allowed to see the prisoner on his own and most especially if he wished to have his confession heard. Captain Stanley said he had no power to allow Father Aloysius to be alone with Connolly, as it was against regulations. The situation seemed to be at an impasse, as Father Aloysius refused to minister to Connolly in the presence of soldiers and Captain Stanley refused to break army regulations.

Only when General Lowe happened on the scene was the matter resolved. Initially, Lowe was also reluctant to go against regulations, fearing the presence of the priest might afford Connolly an opportunity to escape – unlikely, considering the Citizen Army leader was incapacitated with a badly shattered ankle. Father Aloysius 'reminded General Lowe that I was there solely as a minister of the church and had no political axe to grind and that if I was to carry out my priestly duties I would require, and insist, on privacy'.

General Lowe eventually relented and allowed Father Aloysius the privacy he demanded, placing the two soldiers on guard outside the door. When Father Aloysius saw Connolly alone, he made it clear he was there solely in his capacity as a priest. Connolly remarked that he had heard of 'the great work carried out by the priests and nuns during the week of the fighting and he viewed them as friends of the workers'.

Connolly asked about his Citizen Army comrade, Sean Connolly, who he admired greatly. He was saddened to learn that he had been shot dead. He then asked that his confession be heard. Soon after leaving Connolly's room, Father Aloysius ran into Captain Stanley, who asked him to visit the Sinn Féin ward in the Castle, to say a few words to the men and possibly take messages back to their families. He gladly took up the invitation, and Captain Stanley offered to distribute any prayer books the Capuchins sent in to the prisoners.

In fact, Father Aloysius came to recognise Captain Stanley as 'a decent and upright man who was kind-hearted in his care of the prisoners'. Stanley admitted to Father Aloysius that he 'respected the convictions and courage of the Volunteers'. He was anxious to do every service he could for the men, including Connolly, who also confirmed that the British officer had treated him with kindness.

That same morning, General Lowe asked Father Aloysius to meet General Maxwell, who, he said, had been very impressed by his and Father Augustine's work the previous day around the surrender of the Volunteers. Maxwell felt that the friars' endeavours had prevented what might have been 'a bloodbath of immense proportions'. Father Aloysius agreed to meet Maxwell, who duly expressed his appreciation of what he and Father Augustine had achieved the previous day.

In the afternoon, Father Aloysius went back to the Castle again to request a permit to visit any prisoner who might want his services. The permit was readily granted by Lord Powerscourt, the Assistant Provost Marshall. Powerscourt and some other officials in the Castle paid tribute to the bravery of the Volunteers, one of them remarking that the men 'are the cleanest and bravest lot of boys he ever met'.

Father Aloysius also had great praise for Powerscourt, whom he met on occasions when he visited Connolly. Powerscourt was, it seems, particularly anxious for him to visit the wives of the prisoners and assure them their husbands were being well looked after.

On the evening of the following day, Tuesday, Father Aloysius recalled:

*I had just gone to bed – fairly exhausted and expecting a good rest when I was called
to learn a military car was at the gate and a letter was handed to me telling me that
the prisoner Pearse desired to see me and I had permission to see him.*

As the car drove towards Charlemont Bridge, it came under sniper fire and the
driver was forced to take another route to the jail. On the journey, the driver
called to Mrs MacDonagh and Mrs Pearse, to inform them they would also be
brought to the jail in due course to see their loved ones prior to their executions.

Arriving in Kilmainham, Father Aloysius was informed that Thomas Mac-
Donagh also wished to see him. He spent a number of hours with the men as
they prepared for their deaths. He maintained that those hours 'were some of the
most inspiring and edifying' of his life. He recalled telling Pearse he had given
Holy Communion to Connolly earlier that day. Pearse, he said, was very pleased
to hear the news and said, 'Thank God. It is the one thing I was anxious about.'

Father Aloysius heard the confessions of MacDonagh and Pearse and gave
them Communion. He maintained both men were happy and they had no trace
of anxiety or fear. Pearse wrote some notes to his mother and asked Father
Aloysius to give them to an officer to have them delivered after his death.
Around three o'clock in the morning, visitors were ordered to leave the jail.
Father Aloysius recalled 'asking permission to stay with the prisoners up to
their execution', but his request was denied.

Though he would have wished to stay, he left in the knowledge that he had
done his best for both men. When he reached Church Street, he said mass for the
repose of their souls.

The following morning, Wednesday, Father Aloysius lodged a complaint about
not being allowed to remain with the prisoners until their deaths. He also drove
out to see Mrs MacDonagh with the sad news and then visited St Enda's school
to inform Mrs Pearse. She was convinced she would also lose her other son,
Willie, who, she said, 'would never be happy without Pat'.

That night, another message came to Church Street, requiring the friars to attend
the jail in preparation for the executions of Willie Pearse, Joseph Plunkett, Ned Daly
and Michael O'Hanrahan. Father Aloysius was shocked at this turn of events, as he

expected that there would be no further deaths. On the Friday morning, Major John McBride was executed and was attended by one of Father Aloysius's colleagues.

The following Sunday afternoon, Father Aloysius received a message saying that John Dillon, the deputy leader of the Irish Parliamentary Party, wished to see him. He took a car to Dillon's house on North Great George's Street and, though Dillon said 'he disagreed with the politics of the rebels he greatly admired their courage and respected their convictions. As far as he was concerned the men were all good Irishmen who deserved respect.'

Dillon borrowed Father Aloysius's car and drove to Dublin Castle. There he managed to send a telegram to the party's leader, John Redmond, in London, pleading for him to work towards having the executions stopped. That same night, the friars received word that four more men – Éamonn Ceannt, Con Colbert, Sean Hueston and Michael Mallin – were to be executed. All four were attended to by fathers Augustine and Albert. Father Aloysius recalled:

I went back to Dillon and advised him to go to London and raise hell in the House of Commons which he did the following Wednesday. His protestations convinced Prime Minister Asquith to promise there would be no more executions.

The following day, Thursday, he met Captain Stanley in Dublin Castle. Stanley assured him that he expected there to be no further executions. However, around nine o'clock that evening, Stanley arrived at the Friary in Church Street to inform Father Aloysius that his 'services would once again be needed some hours later but he was not in a position to expand on that request'.

At one o'clock the following morning, a car arrived to take him to the Castle. Father Aloysius recalled:

I heard Connolly's confession and gave him Communion again. Then I left while he was given a light meal. I had a long talk with Stanley in the Castle Yard and he told me he had been very impressed by Connolly.

Before Connolly was taken to Kilmainham Gaol, Father Aloysius reminded him that the men appointed to execute him probably knew very little about him. They were, as soldiers, simply obeying orders. He hoped Connolly had no anger towards them and asked him to forgive them. Connolly responded, 'I do father. I respect every man who does his duty.'

Connolly was laid on a stretcher and brought to a car. Father Aloysius travelled with him, and they spoke for the last time. Once in the yard at the Gaol, James Connolly, an Edinburgh man who loved Ireland, her working class and the republic, was placed sitting on a chair and the order to fire was given. Father Eugene McCarthy, who was also in attendance, anointed him. Father Aloysius recalled:

> *I had stood just behind the firing line. It was a scene I should not ask to witness again. I had got to know Connolly – to wonder at his strength of character and marvellous power of concentration. I got to regret that I had not known him longer and now, I had to say goodbye. All I could do was to return home with a heavy heart and to offer the holy sacrifice for his soul.*

In his summation, Father Aloysius asked all Irish people to forget what was 'painful but remember what was heartening and inspiring'. He reminded us that Ireland is an ancient and glorious nation and if we, as a people, have a divergence of views, we should calmly resolve all differences.

As conflict raged around him, Father Aloysius bravely shunned real danger to help those who were suffering and scared. He diligently carried out his priestly duties caring for the people of the city, displaying outstanding courage and compassion in his work as Chaplain to the republican heroes.

Chapter 11

Frank Thornton: An Extraordinary Life in Irish Republicanism

The activities of the Intelligence Department continued to expand. By the end of 1920, Battalion Intelligence Officers were appointed in every active area in Ireland. They reported to their Brigade Intelligence Officer who, in turn, reported to the Intelligence Headquarters in Dublin. Michael Collins was in regular communication with every active Brigade Intelligence Officer in Ireland, and his files show in what an elaborate manner he entered into every detail of their work.

(Frank Thornton)

One of the most notable statements in the Witness Statements archive is from Frank Thornton, a man who dedicated his life to the republican ideal. Thornton moved in exalted company and was a highly influential IRA Deputy Assistant Director of Intelligence, working directly with Michael Collins. His story covers the full gamut of the Irish revolutionary era and beyond, and his contribution to the republican cause deserves to be told in all its detail.

Frank Thornton was born in Drogheda in 1891, into a dedicated republican family. His grandfather was an old Fenian, and Thornton recalled his mother preaching Fenianism in their house. He left Ireland in 1912, travelling to Liverpool to find work as a painter in the Harland and Wolff shipyard, where his main job as a foreman was to camouflage merchant ships. He soon joined the Gaelic League, which had its Liverpool headquarters in Duke Street.

Thornton recalled enrolling in the Irish Republican Brotherhood in February 1913. That year also saw the foundation of the Irish Volunteers in Dublin, and a Liverpool branch was quickly set up, enrolling about 1,200 members. The leadership there hired Irish ex-British Army servicemen to train the men and NCO courses were also started. They paraded at a park close to Aintree racecourse, which was also used by the GAA as playing grounds. The GAA was very strong in Liverpool at that time, and Thornton founded the Tir-na-nÓg Football Club and took on the job of Assistant Secretary of the County Board.

He recalled the 1914 hurling final between England (represented by London) and Scotland, held in Liverpool on the August bank holiday Monday, the very day the Great War started. Michael Collins was a member of the victorious London team. A number of exhibition games were also played, with teams coming across from Dublin for the event, accompanied by the O'Toole Pipe Band.

The previous week had seen the Howth gunrunning incident in Dublin and the deaths of civilians at Bachelors Walk, and a protest march through the streets of Liverpool was staged on the Sunday. The Volunteers paraded behind the band and a large amount of money was collected from onlookers, later used to buy arms. As the band members returned to Lime Street railway station on the Monday evening to begin their journey home, they clashed with some British ex-servicemen before eventually boarding the train for Holyhead.

The following month, following John Redmond's speech at Woodenbridge, the Irish Volunteers split. The vast majority of members of the Liverpool branch chose to leave the ranks and join Redmond's newly formed National Volunteers. Thornton, undaunted by this turn of events, became Captain of 'B' Company of the Irish Volunteers, and set out to build up its numbers. He recalled that their training was closely watched by the authorities, but they succeeded in keeping the organisation intact.

They also secured substantial quantities of arms and ammunition, purchasing them from local stores and from British soldiers. These arms were sent to Ireland by many different and devious methods. For example, Thornton recalled, 'funerals often took place, where, instead of a corpse, the coffin was filled with either arms or ammunition and the consignments were always successfully delivered to their destination'.

Thornton organised a lecture in November 1914 by Piaras Beasley, to commemorate the Manchester Martyrs. Meeting Beasley at the Wallasey ferry, Thornton was surprised to see him attired in full Irish Volunteers uniform. As they made their way to the lecture venue in Duke Street, they encountered hundreds of soldiers and naval men, all of whom came to attention and saluted Beasley, believing he was their superior officer. Thornton later learned that Beasley, who was from Liverpool but had moved to Dublin, managed to travel everywhere for free when back in his native city, because he was always attired in his full Irish Volunteers uniform. No one ever noticed he was not a member of the British military.

The onus was on Thornton to train his men properly and, with that in mind, he secured the basement of Cahill's tailor's and outfitter's shop on Scotland Road. After renovating it, the men engaged in target practice, using miniature rifles and revolvers. The basement, whose entrance was at the back of the building, was never discovered by the authorities. During the War of Independence, it was used as a receiving centre for arms and ammunition, which were sent across to Ireland.

The procurement of arms and ammunition to send to Ireland was a major element of the Volunteers' activities in Liverpool, though the shipments did not always go according to plan, as Thornton recalled. On one occasion in 1915, he and Joe Gleeson, another Volunteer, were making their way to Garston Docks in a taxi, with a box of rifles on top of the vehicle. Travelling down London Road, the taxi got involved with another car and hit a tram standard in the centre of the road. Of course, a crowd gathered, as well as police, and Thornton recalled Gleeson quickly hailing another taxi. Gleeson then:

> ... *tipped a policeman on his shoulder and said: 'Hey, mate, give us a hand to get this box on top of the other car, we are in a hurry to catch our boat at Garston.' Two policemen, Joe and myself tilted the box of rifles from the wrecked taxi onto the second car and off we went to Garston and safely deposited our stuff in the boat that was sailing that night.*

In August 1915, Thornton received instructions to make arrangements with the Irish-owned City of Dublin Steam Packet Company to have one of their ships draw alongside the *St Paul*, an American liner carrying the body of the old Fenian leader, O'Donovan Rossa, as it sailed up the Mersey. Members of Clann na Gaedheal in America were, it seems, anxious to ensure the body did not touch English soil on its last journey home. The Steam Packet vessel was ready for the handover, but the *St Paul* was late arriving due to poor weather conditions, and so it wasn't possible to effect the transfer. However, the problem was solved when, according to Thornton:

We mobilised fifty members of our Volunteers in Liverpool both from 'A' and 'B' Companies and boarded the St Paul at Prince's Landing Stage and carried O'Donovan Rossa's body from Prince's Landing Stage to the Nelson Dock on Irish shoulders and I think that by this means we carried out the wishes of everyone concerned. We boarded the St Paul at Prince's Landing Stage that day, and carried O'Donovan Rossa's remains right along Dock Road, the journey being over two miles. I think it can be safely claimed that by this method O'Donovan Rossa's body had landed in Ireland when we took it on our shoulders at Prince's Landing Stage.

Thornton was in command of the Volunteers party that accompanied the body on its crossing to Dublin. He escorted it to the Pro-Cathedral before taking part in the funeral to Glasnevin.

One Thursday evening towards the end of 1915, Thornton was arrested and charged with being in command of a body of men to whom he issued firearms. One of his men had been caught in possession of a gun. The police held and questioned Thornton for forty-eight hours before charging him. He engaged Austin Harford, a well-known solicitor in Irish political circles, to represent him, and they succeeded in having the charges dropped because of insufficient evidence. It transpired that while he was in custody, the police raided Thornton's home, but found no incriminating evidence there.

However, when he reported back to his job in the shipyard, he was told by a sympathetic general manager that he no longer had employment there, because the authorities had deemed him a danger to the realm. Thornton later claimed he wasn't too upset about being sacked, as he had already been advised by the Volunteers headquarters in Dublin to ready his unit for transfer to Dublin at short notice.

He journeyed to Dublin for further instructions. While there, he was in contact with George Plunkett concerning the proposal to turn his Kimmage estate into a Volunteers training camp. At the beginning of January 1916, the men of 'A' and 'B' Companies of the Liverpool Volunteers gave up their jobs and reported for full-time duty in the Kimmage Camp. Thornton's two brothers, Hugh and Paddy, were among those to travel. For most of the Volunteers, it was time to leave Britain anyway, as the authorities were pursuing all men of military age for conscription into the war.

It did not take long to have the camp at Kimmage up and running and organised on a military basis. Within a few weeks, other units arrived from London, Scotland and Manchester. George Plunkett assumed the role of Commanding Officer, and the men were put to making pikes as well as charges for shotgun cartridges. Some men loaded cartridges with extra gunpowder and special pellets, while others made canister bombs.

From late January to March of 1916, Thornton was attached to the staff of the Limerick Brigade. During his stay in Limerick, Tom Clarke arrived after being accidently wounded in the right arm and Thornton had the task of filling his pipe for him. Seán MacDermott arrived in March. On the eve of St Patrick's Day, MacDermott brought all the officers and NCOs to the Fianna Hall and:

... without actually saying it in so many words that a rebellion was not far off he left nobody in any doubt that they should be ready and prepared to do their duty when called up to do so.

Thornton was instructed to report back to Kimmage within the week. Meanwhile, he had to escape being picked up by police in a raid on his digs. Thankfully, he had received a tip off and by the time the police arrived to arrest him, he was in a car and driving to Dublin.

As soon as he arrived back in Kimmage, he was ordered to accompany a number of other Volunteers on a car journey from Dublin to Caherciveen, to seize a wireless station at Valentia. This was the week leading up to the Easter Rising, and the plan was for the station to transmit false signals designed to convince the Royal Navy that a German attack on Scottish naval bases was imminent. However, Thornton was taken out of the car at the last minute and put in charge of 26 North Frederick Street, which was being used as an auxiliary camp to Kimmage.

That journey to Caherciveen was ill-fated as the driver, Tommy McInerney, took a wrong turn at Killorglin and mistakenly drove off the pier into the water. While McInerney survived the accident, 'three other Volunteers, Con Keating, Daniel Sheehan and Charlie Monahan, drowned and so became the first victims of the Rising'.

On Easter Monday morning, Thornton reported for duty with his unit to Liberty Hall. He was left with a dozen men under his command to hold the building until they could arrange transport for all supplies and ammunition to the GPO. By six o'clock in the evening, his ranks had swelled to around 200 men.

Some time later, they all arrived at the Post Office, where they were met by James Connolly. He instructed Thornton to take twelve men from the ranks and await further orders, while the balance of the men marched to Fairview after some rest and rations. Thornton and his men also rested and had tea in the restaurant before being ordered to go to the Express office to reinforce Sean Connolly's unit there.

He was instructed to proceed via Fleet Street and Temple Bar, fanning his men out on both sides of the road. He recalled approaching Crown Alley and an old woman warning them that British soldiers were occupying the Telephone Exchange. Thornton admitted ignoring her warning and continuing to approach the building. Suddenly, machine gun fire opened up, as well as rifle fire from other buildings in Crown Alley. Thornton recalled that 'instead of retreating, I gave the order, "Forward at the double," and so we reached the quays with only one casualty'.

Arriving on the quays, Thornton and his unit came under fire from Volunteers on the opposite side of the river, and it took some time for them to identify themselves, by means of a white flag. Leaving the quays, they returned to Westmoreland Street and occupied another building, before sending a messenger to the GPO to report what had happened.

Thornton received a reply from James Connolly, congratulating him and his men on their actions and for advising him that the Telephone Exchange building was in the hands of the enemy. Thornton now received new instructions – to take over a suitable building in Fleet Street and commence sniping at Trinity College and the Bank of Ireland.

Thornton's unit occupied Delahunty's pub on Fleet Street. This offered easy access to the College restaurant, enabling the men to get on to roofs and upper windows without being detected. Additional men arrived during the night, and Thornton understood he and his men were to act as a covering party for a unit coming from the GPO with orders to take over Trinity College. Unfortunately, that plan was never activated.

The following morning, Tuesday, Thornton received orders to evacuate the building and return to the GPO, from where he and his men were sent across the road to occupy the Imperial Hotel, above Clery's. Having done so, his unit proceeded to bore through to buildings on either side of the hotel. Later that night, they managed to make contact with Brennan Whitmore and his unit, on the hotel's right flank towards Talbot Street.

Thornton and his unit, composed of men from the Citizen Army and the 2nd Battalion, Dublin Brigade, spent the rest of the Rising in the Imperial Hotel. Their orders were to hold the hotel until it was either blown down by shell fire or burned down. During their time here, they came under a constant barrage from the British. On the Tuesday night, Thorntons's unit was reinforced by twelve men led by Frank Henderson and Oscar Traynor, all of whom arrived from Fairview. The party included Noel Lemass, brother of the future Taoiseach Sean Lemass, and Ned Boland, brother of Harry Boland. That same night, a number of men arrived from the GPO to requisition blankets, mattresses and food. Thornton recalled:

A communication wire had been fixed by us to the GPO and messages were hauled backwards and forwards across the street. The box was riddled with machine gun bullets in its passing back and forth, and the rope severed later in the week.

Thornton then called for volunteers to dash across the road to deliver and pick up dispatches. Noel Lemass volunteered and reached the Post Office successfully in spite of machine gun and sniper fire. On his return journey, he almost reached safety, but as he neared the footpath, he was wounded in the leg and fell. Ned Boland and Jack Whelan immediately dashed out from the door of the hotel and pulled him to safety.

Thornton also received an order from James Connolly to erect the Irish Citizen Army flag, 'The Plough and the Stars', on the roof of the Imperial Hotel. This he managed to do, despite being under constant fire, and it remained there even when the Rising was over.

On the Wednesday morning, Connolly sent IRB leader Sean McGarry over to inspect the post. He insisted on going out on to the roof of the hotel, despite Thornton warning him of the obvious dangers. He climbed up a ladder and out through a skylight and, while pulling himself up on to the roof, he was met by a hail of bullets. He fell back down on top of Thornton, lucky to survive the incident.

The action around Sackville Street continued to intensify, and Thursday was a particularly taxing day for Thornton and his men. The British attempted to shell the GPO with an eighteen-pound gun positioned near the Parnell Monument. The gun crew were sniped so effectively while trying to get the gun into position that a number of them were killed and wounded. Reinforcements rushed out to help and managed to fire the gun, though the shell failed to hit the post office. It hit the YMCA building instead, which was occupied by British forces. Thornton believed the British 'must have thought it was our troops that were shelling them, because they immediately evacuated the YMCA, coming under fire and suffering heavy casualties'.

As Thornton and his unit's position became increasingly dangerous, there was a moment of some levity on the Thursday. He recalled:

While a number of our men were resting in an annex at the back of the hotel, a large tank which was built out on the side of the building, overhead this annex, was hit by a HE shell and just disappeared, the water falling down in one huge lump on to the annex and washing our men out of it on to the main passage in Imperial.

That same day, a shell came over the top of the Imperial Hotel and smashed into the offices of the *Freeman's Journal*, blowing a large hole in the upper portion of the building. Soon after, a shell came through the back window of the hotel, exploding in a room that was occupied by a sniper. He was found still sitting at his post, dazed but unhurt.

In the early evening, the Tricolour flying on the corner of Henry Street was half shot down, but didn't fall all the way to the ground. With a typical act of bravery and determination, someone pushed it back up and lashed a piece of timber to it, despite being under heavy fire.

By Thursday evening, the shelling had become very fierce. Shells that missed the GP fell on nearby buildings, including the Imperial Hotel. The barrage was compounded by heavy machine gun fire and incendiary bombs. That night, a shell fell on Hoyte's store, just to the back of the hotel. The store held a number of barrels of methylated spirits and turpentine, which were blown sky high. A number of them landed on the roof of the hotel, badly injuring some Volunteers.

The situation was becoming more desperate as the barrage from the enemy grew ever stronger and closer. The Volunteers were forced to vacate the upper floors of Clery's store and the hotel. Orders came through from the GPO to 'defend every floor and the building should not be evacuated until it had been rendered useless to the British'.

Thornton ordered the main body of his unit to link up with Brennan Whitmore's unit on the right flank of the hotel. He kept five men with him to defend the building itself from its first floor. They remained in position until the ceiling began to fall around them and then made their way down a burning ladder and gradually worked their way out of the building. Badly burned, they reached the corner of Talbot Street.

Unable to make contact with a burning GPO for further instructions and with few other options available to them, Thornton and his men escaped though a billiard hall to Cathedral Lane and occupied a building there until news came of the surrender. The Easter Rising had come to an end, with a decisive victory for the British. Thornton's determination to continue the struggle didn't waver in the slightest however – for him, the conflict with the British forces in Ireland had really only started.

With the fighting over for now, there was nothing for Thornton to do but surrender. He and his comrades were marched down to the Custom House, where they were to remain for two days, sitting on cold flagstones. Eventually, he was charged and found guilty by court martial, together with Seán MacDermott, Harry Boland and Gerald Crofts. The charge against Thornton was that he masterminded the attempt to blow up the Magazine Fort in the Phoenix Park during the Rising. He had had absolutely nothing to do with this, but nevertheless, he was found guilty. He was also charged with causing great losses to the British Army in Dublin during the rebellion.

After a week in Mountjoy prison, Thornton was sent to Dartmoor prison in England and eventually, in December 1916, on to Lewes prison. He was released under the general release of prisoners in June 1917. He recalled the journey home, when Eamon de Valera insisted, despite the protestations of the ship's captain, 'on all of his men occupying the first-class compartment as they crossed the Irish sea'.

They shared the trip with a contingent of British soldiers, and Thornton and Harry Boland spent the time teaching them the air of 'The Soldier's Song' – as the ship neared Dún Laoghaire, most of them were able to sing it. Thornton's last abiding memory of the trip was seeing Harry Boland on the lookout for the first sight of land and singing the old song 'The Dawn on the Hills of Ireland'.

Soon, Thornton was back working for the republican cause. He was assigned to the Sinn Féin by-election campaign on 10 July 1917, when Eamon de Valera contested the East Clare parliamentary seat. De Valera's victory marked the beginning of a long political career for the future leader of the new Irish nation and further convinced Thornton that a new era had dawned for all Irishmen and women. Once the election was over, he made his way back to Dublin and reported for duty to Michael Collins. By that time, Collins had taken control of the Prisoners' National Aid Association and was also involved in the re-organisation of the Volunteers.

On the evening of 25 September 1917, Thornton was taking part in a Sinn Féin concert when news of Thomas Ashe's death came through. He walked on stage to make the sad announcement of Ashe's demise and brought the concert to an end as a mark of respect. The authorities who were monitoring the concert tried to arrest him, but he escaped back to Dublin and took part in Ashe's funeral.

Soon after, Thornton was assigned to duty in Louth, where he was ordered to organise parades in every part of the county and to start wearing his Volunteers uniform in public. However, within a couple of weeks, he was arrested in Drogheda. After a trial in Belfast, he was sentenced to six months' hard labour in Crumlin Road Prison. The only other republican prisoner with him in the prison was Sam Heron, brother of Archie, who eventually ended up in Dublin and was heavily involved in the Volunteers' bomb-making factory at 198 Parnell Street.

Thornton immediately went on hunger strike, and was removed to Dundalk jail after ten days. Here he was the only republican prisoner and he recalled seeing a copy of the *Irish Independent* with the headline 'Left Alone to Die in Dundalk Gaol'. Soon, however, a group of prisoners from Kerry arrived and Thornton recalled:

> *A consultation was held and it was decided I was looking too healthy and that I would have to collapse on the ground. This arrangement was carried out the next morning and I was carried into my cell by the rest of the prisoners.*

A doctor was sent for, but before he arrived, Thornton recalled that 'I swallowed six pills of soap and smoked as many cigarettes as I could in order to increase my heart rate and temperature.'

The ruse failed and the doctor deemed him not ill enough to be released. However, the procedure was repeated for a number of days and eventually the Governor, a Mr McHugh, called to see him. McHugh arranged for his release into the care of a Dundalk native, Seamus McGuill, who took him to the Imperial Hotel in the town. Here he was examined by another doctor and allowed some tea and dry toast.

Thornton had been released under the 'Cat and Mouse Act' on the grounds of failing health, but the Act allowed the authorities to re-arrest him should they deem him to have recovered his health. Thornton had a fine beard by that time and decided to visit the barber shop the morning after his release to have it shaved off. While reading the paper and waiting his turn, a man got up from another chair and stood looking at him. The man was none other than the Governor of the jail, who was surprised to see his former prisoner, whom he had believed to be dying just the previous evening, sitting in front of him. After his shave, Thornton decided it was best to leave Dundalk. That evening, he 'caught the train to Dublin after being seen off at the station by half the population of the town and its brass band.'

Thornton was soon back in Dundalk at the head of 800 Volunteers, who provided a guard of honour for Eamon de Valera when he visited the town. He continued his work as a Volunteers organiser for the region and was involved in the foundation of the New Ireland Assurance Collecting Society. Arthur Griffith had been continuously arguing for something to be done to stem the flow of insurance premiums out of the country. It was estimated at the time that some £5 million was being taken out of the Irish economy. Examining Griffith's idea, Thornton, together with Michael Collins, Jim Ryan, Michael Staines, Liam Tobin and Eamon de Valera, set about bringing it to fruition.

Thornton was appointed Divisional Inspector for the New Ireland Assurance Company in the northeastern region, while Liam Tobin took charge of the Cork area and Dick Coleman oversaw the Dublin region. Their new jobs provided them with excellent cover for their Volunteers activities. Every man appointed to a position of trust in the new company was a Volunteer, which allowed for the setting up of a nationwide intelligence unit. Company representatives also played important roles in collecting funds for the Dáil Éireann Loan Scheme initiated by de Valera's Provisional Government in 1919. The company's head office at 56 Bachelor's Walk became one of the calling stations for people coming to Dublin to deposit that money.

It was only a matter of time before the authorities caught up with Thornton. One day while he was in Dundalk in the company of Dan Breen, who was in town to visit the jailed Sean Treacy, Thornton recalled that, surprisingly, 'the police ignored Breen who was about to pull a gun on them and arrested me before frog-marching me to the barracks'.

Once again, he was sent to Belfast jail for a period, before being returned to Dundalk jail, where he joined Treacy, Terence MacSwiney, Dick McKee and Oscar Traynor, amongst many other republicans. He recalled an unusual incident while there around March 1918, when Diarmuid Lynch, one of the inmates, was notified he was to be deported to America. He applied for permission to get married before leaving the country, but was refused by the authorities. The men decided to take matters into their own hands and arranged for a local curate to carry out the marriage in the jail without the Governor's knowledge. Thornton's sister Nora and Terence MacSwiney's wife Muriel made the necessary arrangements with the bride-to-be, Kathleen Quinn. On the arranged day, 24 April 1918, Ms Quinn and her sister Carmel arrived with a priest, Father Ryan, to visit Thornton, Dick McKee, Mick Brennan and, of course, Diarmuid Lynch. Thornton gleefully recalled:

The priest carried out the marriage ceremony by simply putting his arms around the bride and groom as if he was in a deep conversation with them and married them while I was designated to make sure the warders did not interfere in the proceedings.

Michael Brennan acted as best man, while Carmel Quinn was the bridesmaid. Later that night, Father Ryan brought the register into the jail under his coat for Michael Brennan's signature. The Governor was less than impressed when the men informed him the wedding had taken place without his knowledge.

The following June, the men were all transferred to Belfast jail and, on 15 August 1918, were released. However, Frank Thornton's freedom was to be short-lived, as the authorities decided he posed a danger to the state. He recalled:

I remember that morning well; it was a lovely summer morning and I was looking forward to spending a couple of days with friends in Belfast, but immediately I got outside the wicket gate of the prison, I was touched on the shoulder by an RIC Inspector who read out a Deportation Order signed by Mr Short, the Chief Secretary. This Order stated that I was guilty of some plot with the Germans and, as a consequence, I was to be deported from Ireland.

Initially, Thornton was sent to Arbour Hill prison where he spent a few days. Then a sergeant and a corporal, together with twenty other men of the Welsh Fusiliers, escorted him to a London North West cargo ship berthed at the North Wall in Dublin and accompanied him across the Irish Sea, on the first leg of a journey to Reading Jail.

He recalled arriving at Euston Station in the early hours of a Sunday morning and being met by a lorry, which brought them to Paddington Station. There they all went into a restaurant catering for troops and Thornton sat at a table just inside the door while the soldiers went to the counter to order breakfast.

Thornton was ordered out by a lady who told him only soldiers were allowed in, and he saw his chance to escape. Finding himself outside the restaurant, he turned right and walked quickly to the nearby underground station. However, as it was early Sunday morning, the gates were locked.

Forced to go back to the restaurant, he was met by the sergeant and corporal, both of whom had noticed he was missing. Thinking quickly, Thornton, in his own words, 'kicked up a terrible row', complaining that the woman in the restaurant had kicked him out. The soldiers accepted his explanation. Thornton realised that had he turned left instead of right after leaving the restaurant, he could have slipped away into London's myriad of streets and made his escape.

Eventually Thornton and his escort boarded the train for Reading, arriving there about 10am, only to find there was no conveyance at the station. They had no choice but to walk. About halfway to the prison, the Sergeant suggested they stop for a drink in a local pub. It seems there was no objection, and in fact they had three drinks, with the Sergeant calling for the first round, followed by the Corporal and then Thornton himself. Convivial as the company was, Thornton recalled that 'all the time at the back of my mind was that some opportunity might present itself of getting away. However, that didn't happen and we finally arrived at the gaol.'

The Sergeant spoke to a man behind an iron grille and confirmed they had brought a prisoner from Ireland, only to be told that no prisoners were accepted on Sundays. Everyone agreed there was nothing for it but to return to the pub. As they walked away from the prison, however, they were met by the Governor arriving in his car. He quickly fixed the matter up and admitted Thornton to the prison, but not before, as Thornton recalled, 'each and every one of the soldiers shook [his] hand and wished [him] well'.

Thornton remained in Reading jail until March 1919, when he returned to Ireland. Once home, he joined the newly formed IRA Intelligence Unit under the leadership of Michael Collins and began a new phase of his career in the republican movement. He eventually became a Deputy Assistant Director of the Intelligence Unit, but not before spending some time in the field helping to fine-tune the intelligence organisation in the northwest of the country.

Thornton eventually made his way to Dublin, arriving there on 19 December 1919. That same day, the IRA had attempted to assassinate the Lord Lieutenant, Lord French. Thornton had orders to report to Vaughan's hotel, where he met Joe O'Reilly and Tom Cullen. They went to 88 Phibsboro Road, where Dan Breen was in a bad way after being wounded during the failed attack on French.

A doctor was summoned to tend to Breen's wounds, but by that time, the authorities were searching all the houses in the area. To get the badly wounded Breen away, a taxi belonging to another Volunteer, Joe Hyland, was hired. There was no other option but to run the gauntlet of British soldiers who had arrived at the end of the Phibsboro Road. With Joe O'Reilly and Dan Breen inside the car and Thornton and Cullen standing on the running boards, they made their escape to a safe house on Grantham Street, where Breen remained until his wounds healed.

Thornton's reputation since 1915 as a loyal, trustworthy and brave republican activist made it inevitable that he would ascend to a position of importance. Soon after the incident on Phibsboro Road, Thornton was transferred by Michael Collins to GHQ Intelligence Unit, to work under the command of Liam Tobin.

In early January 1920, Thornton went to Belfast to gather information on an Inspector Redmond, who had been transferred to Dublin to run intelligence operations in the Dublin Metropolitan Police. Thornton recalled that 'although we knew of his arrival from one of our Agents in Belfast, we still had no description nor had we anyone to identify him here in Dublin'.

Arriving in Belfast, Thornton was introduced to a Sergeant McCarthy, a Kerryman stationed at Chichester Street Police Station. Thornton, posing as a cousin of McCarthy, stayed the night as a guest in the station, hoping to acquire a photograph of Redmond. He recalled:

The Police Amateur Boxing Championships were taking place in the Ulster Hall and practically all the Police Force off-duty were in attendance including the District Inspector, in whose office was a photograph of Redmond. Getting my direction from McCarthy, I had no trouble in slipping into the DI's office, and annexing the photograph, which I brought back to Dublin the following day.

A day or so later, Redmond was identified on Harcourt Street in Dublin and assassinated.

Thornton recalled the arrival of Liam Devlin in 1920 to Dublin from Scotland, where he had been involved with Sinn Féin and the Volunteers. Devlin purchased a public house opposite the Rotunda Hospital on Parnell Street and, through some mutual friends, came into contact with Sean O'Muirthuile, the then-Secretary of the Gaelic League and a close friend of Michael Collins. O'Muirthuile introduced Devlin to Collins and Devlin offered the full use of his new establishment to the IRA. Collins accepted the offer and soon the public house became his unofficial headquarters.

Thornton, Collins, Piaras Béaslaí, Liam Tobin, Gearóid O'Sullivan, Tom Cullen and Joe O'Reilly met every night in the pub to discuss the events of the day and plan for the future. Any column leader or brigade officer who came to Dublin usually reported to Devlin's, where they were provided with a meal by Mrs Devlin and a bed for the night if required. Thornton said having a headquarters in the heart of the city was 'often very helpful to the Intelligence Unit and the fact it was a public house served as a perfect cover for many of its activities'.

Collins left Devlin's almost every night on his Raleigh bicycle, while Thornton, Cullen and Tobin journeyed across town to Rathmines where they shared a flat. There were nights when they all had to stay in Devlin's because of enemy activity in and around Parnell Square or because they had an operation planned for early the next morning.

They had a number of narrow escapes while staying in Devlin's. One night in particular, the British raided houses on Parnell Square. Thornton and his comrades kept a sharp look out, and about an hour after the operation began, they heard the movement of soldiers on the roof. Though they endured a nervous few minutes, the enemy made no attempt to search the houses on Devlin's side of the Square. It later transpired the soldiers on the roof were a covering party for the raiding party in the Square. Little did they realise the men they were looking for were right underneath them all the time. Another night, while they were in an upstairs room, a British military patrol was downstairs in the pub searching all the customers and left without going upstairs.

Thornton recalled how Collins and his Intelligence Unit managed to infiltrate the Dublin Metropolitan Police from around the middle of 1920. He was ordered by Collins to report to a house on Rathgar Avenue where he met Sergeant Matt Byrne of Rathmines Station and Sergeant Mannix of Donnybrook Station. He had a lengthy discussion with the two men and concocted an elaborate scheme of organising the DMP into a useful asset to the IRA. The Intelligence Unit very quickly succeeded in enrolling a number of DMP men in stations like College Green, Donnybrook, Kevin Street and Fitzgibbon Street.

When the Crown forces went on raids in the city, they usually took a DMP man or two with them, and more often than not, the DMP were advised in advance that a raid was about to take place. DMP informants passed that information on to the IRA, allowing them to move their personnel out of danger. There were times, according to Thornton, when a DMP man was able to cover up for an IRA man, saying he was a friend and of no consequence to the authorities.

Thornton described Sergeant Mannix as one of the more prolific informants, who had the trust of Collins and the Intelligence Unit. He detailed a number of instances when Mannix saved IRA men while accompanying the British on raids across the city. On one occasion, Mannix managed to 'hide some important documents in his tunic after two IRA men dropped them when they were briefly apprehended and detained in Ballsbridge'.

Mannix also secured information about payments being made by the British Secret Service to a man working as an Inspector on the Dalkey tram line. As a result of that information, the man was escorted off his tram car and taken out to Killiney Golf Links, where he was shot dead.

By the middle of 1920, the British realised that the terrorism of the Black and Tans, with their burning and looting, was failing to subdue the IRA and the Intelligence Unit. They concluded they would have to specifically target IRA Headquarters staff and hope to eliminate them one by one. The British therefore set up a full-time Secret Service operation outside of the Army, based in Dublin, with a functioning headquarters and satellite offices. They built up a formidable organisation and managed to secure some very valuable intelligence across the city.

The battle of wills between Michael Collins and his Intelligence Unit and the British Secret Service intensified during 1920 and into the following year.

This brought with it serious and deadly consequences for many people on both sides of the conflict, including the deaths of fifteen British agents on 21 November 1920, a day that has gone down in the annals of Ireland's modern history as 'Bloody Sunday'.

While Collins patently had the lead role in the intelligence war against the British, he always valued and depended on the experience of many fine and committed men around him. One of these was Frank Thornton, a man who regularly placed himself in danger during the revolutionary era for the cause of Ireland's freedom.

Chapter 12

Vincent Byrne: Committed to the Republic and the Squad

Up to the year 1919, the Detective Branch of the DMP, known as the G-Division, had full sway in Dublin, and could arrest anyone who was active in the national movement and have them flung into jail; also, their spies and informers were giving information ad lib, without fear of punishment. It was obvious that it was little use having a Volunteer army if this state of affairs was allowed to go on, as any officer or Volunteer did not know, from hour to hour, when he might be arrested. So, the 'big fella' Michael Collins, set up an Intelligence department to find out who were the men selected by the British administration to do this work. It was well-known that certain G-men were on this work, which was called political work. I believe these men were requested to cease their activities, but events proved that they became more zealous than ever. Instructions were received from the Director of Intelligence through his deputy, Liam Tobin, that these same men were a menace to the movement and would have to be got out of the way.

(Vincent Byrne)

During the War of Independence, a cohort of young men emerged within the republican movement who went beyond the normal call of duty, fearlessly obeying orders that put their own lives in danger and left them constantly looking over their shoulders in anticipation of arrest. One of those brave young men was Vincent (Vinnie) Byrne, a Dubliner who fought in the Easter Rising as a mere boy of fifteen. Byrne went on to become an important member of Michael Collins's infamous assassination squad often referred to as 'The Twelve Apostles'. His witness statement to the Bureau of Military History makes for fascinating reading.

During 1919, the Detective Branch of the Dublin Metropolitan Police, known as G-Division, had complete control in the city and could arrest and incarcerate anyone they wished. They had a network of spies and informers across the city, which made it very difficult for the Volunteers to operate. Michael Collins set up an Intelligence Unit in 1919, which he led, primarily to identify members of G-Division and take action against them.

Instructions came down from Collins, through his Deputy, Liam Tobin, that prominent detectives in G-Division were to be eliminated. To this end, a number of men from the IRA 2nd Battalion were selected to attend a meeting. It was made clear there was no compulsion attached to any man – he could volunteer for the job at hand or not. Indeed, some men conscientiously objected, saying they had no problem confronting the enemy in open warfare but were not inclined to participate in clandestine operations.

Byrne recalled that the first operation by this new group of Volunteers was carried out on 30 July 1919, when Detective Smyth was shot on Millmount Avenue in Drumcondra. He did not die immediately, but succumbed to his wounds some days later. That killing was followed by the assassination of Detective Hoey on 19 September 1919, on Townsend Street, as he was about to enter Brunswick Street (now Pearse Street) police station. Byrne also recalled two other G-Division men being assassinated around that time. One, whose name was Kells, died on Pleasants Street and another man died on St Stephen's Green, near the corner of Cuffe Street.

Byrne recounted how he became part of the squad. It all began on a cold November evening in 1919, when he visited Mick McDonnell's house in Richmond Crescent. He sat around the fire here in the company of his best friends, Jimmy Slattery and Tom Keogh. He was asked by McDonnell if he would be willing to shoot a man, and Byrne replied, 'It's all according to who he was.'

When McDonnell suggested John Barton, it only took a second for Byrne to reply, 'I wouldn't mind as he raided my house.'

He had previously encountered Barton in 1916, having been arrested, questioned and fingerprinted by him over his involvement in the Easter Rising.

McDonnell replied, 'That settles it. You may have a chance.'

They agreed a plan, McDonnell telling Byrne and Slattery to make their way to College Green the following day at about 5.30pm. Both men worked together at The Irish Woodworkers in Crow Street. When they returned to the workshop the following day from their dinner break, they had their guns with them, primed for the assassination attempt. After finishing work, Byrne and Slattery made their way to College Green to meet McDonnell and Keogh.

Byrne and Slattery walked up Grafton Street and before long, they spotted Barton walking up the other side of the street. He seemed to have noticed the young Volunteers and he stopped a number of times to look into shop windows and glance across the street. Reaching the top of Grafton Street, he dallied awhile to look into a bookshop before crossing the street to walk down the other side. He still seemed aware of Byrne and Slattery, who kept a distance behind him. When they reached the bottom of the street, however, he disappeared from view.

They soon spotted Barton again as he crossed the road to Trinity College. Here they picked up McDonnell and Keogh, who had been joined by three other Volunteers – Paddy Daly, Joe Leonard and Ben Barrett. Barton continued into College Street, keeping to the right-hand side and mingling with people making their way home from work. It was proving very difficult to keep a clear view of Barton, and Byrne recalled:

> Barton got as far as the Crompton monument and was in the act of stepping off the path to cross over to the police station in Brunswick Street [now Pearse Street] when fire was opened on him. He went down on his side, falling to the right slightly. Then he turned towards his left and raised himself a little on his right knee and said: Oh, God, what did I do to deserve this?

Now Barton pulled his gun and fired up College Street. Byrne and McDonnell ran up College Street and were confronted by a policeman at the corner of

Westmoreland Street, who recoiled when Byrne drew his gun. Meanwhile, the stricken Barton was taken by ambulance to Mercer's Hospital, where he later died.

Byrne and his comrades engaged the enemy again on 19 December 1919, planning to assassinate Lord French, the Lord-Lieutenant of Ireland. A hate figure for republicans, he had openly supported the conscription of eligible Irishmen into the British Army and advocated the use of the military to bring it about. There had been a number of previous failed attempts to assassinate French. One plot, to shoot him as he attended a function at the Provost's house in Trinity College, was called off at the last minute. Another attempt was planned when French took the salute at a victory march in College Green, but again it was aborted, for fear of innocent civilians getting hurt.

A proposal was made that Byrne, Tom Keogh and Jimmy Slattery should determine if it was possible to assassinate French inside his place of residence, the Vice-Regal Lodge in Phoenix Park. It was known that French took a walk around the grounds every day and the plan was for the three of them to climb over the railings and hide in the bushes, where they would be in a position to shoot him:

> We scouted round the whole area to see if there was any chance of carrying out the job. We were unarmed. When we had finished our scouting, Tom Keogh said: 'Well, lads, what do you think of it?' I replied: 'I am no Robert Emmet.' So, we all agreed none of us were Robert Emmets.

They concluded that because of a strong police presence, it would be far too dangerous to make an attempt on French's life there. However, the chance to strike came quicker than expected and what transpired proved to be one of the most daring escapades of the independence war.

On the night of 18 December 1919, Byrne was sitting around a fire in the Sean Connolly Sinn Féin Club on North Summer Street, chatting with other members. A fellow called Paddy Sharkey mentioned his father, an engine driver on the railway, was due to travel to Roscommon the following morning, 'to bring ould French back to Dublin'. This of course was music to Byrne's ears and he asked Sharkey what time his father expected to be back in Dublin, to which he replied, around midday. Byrne went quickly around to Mick McDonnell's house with this important piece of information. An excited McDonnell said, 'That's the best bit of news I've heard in a long time.' He instructed Byrne to report back to the house at ten o'clock the next morning, 'as we might have a go on French'.

The following morning, Byrne, Tom Keogh, Martin Savage, Paddy Daly and Joe Leonard reported to McDonnell's house. McDonnell instructed Byrne to go to the arms dump and bring down a number of grenades. When he returned, the party had been joined by Dan Breen, Seumas Robinson and Sean Treacy. Byrne stated that Sean Hogan may well have been present as well.

When they were about to depart, there was a discussion as to whether Byrne should be included, as some considered him too young and inexperienced. It was eventually decided that he should come along, and he duly took possession of a bicycle and some grenades. The party cycled up the North Circular Road and out to Ashtown. They stopped at Kelly's pub and ordered soft drinks, going over the plan for the ambush. Byrne recalled:

> When I had finished my glass, Mick called me and told me to get my bike, cycle towards the station and see if there was any sign of the train, or if there were any military or police there. I got my bicycle and started to cycle down the road towards the station. I had only gone about two hundred yards when I heard the sound of motor cars coming. There were four cars in all. I wheeled around, cycled back as hard as I could and reported to Mick McDonnell about the military passing me going to the station.

Soon the men heard the sound of the train arriving in the distance. Daly, Leonard, Hogan, Treacy and Robinson took up positions behind a hedge near the road. Mick McDonnell, Dan Breen and Tom Keogh rushed into the yard of the pub and took a big farm cart. They pulled it to the side of the road, only for it to get stuck in the mud. The rest of the unit assumed positions at the intersection of the Navan Road and the road to the railway station. Around the same time, an Inspector and a policeman arrived and stood in the centre of the crossroads, to ensure that French's convoy would have a clear passage.

Eventually, the convoy approached, and the men behind the bushes opened fire on it. The first car contained the well-known Detective Sergeant Halley, who fired back with a revolver. Byrne recalled: 'As the car came clear of the corner, I let fly my grenade, which hit the the back of the car and exploded. The next thing I saw was the peeler being blown across the road.'

The second car stopped opposite the hedge where other Volunteers were hiding, while a third car accelerated past them, even though it was coming under a hail of fire. The fourth car, an open Sunbeam, had a soldier driving it and another lying across the backseat firing with a rifle.

Byrne recalled bullets whizzing past his head and very soon he heard Martin Savage shout that he had been hit. Within seconds, the Sligo native was lying dead on the road. The second car by then had smoke coming out of it and Byrne noticed the driver waving a handkerchief. The driver exited the car, but was unable to say where Lord French was. As the soldier, a Corporal Applesby, was of little interest, he was allowed to leave.

The ambush had been a failure, and the Volunteers cycled back into the city in pairs. Dan Breen, nursing a leg wound, had to lean on Paddy Daly, and Byrne, in a state of shock, recalled, 'I started talking to myself, in the strain that we would never see town. I honestly believed we would never see the city.'

However, the unit was not intercepted by the military or police and Byrne was home for his dinner within nine minutes. The stricken Dan Breen was eventually brought to a safe house on the Phibsboro Road, and it took some time for him to recover from his severe wound.

Unfortunately, the men had to leave the deceased Martin Savage behind, which caused his comrades a great deal of grief and sadness. A grocer's assistant, on the morning of the ambush Savage left the shop to bank some money for his employer. Instead of going to the bank, he went out on the job with his comrades. A newspaper report later stated that a large sum of money was found on his body by the authorities.

On 31 January 1920, Detective Inspector Redmond, who had been transferred to Dublin from Belfast to take over the Dublin Metropolitan Police intelligence operation, was shot dead. The Inspector had bragged that he would show those in Dublin Castle how to smash the IRA. The unofficial Squad (it would not gain official status until March 1920) first went after Redmond one evening on Dame

Street as he left Dublin Castle, but they failed to kill him. The following night, Redmond left the Castle about the same time and walked to Grafton Street and along St Stephen's Green. Turning on to Harcourt Street, he was gunned down just outside the Children's Hospital by a group led by Mick McDonnell.

In the early weeks of February, a raid was carried out on the Great Northern Railway. Tom Keogh worked for the company and he reported to Mick McDonnell, his step-brother, that he had loaded two wagons with gelignite in the course of his work that day. That evening, men from the 2nd Battalion in the city were mobilised and told to report to Oriel Hall on Oriel Street at 11.30pm. Those who possessed small arms were instructed to carry them. Some twenty to twenty-five men turned up at the appointed time.

Byrne and Slattery were sent out on bicycle patrol to keep an eye out for police or military, while some of the men got over the wall at the side of the Hall and made their way to the nearby railway wagons, directed by Tom Keogh. Other men remained outside the railway wall in their stocking feet. The job began, as the men raiding the wagons carried the gelignite to the wall and handed it over to the men in stocking feet. These men ran along Oriel Street and across Seville Place into Lower Oriel Street and down to the house occupied by another comrade, Paddy Ennis. Here it was concealed under the floorboards.

The next morning saw the beginning of military activity in the area, which lasted for several days. Every house in the vicinity of the railway was searched, even that of Paddy Ennis, but nothing was found. The gelignite was eventually used by the IRA in the making of hand grenades.

On 18 February, Byrne and some members of the Brigade and Squad were mobilised for the attempted rescue of Robert Barton, who had been on trial in Ship Street barracks. Byrne and Mick McDonnell waited outside the barracks on McDonnell's motorcycle and sidecar, expecting Barton to be transferred to Mountjoy jail. When the first car emerged from the barracks, they let it go on, but when a second one emerged, McDonnell believed Barton was in it. McDonnell and Byrne sped off in the direction of Berkeley Road, on the route to Mountjoy. At a given signal as the military car approached, two other men pushed a handcart and a ladder out onto Berkeley Road, stopping the car. Byrne recalled:

We rushed over, revolvers drawn, to find to our dismay that the only occupants of the van were two British soldiers who were unarmed; it was a Red Cross car. There was an officer in charge of the car. In the running over to the car a shot rang out and the officer shouted: 'One of your own men,' which was true.

Henry Kelly, when pulling the gun out of his pocket, shot himself in the foot. The soldiers were allowed to proceed on their journey, and Kelly was taken away in the sidecar. It transpired later that Barton was brought to Mountjoy under heavy guard escorted by two armoured cars. He later escaped from the prison, leaving a note for the Governor saying, 'Owing to the discomfort of the cell, the occupant felt compelled to leave.' He also requested the Governor to hold on to his luggage until he sent for it.

The following day, information was received that military stores had arrived by ship into Dublin and were being stored behind the B and I Shipping Company's offices at Sir John Rogerson's Quay. The 2nd Battalion carried out a raid on the premises around 10.30 that night. Byrne recalled that one of the men scaled the railings and smashed a window, allowing him to slip open the catch and get into the building, and open the door from the inside. Some men were posted outside to keep watch for any military or police, while others began searching the stores. Since no one was sure what they were looking for, all likely cases and boxes were opened. Byrne recalled:

I remember opening a case and finding that its contents consisted of sticks of black liquorice. Needless to say, I filled my pockets and had a good chew for a day or two. The next case I opened contained small tins of café au lait, so I helped myself to a tin and had a nice cup of coffee for my supper when I got home.

In a postscript to the raid, Byrne recalled he heard shots as he made his way home. He thought at the time that the shots had come from the St Stephen's Green area, but did not see anything warranting his attention. The following morning, he heard that two of his comrades, Paddy and Gay McGrath, had been accosted by some policemen. They were armed and opened fire on the brothers, wounding Paddy, who was taken to Mercer's Hospital, where he was put under armed guard. That evening, a party of Volunteers raided the hospital, overpowered the guard and spirited Paddy out of the building.

Members of the Crown forces were always in the sights of the Squad and every opportunity was taken to carry out ambushes or attacks on them. One individual who came to their notice was a Captain Hardy of the Auxiliaries, stationed in Dublin Castle. Byrne recalled that Hardy 'walked with a limp and had a reputation as a cruel and brutal interrogator of republican prisoners'.

It was decided that Hardy should be shot. However, he rarely left the Castle and when he did, it was under heavy escort. Information was received that he had gone to England, but was due to return on a particular Sunday morning, arriving in Dún Laoghaire by mailboat from Holyhead. Byrne, Tom Keogh and Jimmy Slattery were ordered to go to the port and attempt an assassination of Hardy. As it transpired, Byrne overslept and was late arriving at the appointed meeting place, the corner of Holles Street and Merrion Square. By then, Keogh and Slattery were already on their way to Dún Laoghaire.

Byrne decided to go home. As he walked through Merrion Square, he heard the rumble of an armoured motor vehicle approaching from the city, with its searchlight flashing from side to side. With the overnight curfew still in place, Byrne had to escape the attentions of the vehicle's searchlight:

I immediately threw myself on to the ground, at the same time hugging my body as close as possible by the small stone base on which the railings were standing. I shall never forget that morning! As I lay there, the searchlight played about three feet away from me. I said to myself: 'So this is the end.' But, lucky for me, the operator turned it to the other side. I breathed freely again, for I believe while I was on the ground I was afraid to breathe.

Having had a narrow escape, Byrne proceeded along Clare Street. As he was about to turn into Kildare Street, he ran into two policemen, who called on him to stop. He ran, pursued by the policemen. Stopping at Frederick Lane, he pulled out his gun and fired at his pursuers, who returned fire.

As he lived in the locality, he knew every nook and corner of the place. Eventually, he managed to get to his home in South Anne Street, learning later on in the morning that houses in the area had been raided.

As for Captain Hardy, he was collected at the port by an armoured car, thereby evading his would-be assassins. Byrne, Keogh and Slattery later came to the conclusion that the armoured car was the very same one that Byrne had managed to evade in Merrion Square.

Early one morning, a Dublin Castle horse-drawn mail van was ambushed in Parnell Square. Byrne, Tom Keogh and Jim Slattery, among others, were involved in the raid. As the van entered Parnell Square, Slattery and Keogh stepped off the pavement and caught the horse by the reins. Byrne ordered the driver and post-man to get down, leaving Slattery to drive the horses and van away to a building near Mountjoy Square.

There, the mail was searched by the whole of the Intelligence Staff, includ-ing Liam Tobin and Frank Thornton. Byrne and Keogh arrived and helped in the search. Some leather bags with official correspondence were dealt with by senior intelligence officers. Byrne recalled that they came across crisp pound notes in some of the letters, as well as passport applications with postal orders attached.

When the Intelligence Staff left, after taking what they deemed to be important, Byrne and his two colleagues remained to burn the rest of the haul. However, they gathered up all the postal orders, most of which were blank, and divided them equally between themselves. They agreed to cash them that day in various post offices. According to Byrne, they had a successful day and divided a substantial sum of money equally that evening.

Byrne and Jimmy Slattery left their jobs as carpenters on 9 March 1920, when the Squad was given full-time status. The official Squad, at the outset, comprised of twelve men and they quickly became known as the 'Twelve Apostles'. They came under the control of the Director of Intelligence or his Deputy and under no other authority. The men all ceased their work with their companies and bat-talions. The first Commander was Mick McDonnell.

Sometimes, the Squad was strengthened by members of the Intelligence Staff, the Active Service Unit, munitions workers and members of the Brigade as occasions demanded. The Squad was also assisted by Dan Breen, Seumas Robinson, Sean Treacy and Sean Hogan of the Tipperary flying column, as well Mick Brennan from Clare. Jackie Dunne of the Quartermaster General Staff, and Jimmy Brennan of 'C' Company of the 2nd Battalion were also involved.

The members of the Squad left their regular employment and were paid the same wages as they had earned with their former employers. The first full-time Squad was made up of Mick McDonnell, Tom Keogh, Jimmy Slattery, Paddy Daly, Joe Leonard, Ben Barrett, Vincent Byrne, Sean Doyle, Paddy Griffin, Eddie Byrne, Mick Reilly and Jimmy Conroy.

The Squad's first arms dump was located in Mountjoy Court, in a converted lock-up garage belonging to Mick McDonnell, where he kept his motorcycle. 'B' Company of the 2nd Battalion also had a dump nearby, and one morning, the area was closed off by the military. Barriers were placed on the streets by around 100 soldiers, accompanied by two whippet armoured cars and a three-ton lorry with a searchlight, which moved from place to place after dark, playing on the houses and streets.

Everyone was searched going in and out of the area for three days, and Byrne recalled that they could do nothing but look on and hope their arms dump was not discovered. When the military eventually left, Byrne, Keogh and Slattery took a chance on checking the garage and were relieved to find everything intact, though 'B' Company's dump had been discovered. They decided to take no chances, however, and cleared out the arms and ammunition. They made the correct decision because the military returned some days later and discovered the garage.

The Squad relocated its headquarters to a building on Middle Abbey Street, facing Stafford Street. A sign saying 'Moreland's, Cabinet-Making and Upholstering' was placed on the gates. The ground floor was used as a cabinet-making shop, which of course was only a ruse. The second floor consisted of two large stores, one of which had an opening window, which could be useful in the case of a raid. A secret passage was constructed within the building itself to act as a barricade.

Some pretence of cabinet making had to go on, and Byrne collected a tool kit from Messrs Booth of Stephen Street. When he picked it up, he handed the assistant a note that read, 'Taken in the name of the IRA.' He made a work bench and acquired lots of wood shavings to give the place some authenticity and create the impression of work being done.

Moreland's was never raided. The Squad's guns were hidden in an old ground-floor lavatory, which had its door bricked up. Access was by means of an ingenious mechanism of two nails and a mail bag lowered through the floor of another lavatory directly above the ground floor one.

According to Byrne:

The 'big fella', Mick Collins, visited us at least twice a week. Notwithstanding the enormous amount of work he undertook, he found time to visit his squad. The morale effect of his visits was wonderful. He would come in and say: 'Well, lads, how are ye getting on?' And pass a joke or two with us.

Byrne reiterated in his statement just how loyal everyone was to Collins. He was, he said,

... loved and honoured by each and every one of us, and his death was felt very keenly by the squad. I am proud to say that Mick stood by us in our hard time, and that every single member of the squad stood by him in his hard times, without exception.

One evening early in 1920, the Squad were in Moreland's, playing cards, as they often did during down time. Their game was suddenly interrupted by the sound of gunfire, which seemed to be coming from directly outside the gate. After a little while, Tom Keogh said, 'You had better go down Vincie and find out what all the row is about.'

Byrne recalled:

I threw my jacket off, tucked up my shirt sleeves and, with my overalls on me, I looked the real hard-working fellow. I proceeded to the gate and opened the wicket. Standing outside was a British Tommy. I popped my head out and asked him what was all the shooting. He replied: 'Those bloody Shinners ambushed us.' I said to him: 'that's terrible,' and then I remarked: 'I had better be getting back to my job, in case the boss is looking for me.'

Byrne went back to his comrades and told them what had happened. They later learned that the Active Service Unit had attacked an army lorry at the corner of Swift's Row and Ormond Quay.

On 2 March 1920, the Squad assassinated a British agent named Jameson. Though Byrne was not part of the assassination team, he did give details of the killing. Jameson arrived in Dublin from Scotland Yard and posed as a commercial traveller. He was staying at the Hammam Hotel in Upper O'Connell Street, and quickly became known to Collins and his Intelligence Unit. Jameson contacted Collins and offered him all the arms he wanted and Collins played along with him.

One evening, Jameson was met by a Squad member, who escorted him to see the 'big fella'. They boarded the tram to Glasnevin and, unbeknownst to Jameson, so did other members of the Squad. They arrived at the terminus and walked along the Ballymun Road for some distance before Jameson was shot dead.

Three weeks later, on 23 March, the Squad was in action again when a sergeant in the British Army by the name of Molloy made contact with the Intelligence Unit, asking to meet Liam Tobin. That evening, Frank Saurin of the Intelligence Staff took him for tea in the Cairo Café on Grafton Street. Byrne was detailed to follow them to the café and he took a seat at a table beside them, so that he could identify Molloy in the future.

After a while, Saurin acknowledged Byrne and asked him to join them. He introduced him to Molloy, saying to Byrne, 'Our friend is anxious to meet Liam Tobin and I am sure you can arrange it.' Byrne indicated that he could do so. He recalled Molloy saying he could be very useful to the movement. After having tea, they agreed to meet the following evening at the corner of South King Street and Grafton Street. The following evening, Byrne and members of the Squad went to the appointed meeting place and saw Molloy waiting. The Squad members observed him from a distance for three quarters of an hour before he moved off down Grafton Street. Byrne recalled:

We made several attempts to get him, but, owing to the large number of people in the street, it was very difficult. He turned into Wicklow Street and proceeded as far as the corner of South William Street. Here we opened fire and he fell dead.

While they were making their getaway, civilians started shouting, 'Stop them,' and some bystanders attempted to do so. This, according to Byrne, was the first time this ever happened. He was of the opinion that the people on the street believed the shooting had been carried out by Auxiliaries or British military dressed in civilian clothes. The public was on edge at that time because, only four days previously, Tomás MacCurtain had been shot dead in Cork by members of the RIC dressed in civilian clothes.

One of the more high-profile assassinations of the War of Independence took place on 26 March 1920, with the shooting dead of Alan Bell, a British agent sent to Ireland to examine bank accounts held in the name of Sinn Féin. His assassination highlighted the lengths Collins and his associates were prepared to go in order to preserve Sinn Féin's finances, which were so important to the successful prosecution of the conflict.

Information was received from the Intelligence Unit that on a particular afternoon Alan Bell was due to visit the Four Courts. Byrne and Mick McDonnell were delegated to carry out the hit on Bell. They took up a position at the corner of Chancery Street and Ormond Quay, with an Intelligence officer posted on Grattan Bridge. He was to give a signal by waving his handkerchief when Bell's car passed him on the bridge, and Byrne and McDonnell planned to throw a grenade at the car as it passed them. The signal eventually came and Byrne and McDonnell expected the car to travel up Chancery Street, but instead it travelled away up the quays.

Two days later, six Squad men went out to Monkstown to make another attempt on Bell's life, as it was known he was living there. When they arrived, however, some five or six 'G' men were standing outside the house and it was decided not to pursue the attempt.

It was learned that Bell came into town every morning by tram and usually alighted on Grafton Street. Byrne and his colleagues scouted the area on a number of mornings, but failed to locate Bell. They did, however, notice that one of the men who had followed Byrne and Slattery some days earlier along Dame Street was conspicuous by his presence on Grafton Street every morning, clearly anticipating an attack on Bell. It seemed that they would need to devise another plan.

On 26 March, Tom Keogh cycled out to Monkstown while other Squad members, together with Intelligence officers, were despatched to Aylesbury Road to await developments. Keogh was to determine which tram Bell took into town and follow it. When it got to Ailesbury Road, he was to signal to his waiting colleagues that the agent was on board.

Bell boarded a tram in Monkstown and Keogh kept pace with it into the city and gave the signal on Ailesbury Road. The Squad members boarded the tram and Byrne recalled:

I was detailed to go on top. My job was to cut the trolley rope when I heard any
commotion going on below. When we got as far as Simmonscourt Road, Bell was
pulled off the tram. The conductor ran up the stairs shouting: 'There's going to be a
man shot!' I said to him: 'Oh, let me down off this tram' – at the same time cutting
the trolley rope.

After shooting Bell, the Squad members ran up Simmonscourt Road, with some
men veering off to Donnybrook and others to Clonskeagh.

The following month, information was received that a 'G' man by the name of
Dalton was carrying out what the authorities in Dublin Castle called 'political
work'. On 20 April, the Squad received orders to eliminate Dalton. Byrne and a
number of his comrades made their way to the Black Church at St Mary's Place,
off Dorset Street, and were joined by a number of Intelligence officers. They all
took up positions on each side of the Black Church to wait for the target. Dalton
arrived, accompanied by an escort, and as they crossed to Mountjoy Street, the
men detailed to carry out the assassination shot him dead. Byrne recalled it was
a miracle the escort escaped injury or death, but that it was just as well, as he was
not a wanted man.

The Squad was involved in an intelligence war, which required a certain
amount of patience. There were times when they were frustrated by plans going
awry, but they just had to accept it and move on to the next job. Not all assassination attempts were successful, and Byrne detailed two operations in particular
that failed.

The first involved the tracking of a detective by the name of Coffey. A dedicated
'G' Division man, Coffey was engaging in political work and the Intelligence Unit
wanted him eliminated. Coffey lived at Kenmare Place just off the North Circular Road, and one morning the Squad took up positions nearby to carry out the
assassination. Coffey appeared with his escort, but as the men detailed to shoot
him were about to open fire, two women appeared on the scene. They stood very
close to the target and began speaking to him. The Squad had no option but to
call the operation off. The following day, Coffey was spotted patrolling around the
city. The Squad made contact with him around 5.30pm in St Andrew Street, but
the opportunity to shoot him was lost when he disappeared from view.

The second failed assassination attempt revolved around another 'G' Division man called Revelle. The Detective Sergeant, who lived just off the Phibsboro Road, was deemed to be a real danger to the republican movement. He was, it seems, somewhat arrogant and his custom was to sleep at home every night, believing he was immune to attack. Byrne was delegated to follow Revelle and report on his movements. He arrived on the Phibsboro Road at 9am on 7 May and waited around for half an hour until Revelle appeared. When he did, the 'G' man stared long and hard at Byrne before moving off at a strong pace.

Byrne followed Revelle for a while before he disappeared and then re-emerged behind a tramway standard. Byrne recalled pretending to look at his watch and attempting to be as inconspicuous as possible. Revelle moved off and Byrne decided it was not in his interest to follow him, especially when he saw him speaking to a policeman. Byrne jumped on a tram and went to Mick McDonnell's house to make his report. Liam Tobin happened to be there at the time. It was decided to have a go at Revelle the next morning.

The Squad took up their positions the next morning, and it wasn't long before Revelle appeared on his bicycle on Connaught Street. As he came within yards of the men detailed to shoot him, they stepped out in front of him and fired a volley, sending the 'G' man across the street. Thinking the job finished, the Squad members made their getaway.

However, Revelle cheated death because he was wearing a steel jacket. That evening one of the newspapers interviewed him and he was reported to have said, 'I would know one of them very well, as I had seen him the previous morning.' This of course left Byrne in a difficult position. He could not allow himself to be arrested as long as Revelle remained in the Castle, for fear he would identify him.

Byrne did indeed come very close to being captured by Crown forces one day. He and another squad member, Bill Stapleton, were taking their ease, strolling down Fownes Street and looking into shop windows. When they came to the corner of Cope Street, they walked into a military patrol. Byrne recalled that it was the last thing they expected to meet. Both men, of course, had revolvers in their pockets, which put them in a difficult and dangerous situation.

With a British officer watching them very intently, Bill Stapleton, thinking on his feet, said, 'I wonder is this the right number?' Byrne replied, 'Let's try.' The two men entered the building, climbed a flight of stairs and waited at the top for a few minutes. When they came down and re-emerged onto the street, the patrol had moved off. Byrne maintained that had Stapleton not been so quick-thinking, they certainly would have been arrested on the spot with guns in their pockets, or alternatively, they would have had to use them against overwhelming odds.

In July 1920, word came down from the Intelligence Unit that Collins wanted the Squad to eliminate a man called Frank Brooke. Brooke lived in Shillelagh in County Wicklow and was a Director of the Great Southern and Eastern Railway and an advisor to the British military in Ireland. Byrne, Jimmy Slattery and Tom Keogh cycled down to Wicklow and stayed in the Keogh family home while they scouted the demesne where Brooke lived and the general Shillelagh area. As the three were best friends as well as comrades, they decided to enjoy the glorious summer weather for a few days in Keogh's home area. However, it wasn't long before a letter arrived from their immediate boss, Mick McDonnell, admonishing them for staying beyond the time agreed and ordering them back to Dublin.

They were back in Dublin a few days when information was received that Brooke would be at a railway office in Westland Row at a certain time. Four Squad members, led by Paddy Daly, made their way to the office. While one man waited in the hallway, the others went upstairs. They shot Brooke dead as a train arrived in the station, the noise of the train masking the shot.

On 17 October 1920, the Squad carried out another successful assassination in the heart of the city. The target was an RIC Sergeant named Roche, a Tipperary man who had come to the city to identify the body of Sean Treacy, who had died in a shootout on Talbot Street. Roche left the Castle in the company of Dave Neligan – a G-man who Collins called his 'spy in the Castle' and a future Commandant in the National Army. Neligan excused himself to go into a shop, which was the cue for the assassins to step in. As Roche sauntered on down towards the corner of Strand Street, they opened fire and shot him dead.

Byrne recalled the delivery of a Thompson gun to Moreland's, and Tom Keogh following the instructions on an accompanying pamphlet to assemble it:

As we did not know what was going to happen, we all stood behind him in case of danger. Keogh started to load the drum, and when he had it fully loaded, he slipped it on the gun. He started to fidget around with it, when all of a sudden there was a burst of fire. In fact, it nearly drilled a hole in a brick wall.

The Intelligence Unit had been collecting the addresses of British Intelligence officers living across the city. When it was completed, Collins decided to act against them, and the operation was planned for 9am on Sunday, 21 November 1920. The Squad and the Intelligence Unit, aided by men from various Volunteer battalions around the city, were to participate.

Byrne was ordered to lead the raid on 28 Upper Mount Street. When they arrived at the house, he detailed five men to keep guard while he went to the door with Tom Ennis and rang the bell. A servant girl opened the door and Byrne, jamming the door with his foot, asked to see Lieutenant Bennett or Lieutenant Aimes. She let them in and directed them to the rooms where the men were sleeping. One was in the parlour and the other in a back room.

Ennis went to the back room while Byrne went to the parlour, accompanied by Sean Doyle and Herbie Conroy. As he opened the door, the officer was in the act of going for his gun under his pillow. He was ordered to put his hands up, which he did. Doyle pulled a Colt .45 from under the pillow while Frank Saurin of the Intelligence Unit entered the room and began his search for papers. Byrne ordered the man out of bed, and he asked what was going to happen to him. Byrne replied, 'Ah, nothing,' and marched him out of the room.

As they were entering the back hall, they heard a hell of a row going on somewhere outside, with heavy revolver fire. The front doorbell rang and the man covering the door looked at Byrne. Byrne told him, 'Open the door,' and in walked a British soldier, who seemed to be a despatch rider. He was ordered to put his hands up, which he did, and Byrne left him under guard in the hall. Byrne recalled:

I then marched my officer down to the back room where the other officer was. He was standing up in the bed, facing the wall. I ordered mine to do likewise. When the two of them were together, I said to myself: 'The Lord have mercy on your souls!' I then opened fire with my Peter. They both fell dead.

As they left the house, they came under fire from a house across the road. They retreated as quickly as they could. As they neared Lower Mount Street, the gunfire was very heavy. Byrne recalled Tom Keogh dashing across the road and, as he did so, dropping one of his guns. Undeterred, Keogh quietly turned back and picked it up.

The raiding parties then made their way to the quays at the South Wall, where they were to take a boat across the river. When they arrived, however, the boat was on the other side, but it crossed back over and Byrne and his colleagues boarded it and made for the relative safety of the city's northside. He eventually arrived at 17 Richmond Street and made his report to the waiting Sean Russell.

The Squad was back in action on 28 January 1921, when it was instructed to assassinate a man by the name of Doran, who worked as a porter in the Wicklow Hotel. The Intelligence Unit had credible information that Doran was a police informer and had passed on information about the movements of various men staying at the hotel. He had been warned to desist from that practice, but had refused to take heed of the warning.

On that morning, Byrne and a number of comrades made their way to Wicklow Street and waited for Doran. They knew he was in the habit of sweeping in front of the hotel every morning between 8.30 and 9am. When he came out, the men opened fire and Doran fell dead on the path. In Byrnes's view, Doran was just another informer out of the way.

The burning of the Custom House in Dublin was carried out on 25 May 1921, and though it was a propaganda coup for the IRA, it was, in the end, a military disaster. Some 100 men took part in the operation, including about seventy-five from the 2nd Battalion of the Dublin Brigade, under the command of Tom Ennis. The Squad members were under the command of Paddy Daly and Tom Keogh and the Active Service Unit was commanded by Paddy Flanagan.

The orders were that, after the civil servants had vacated their offices for lunch, the whole building was to be saturated with petrol. Tom Ennis would give a signal by blowing a whistle, and the men were to set the building alight. Byrne's task was to set alight some offices on the second floor. When he got to the first office, he recalled:

I opened the office door and sitting inside were a lady and a gentleman, civil ser-
vants, having tea. I requested them to leave, stating that I was going to set fire to the
office. The gentleman stood up and said: 'Oh you can't do that!' I showed him my gun
and told him I was serious. I said to him: 'You had better get out at once, unless you
want to be burned alive.' The lady then asked me could she get her coat, and I replied:
'Miss, you'll be lucky if you get out with your life.' They then left.

Byrne gathered up all the ledgers and paper he could find in the office and doused
them in petrol. On hearing the signal, he stepped outside, lit a ball of paper and
threw it into the room, setting it ablaze.

Unfortunately for Byrne and his comrades, the operation then began to
unravel. The caretaker was shot dead when he attempted to call the police. A
watching policeman notified the authorities, and some sixty Auxiliaries turned up
in lorries and an armoured car. A thirty-minute gun battle ensued and a number
of IRA Volunteers and civilians were killed or wounded.

Byrne was confronted by two Auxiliaries and attempted to shoot his way out
of the building, but ran out of ammunition and had to give himself up. He was
struck a number of times with a rifle and ordered to walk over to the nearby
Brooks Thomas premises. Asked what he was doing in the building, he recalled
replying, 'I was on a message for my boss, sir.' He was struck again and told not
to stir from the spot, as the two Auxiliaries left him and turned their attention to
a dead civilian lying nearby.

Across the road he could see many of his comrades under guard, but did not
hail them. A big crowd of civilians stood outside the entrance to Brooks Thomas,
and Byrne moved slowly and quietly towards them. As he mingled into the crowd,
he noticed the strong smell of petrol coming from his hands. He took some cigarettes from his pocket, wet them and rolled them very well into his hands, thereby
giving off a strong smell of tobacco. Soon, he came before an officer and asked
if he could go home. The officer asked him what he was doing there, and Byrne
recalled saying:

'Sir, I was on my way to Brooks Thomas to buy some timber.' He then ran his hands
all over me and pulled out a carpenter's rule and a few pieces of paper out of my
pocket. The papers showed different sizes of pieces of timber, which I usually carried

as a decoy. Handing me back my rule and papers, the officer said: 'Get to hell out of this.' I said: 'Thank you, sir.'

Some weeks later, the Squad was given another assignment – to assassinate a British Intelligence officer known as the 'Frenchman', who was staying in the St Andrew's Hotel on Exchequer Street. While he was not long in the country, he had a bad record, and it was believed he had taken part in the shooting of some Volunteers in the south of the country.

The Squad took up their positions in Exchequer Street one particular morning, while the men detailed to shoot the 'Frenchman' stood at the corner of Drury Street. The target left the hotel around 9.30am and, as he approached the corner of Drury Street, he was shot dead.

During the last few weeks prior to the truce in July 1921, Byrne and those of his colleagues who had not been arrested after the Custom House burning contented themselves with smaller-scale operations, like the burning of two railway carriages carrying supplies for the British military and raiding a couple of mail vans. The Truce brought about an end to the work of the Squad, and life for Vincent Byrne was set to change for ever. For the previous two years, he had placed himself in real danger, at the heart of the clandestine war against the might of the British Empire. He had proved his worth in the field as a shrewd and courageous member of a group of young men that occupies a revered place in the annals of Ireland's modern history. Vincent Byrne went on to serve his country as a respected officer in the National Army.

Chapter 13

Seán Moylan: Committed Republican and Outstanding Military Leader

Irishmen, they could not accept the view that they were a lesser breed, that their country was fated to remain a Province. Blindly, instinctively, they held to this refusal; out of it, because they were intuitively right, came light and guidance and strength to achieve. Ireland would never again be quiescent under foreign rule.

(Seán Moylan)

On 12 November 2007, the *Irish Examiner* reported on a commemoration held the previous day in Kiskeam, County Cork. It was the fiftieth anniversary of the death of the great IRA Commandant, and later national politician, Seán Moylan. The article stated that Moylan shared a political vision with some of the major figures of the revolutionary era, such as Sean Lemass. According to the then-Minister of Justice Brian Lenihan, who gave the keynote speech at the commemoration, Moylan and Lemass went on to lay the foundations for a remarkable transformation in Ireland's economic fortunes throughout the 1960s.

Lenihan rightly pointed out that Moylan was not only an outstanding military leader during the War of Independence, but he also left a legacy of achievements as a politician and statesman that enriched the economic, educational and social fabric of the country. Lenihan went on to say that Moylan:

... left us with a set of personal qualities of integrity, honesty, nobility and forthrightness that provide an enduring standard for all holding high office. That is a measure of the contribution which this extraordinary republican made to the profession of politics in this country.

Seán Moylan was born on 19 November 1888, in Kilmallock, County Limerick. In his extensive statement made in 1953, he recalled his early upbringing among people who were dedicated to the republican ideal.

Moylan opened his statement with a personal recollection from when he was a small boy, of meeting a man called Patrick Pickett, his grandmother's brother. Pickett, a revered man among his people, had taken part in the Fenian Rising at Kilmallock in 1867, and had been ordered to intercept a police dispatch rider travelling between Bruff and Kilmallock. After disarming the rider, he took his horse and the dispatches and handed them over to his commanding officer at Kilmallock. For that action, Pickett was sent to Limerick jail.

While he was in prison, another man was convicted of the attack on the policeman and sent to Australia for five years as punishment. When an amnesty was introduced and Pickett was released from prison, he heard that an innocent man had been convicted of his crime, and he promptly presented himself at the local RIC barracks and confessed to it. The truth of Pickett's statement was eventually confirmed, and the innocent man was brought back to Kilmallock and given £300 in compensation.

In view of the amnesty, it was decided Pickett should not be tried for the incident. He was released, and subsequently emigrated to America. He was a man of integrity who, like his Fenian brethren, could be counted on to uphold the values of that community. Seán Moylan went on to live his life abiding by those same principles.

Family circumstance saw Moylan move to Newmarket in County Cork. Here there was no tradition of Fenianism and the people were not really interested in the politics of the past or the nationalist future. In fact, the most prominent people in Newmarket were unionist in their outlook. He recalled the local bank manager and his assistants being of that disposition, as were the local stationmaster, the petty sessions clerk and the postmaster.

There was a tradition in Newmarket of holding a concert once or twice a year to raise funds in support of the local harriers and invariably the evening was brought to an end with the singing of 'God Save the King'. On one occasion, Moylan's younger brother, Joe, sang a rendition of 'God Save Ireland' in opposition to the anthem. This led to the hall descending into chaos and the nationalists in the audience milling out on to the street, cheering and laughing. It turned out to be the last ever foxhound concert, and Moylan said that he noticed the first signs of political change in the community that evening.

He returned to Kilmallock, where he was apprenticed as a carpenter. When the Gaelic League set up a branch in the town, he enrolled as a member and came into contact with people who discussed the merits of Sinn Féin and Arthur Griffith. Moylan had barely heard of Sinn Féin at the time, but asking questions of those in the know, he soon realised it was a political movement he could relate to.

Moylan joined the Irish Volunteers in 1913, but was not impressed by those who joined with him. He believed many of the recruits saw the organisation as just another arm of the Irish Parliamentary Party.

With his apprenticeship complete, he moved back to Newmarket in April 1914, to start a business of his own. In June of that year, a Volunteer company was set up in Newmarket and initially attracted some 200 recruits. According to Moylan, most of them had no idea about soldiering or a soldier's way of life. In fact, he described them as 'a gay irresponsible crowd of young men attracted for the moment by the drilling, marching and shouted orders'. However, he stated that some were eventually to become first-class material for military purposes and they went on to prove themselves in the IRA.

The nightly drills before the outbreak of the First World War were attended by the more unionist-minded members of the community, who hoped the young men they were watching would eventually join the British Army to fight in the trenches in Europe. Unfortunately for the Volunteers organisation, the early enthusiasm soon dissipated and, by the time war was declared in the first week of August 1914, only eight men remained in the company. Of that number, Moylan recalled, one was killed in action on IRA duty in 1921, another was sentenced to death in the same year and two others died prematurely of wounds and disease while on active service.

Late in 1914, a Volunteers organiser, Tom McCarthy, arrived in the area. He stayed around for a few months, working hard to convince men that a fight was necessary to attain independence, but met with little enthusiasm. The 1916 Easter Rising mostly passed the Newmarket community by, and Moylan said that the lack of interest and enthusiasm may have been down to the absence of clear and explicit orders from Dublin. Had there been more clarity, he said, there would have been attempts to 'fight in pockets around the country but little more than that'. As it was, there was no coherent country-wide Volunteers organisation. There was also a distinct lack of arms.

Regardless of the lack of enthusiasm in Newmarket generally for the nationalist ideal, Moylan and a small few Volunteers met and drilled in secret, sometimes half-heartedly. Another problem, he maintained, was that he and his comrades were living in an isolated, rural district – their only contact with the outside world was via the daily newspaper, which was, more often than not, filled with news of the war rather than any information or comment on the Volunteers.

When the Company received its mobilisation order on Easter Sunday 1916, it met, for the first time, other companies from adjoining areas at the mobilisation point on Barley Hill, near Newmarket. Then, after waiting around all day, the men were ordered to return home and were not called upon again.

Many of those who did parade that day, Moylan recalled, 'emigrated in the following years; some played minor parts in the movement; some disappeared from it; a few were faithful to the end'.

Despite little happening in Newmarket during the rebellion, Moylan believed that many in Cork and elsewhere were willing to fight for their country's independence. He became even more convinced of this in the wake of the Easter Rising. He said that though leaders had died and others had been imprisoned, the ideal of an Irish republic continued to be widely held across the country. When the prison gates were opened in December 1916, and in June 1917, the prisoners returned home as heroes to a most enthusiastic welcome. In his statement, Moylan said that what had initially been an insurrection quickly became a revolution. He admitted that:

> ... *whether I intended it or not I became one of its organisers. I was never again to follow my humdrum occupation, to live my 'quiet uneventful life'. I was to travel many a weary mile, to make good friends and bitter enemies, to develop endless patience and tolerance, to know wounds and hunger and weariness of spirit, to learn how fear is conquered and to stand at last in the shadows of the gallows tree.*

Life for Moylan and many other young men changed dramatically in 1918 as they engaged in a physical training regime. This, he said, played 'an important role in developing each man's character'. They enthusiastically engaged in long-distance cycling on bad roads as well as punishing sessions of drilling and marching.

Moylan believed the IRA did not emerge as a result of 'clearly conceived plans', but was born out of an uprising by the people, with its roots in a long tradition of resistance. He said that it was lucky to have escaped the control of professional soldiers, instead veering from the outset towards traditional guerrilla tactics based on locally organised units. Of course, some control and direction did emanate from Dublin headquarters, but Moylan said that this was more of a general nature rather than specific. He recalled that brigades and companies were really left to make their own decisions and to take the opportunities that came their way to make life difficult for the Crown forces in their areas.

He was convinced that this looseness of organisation was a major source of strength during the conflict with the British, as any setback suffered by a company or brigade in one area did not materially impact on the morale of men in another area. This, in his view, was very important to the IRA's overall prosecution of the war.

The IRA became an almost nationwide fighting force in a very short time, despite a lack of financial resources and equipment. This, said Moylan, was entirely due to the selfless determination of the fighting men in the field. Moylan injected a note of bitterness when he said that, to his knowledge, not a penny or cent of the funds collected by Dáil Éireann through the National Loan schemes went towards financing the Irish Republican Army. In fact, the fighting men were left to finance themselves, depending on the generosity of family members and sympathetic neighbours and friends.

Up to the time of the so-called 'German Plot', Moylan lived at home and devoted his spare time to the IRA, but after May 1918, it was no longer feasible for him to do so, and he was also unable to pursue any work as a carpenter. In effect, he was forced, like other young men, to go 'on the run' and depend on friends to provide him with food and shelter. He recalled needing nothing more than that. He did not smoke and only took a drink, he said, when his 'wearied muscle had to be flogged to meet unexpected demands or as a remedy for complaints caught from soaking rain and chilling winds'. He did, however, often welcome the delivery of a pound note and some underclothing from home.

One of the first consequences of the emergence of the IRA across the country was the retreat of the RIC from more rural and isolated barracks to the bigger and better-protected barracks in the towns. Moylan claimed it left the countryside open to a sense of lawlessness, with age-old animosities over land, water rights and rights of way rearing their ugly heads once more.

With the disappearance of the RIC, the Petty Sessions court system broke down and became almost non-existent. As a consequence, bullying, burglary and riotous behaviour was widespread, and the easy availability of alcohol, especially poteen, contributed to the mayhem. Moylan supported the emergence of Arbitration Courts set up by local Sinn Féin branches to deal with the social problems bedevilling the country at the time. People took notice of the Courts, he said, because behind them was the spectre of the gun and the severe justice often imposed upon those found guilty of offences. The Arbitration Courts had no set procedures, and evidence was often accepted that no traditional court would have allowed.

Moylan discussed how the Volunteer movement dealt with and combatted the existence of bad and unsociable behaviour across the country. The organisation managed to implement a very robust intelligence structure, so that those who carried out crimes or disturbed the peace were quickly identified and apprehended. In most instances, it was sufficient just to issue a warning to the culprits and some cases were settled by the handing over of a sum of money to those who were wronged. A very few cases were settled with the forced deportation of a wrongdoer.

Moylan was adamant that these remedies were effective and resulted in a significant drop in crime across the country. In essence, the republicans took the matter of law and order into their own hands. They could rightly claim that their justice system was not only successful but was also accepted and embraced by the people.

Moylan recounted a number of cases to illustrate how the Arbitration Courts operated. The first concerned the wife of a British soldier forced to leave her rented home by her landlord so he could avail of the higher rents available in the rental market. Before the outbreak of the War of Independence, married quarters attached to the various barracks around the country were sufficient to house the families of married members of a garrison. However, with the increase in violence in the countryside, more and more soldiers' wives were forced to seek housing in the safer, larger garrison towns. As a result, landlords attempted to evict existing tenants in order to let their properties out at higher rents.

The woman in question heard about the Sinn Féin Arbitration Court and brought her case before it. It was a problematic case for the Court, having to defend the wife of a British soldier against an abuse of her rights. They discussed the possibility that the case might be a ruse and the British military would turn up on the day of the hearing. The case went ahead, but with scouts posted all over the area from the previous night, ready to raise the alarm if any military activity was spotted.

When the Court was called into session, the irate landlord pointed out that the case had already been heard by a law court and a decision in his favour had been passed down. Moylan recalled the landlord making it clear that, in his view, 'it wasn't the business of Irish republicans to interfere on behalf of a British soldier's wife and the property was his and he could do as he liked with it'.

The landlord attempted to pander to the Court by expressing anti-British feeling. But the English woman was allowed to make her case, and Moylan remembered her 'as middle-aged, rotund and good-humoured and had the attention of all of those present even if they sometimes failed to understand her strong Lancashire accent'.

Though she was an Englishwoman and a stranger, she was, like many other women in Ireland, poor and in difficulties. When the Court handed down a verdict in her favour, it proved a popular one. Moylan recalled her offering to pay the cost of the Court and he informed her that there was no cost. Beaming and obviously pleased with the decision, she said, 'Young man, when you need a midwife you know my address.'

To show the fairness of the Sinn Féin Arbitration Court system, Moylan recalled another incident involving a dispute between two gangs of poachers over a salmon net. The river Blackwater, noted for its abundance of salmon, passed through his area, though the fishing was well protected by bailiffs and police. In this instance, two groups of men were indulging in the illegal and anti-social activity of poaching. The IRA took a dim view of this, and the men were brought before the Arbitration Court. The men were not only fined, but also had their nets confiscated. The Arbitration Courts signified a refusal to recognise British authority in Ireland, but they did uphold the law and contribute to a sense of order across the country, and that stance, Moylan claimed, had the backing of the people.

All law breakers were swiftly dealt with and, apart from the RIC and the British military carrying out raids and interfering with fairs, markets and football matches, the countryside was relatively peaceful in 1918. Despite the hiatus, Moylan and his comrades continued making plans, putting in place a military organisation capable of taking on the enemy when the time arrived.

There had been only one brigade in Cork city and county in 1917. At the first meeting held to reorganise it, there were less than twenty men present, among them Tomás MacCurtain, Terence MacSwiney, Sean Hegarty and Tom Hales. Yet, within a year, the strength of the Volunteers organisation in Cork, and around the country, had increased significantly. Units in adjoining areas were making contact with each other and formulating cohesive plans for the War of Independence.

Before fully embracing the life of a guerrilla fighter, Moylan turned his attention to the political side of Irish republicanism. With the general election looming in December 1918, he stepped back from his Volunteers activities, as his organisational skills were required in the election campaign.

With the election over, he returned to Cork and his home area, which he described as 'the land of abandoned and destroyed police barracks'. He recalled

The Times of London describing them as 'Tombstones of British Supremacy in Ireland'. While occupied with his political work, Moylan had kept in touch with the military wing of republicanism, regularly meeting with Tomás MacCurtain, his Brigade OC, in the Boggerah Hills around Macroom.

Unfortunately for him and so many more in Ireland, disaster struck around this time, with the outbreak of the 'Spanish flu' pandemic, which took as victims some of the most promising men in the Volunteers movement. Moylan himself was struck down in the winter of 1919, and spent a long month fighting the illness and another month recuperating.

Moylan recalled Liam Lynch, his Brigade Commandant, visiting him just after he returned to duty in early January 1920, and insisting that he resume his post as Battalion Commanding Officer. He was somewhat reticent to do so and pleaded ill health. He later admitted the real reason for his reluctance was that he feared some resentment among the men down the command chain who would face demotion if he resumed his position as their commanding officer. As it transpired, that fear was unfounded. Charlie O'Reilly, who had stood in for him during his absence, willingly and graciously stepped aside and served with Moylan until he was killed in action a year later.

As soon as he returned to his post, Moylan turned his attention to the operational failures that had beset his Battalion during his absence. A number of planned ambushes and attacks had failed because of indiscreet conversations and leakage of information. He decided that, in the future, information would be kept within a very narrow circle. A raid was carried out on the mail to determine where the leaks were coming from. Moylan thought that this would yield prolific information and, as it turned out, his expectations were well and truly exceeded. The information gleaned resulted, he said, in several deportations, a number of warnings and an almost complete drying up of enemy intelligence.

The raid took place on the night before the initial meeting of the newly elected County Council. A dozen men under Moylan's direction skimmed through the letters and put aside, for his perusal, any which they had a doubt about. Moylan recalled it being a long night's work, which finished at around 6am, when they all sat down for breakfast.

Two of the group were newly elected members of the County Council and after breakfast they prepared to set off for their first meeting. They washed and shaved, and one of the men drew the attention of the others to the condition of their shirts and collars, which were dirty and crumpled after the night's work. Moylan remembered seeing among the parcels one that had the label of a well-known laundry in Cork on it, addressed to a police barracks in Portmagee in Kerry. He opened the parcel and found a number of pristine shirts and collars. His two comrades were quickly kitted out and sent on their way, immaculately dressed, to their first County Council meeting.

Moylan had cause to regret that many more laundered shirts and collars had not fallen into his hands. An unseen difficulty arose very quickly in 1920, with an outbreak of scabies. Improper hygiene, lack of underclothing and irregular hours, food and sleep were probably the causes of the problem, which, he said, affected his men in different ways. Many strong, athletic young men were virtually incapacitated by the infestation, with Moylan recalling Seamus Brislane as the first to fall victim to it. Everywhere he went, it seems, he left a trail of infection behind him. When he was finally discovered to be the carrier, the curses put on him by his comrades were, in Moylan's words, 'varied, eloquent and all inclusive'.

The British decided that the mail needed to be protected and had to be escorted every night to the railway station, with the soldiers remaining on the platform until the train had departed. Moylan and his comrades heard that the soldiers were less than happy about this particular duty, and so they continued to raid the mail for the best part of a month, so that the British had to guard every movement of the mail.

Moylan recalled the last raid of the campaign produced much laughter among his men. The mailbags arrived in Newmarket one morning, accompanied by a number of troops on bicycles. The bags were delivered to the post office, and the soldiers waited outside for their own letters. Meanwhile, two or three IRA Volunteers arrived into the office via the back door, held up the staff and disappeared with the bags. The soldiers were less than enamoured when they discovered what had happened, and their 'sulphurous eloquence' remained a treasured memory, according to Moylan, for many people living in the district.

He also recalled the strength of the Battalion was considerably increased during the early months of 1920, and, as a result, an Active Service Unit was brought into being. It did not take long for it to become a cohesive and determined fighting force. The commitment of the men in the Unit was matched, said Moylan, by the civilian population in the area. The railwaymen, for example, refused to handle trains carrying British troops, which often led to the dismissal of the drivers and the guards. Moylan recalled how he spoke, one Sunday afternoon, to the local Sinn Féin Constituency Committee, asking them to collect £1,000 for a fund in support of the railway men. Within a week, he said, the money was lodged with the officials of the men's union. He pointed out that this was not a forced contribution but a spontaneous gift from local people.

In the early months of 1920, a curfew order came into effect across the country and, in the garrison towns, curfew patrols were established to enforce it. The curfew, said Moylan, placed a real burden on the people and restricted their lives. He recalled how:

> ... those working indoors during the day had no opportunity for outdoor recreation, the children's play was stilled and the ordinary friendly intercourse of the village street brought to a complete cessation.

In Newmarket, military patrols appeared in single file, often coming by roundabout ways, in an effort to catch civilians not obeying the order. They were watched, of course, by the IRA, with a view to mounting an attack on them. However, a good opportunity never appeared, which Moylan put down to the activity of informers at work within the community.

Moylan recalled that the Active Service Unit in the area was 'pitifully armed' and could only have hoped for success against well-armed patrols by way of sudden surprise attacks. But he maintained that the attempted ambushes that were laid for patrols had a positive impact – they set the British nerves on edge and ensured that the police and military remained inside a very confined area of control.

Though the Active Service Unit did not manage to engage the enemy during those early weeks of the curfew, there was, according to Moylan, a belief that he and his men were developing their self-confidence and were taking their first steps towards becoming an effective fighting force. He recalled an order from Headquarters in July 1920, to cut the police and military telephone wires in their area without damaging the ordinary telephone communication system. Two of his men, interpreting the order very literally, climbed a padded ladder, in their bare feet, to the roof of the police barracks in Newmarket and cut the telephone wires at the chimney shaft before making a clean getaway.

Moylan obtained some money in July 1920 from personal friends, as well as unexpectedly benefitting from an American relative's bequest. He decided to use the cash to purchase some arms and ammunition for his Battalion and made a trip to Dublin after consulting with his Brigade Commandant, Liam Lynch.

In Dublin, he registered in a hotel and slept in the same room where, four months later, Limerick Sinn Féin member Jack Lynch was murdered by the Black and Tans. The day after his arrival in the capital, he called to another hotel, where an appointment had been arranged with three members of the Headquarters Staff. When he arrived, he found Liam Tobin, Tom Cullen and Fintan Murphy sitting down to lunch as if, he said, 'they hadn't a care in the world'. Moylan was stunned by their audacity, as he was well aware that the three men were constantly watched by British agents. Yet, as he recalled, 'they sat there unabashed in a gathering of which one half at least were sworn enemies'.

He discussed his requirements with the three men, who told him it would not be easy to come by what he wanted. Eventually, they agreed to supply him with six 'Peter the Painter' Mauser pistols (called after Latvian anarchist Peter Piaktow, who used the pistols in the famous Sidney Street siege in London in 1911), two parabellum pistols with ten rounds of ammunition for each, one dozen percussion bombs, a rifle and fifty rounds of .303 ammunition. The whole consignment was delivered to Moylan's hotel by a man called Chris Harding, and the total cost was £120.

Moylan was of the opinion that he had actually paid through the nose for the cache, and eventually found it was an even worse bargain than he initially imagined. The bombs were useless and while the pistols were good, the few rounds of ammunition meant they had to be used very sparingly. The rifle was the best of the lot and, by far, the best value for money.

Despite his misgivings about the guns, Moylan recognised the psychological value for his men of having them. They all displayed a great deal of interest in the guns and eagerly took instruction on how to take them apart and re-assemble them.

A Brigade Council meeting was held a few weeks later in August and one item on the agenda was the distribution of a small quantity of revolvers among the battalion commanders. To his amazement, Moylan was not allocated any of the guns, on the basis that it was known he had secured a cache of arms and ammunition in Dublin. He protested, but his pleadings fell on deaf ears, even though:

> I pointed out that I had taken the risk of going to Dublin and of bringing home the guns, that I had with my own money paid for them, that the revolvers now being distributed were the property of the Brigade and, therefore, that my quota was included.

Moylan was determined to get his share of the guns, even though the revolvers had been parcelled up and put into another room as the meeting continued. After a while, he went outside and, with a table knife, slipped the catch of the window of the room where the guns were and grabbed one parcel. He opened it and removed two revolvers, leaving one and substituting wood and stones for the guns he had taken. He then returned to the meeting. On the way home with Paddy Clancy, he told him what he done. Clancy, he recalled, laughed uproariously.

The guns he took were almost useless and had probably come from some European port where they were for sale to revolutionaries. Moylan was by now convinced that the British were the best source of effective guns and ammunition.

A week after the Brigade Council meeting, Paddy Clancy was killed. His death had a devastating impact on Moylan and other Brigade and Battalion members. A British plane had made a forced landing at Drominagh, near Clonbanin, and a company of British soldiers was detailed to protect it until repairs were made. During the night, poorly armed local Volunteers, without any real plan of action, attacked the soldiers. The British managed to repel the IRA men after several hours of fighting, during which a number of Volunteers were wounded.

The fight, according to Moylan, brought the British military in force into the district. Clancy and his comrade Jack O'Connell were surrounded in a farmhouse by the British. They defended themselves until they had expended all their ammunition. Moylan maintained that his comrades were gunned down as they ran from the house in a desperate attempt to escape, though there are one or two differing accounts of how the two men died.

Moylan recalled his dead comrades as men of courage and outstanding character, and the death of Clancy, a close personal friend, impacted him to his very core. He sadly remembered how:

> ... the sun shone brightly, there was a scent of hay from the meadows, the Irish countryside was beautiful; but for me the world was empty that day as I carried his body over hill and dale and murmuring stream to bury him beneath the haunted mountain on which his eyes first opened.

He returned from Clancy's funeral by unfrequented roads. Most of those who attended the funeral drove back along the main roads and many of them were held up, searched and questioned by British military personnel. All the young men were savagely beaten. The effect of that action, according to Moylan, was only to intensify support for the Volunteers and to add to their numbers.

The following day, Moylan met the Brigade Commandant, Liam Lynch, to discuss difficulties created by Clancy's death, and the operational methods employed by the IRA. The view held by many officers was that there could be no real success if the organisation continued to depend on ordinary Volunteers, who were poorly armed, often hurriedly mobilised and not sufficiently trained or disciplined.

By that time, the British were moving around the country in much greater strength. They could not be successfully attacked by men who were suddenly called away from their ordinary work and expected to use a gun for a few hours, before returning to their daily employment. Moylan proposed that the most suitable men in the Brigade should be called together, given the best arms available and trained to act as regular soldiers.

It was agreed that they would go down that route, and a call went out to the battalions for volunteers. A quota for each battalion and a date for mobilisation was agreed upon. The number of men who volunteered for duty in what would eventually form a flying column was overwhelming. Liam Lynch decided that Moylan should take charge of the new Active Service Unit, a position that would have gone to Clancy had he lived.

With his new position confirmed, Moylan attended a Sinn Féin Constituency Convention. He appealed for financial support, which came the following day in the form of a substantial sum of cash. He passed the money on to the Brigade leadership and it was used to buy arms and step up the training for the men recruited to the flying column. This allowed Moylan to set up a training camp, which continued to operate until the cessation of hostilities in July 1921. The camp was moved around to avoid burdening any one area too much in terms of billeting the men. He recalled most of the recruits in training responded intelligently and energetically to the demands made of them. An esprit de corps was created as each company sought to outshine the others in soldierly flair and effort.

The training the recruits undertook was, in every sense, very intense. They started with close-order drill and went on to the handling of a rifle. Physical training was a major element of the programme and included jerks, running, jumping, wrestling, route marches on roads, where possible, and cross-country marching. There was a course in the care and operation of the rifle and revolver, and recruits were trained in the making and deployment of bombs. Sentry and outpost duties were learned, as was signalling. There was an emphasis on engineering and also First Aid and, by the early months of 1921, a course in street fighting and silent movement at night had been developed. Within weeks, according to Moylan, a cohesive unit of fighting men had emerged, ready and willing to engage the enemy.

Moylan and his comrades began to constantly watch the movements of Crown forces, and it became apparent there was a regular schedule of movement in certain areas. They realised two lorries of Black and Tans travelled weekly between Cork and Mallow, though their hours of travel varied slightly. It was decided that Moylan's flying column should make their first assignment an attack on that patrol. He recalled a meeting of the Brigade Council was held one Sunday to make final arrangements for the attack, expected to take place the following Tuesday.

Moylan was a little late for the meeting, because he had to detour around a party of British soldiers who were searching houses on his route and holding up traffic. When he arrived at the house where meeting was to be held, he discovered it had been burned to the ground. He found a Volunteer crouching behind a fence ready to re-direct him to the new meeting place, which was 300 yards away.

Moylan eventually joined the re-assembled Council members, and found them in an unusually solemn mood, being questioned by a stranger sitting beside the Brigade Commandant. The young man, Moylan recalled, had red hair and blue eyes, and a scar across his face. He was clad in guns and fountain pens and surrounded by maps and notebooks.

He was, as it turned out, a Staff Captain from Headquarters in Dublin on a tour of inspection. Moylan readily admitted that he was 'prepared to dislike this fellow even before he barked a reference to unpunctuality to me'. However, he did recognise his comrades had accepted him and he seemed to have the authority and approval of the Brigade Commandant.

Moylan had a robust and lively interaction with the young man, whom he felt was a very serious individual with a sense of his own importance. He readily admitted he was antagonised by his adversary, and he answered his questions with complete inaccuracy. Both the Brigade Commandant and Adjutant realised what he was doing, but both managed to keep a straight face, with a definite glint of approval in their eyes.

However, first impressions can be deceptive, and during the time the young man spent with the Council members, their attitude towards him changed. It became clear that he was an individual of courage and ability and that he had, in fact, seen much fighting. He went on to make a name for himself throughout the conflict. His name was Ernie O'Malley.

With O'Malley's questioning completed, the attention of the meeting turned to the proposed attack on the British convoy the following Tuesday. Much to the disappointment of Moylan and his comrades, the Brigade Commandant informed them that it would not take place. He proposed, instead, an entirely different operation, as new information had been brought to him by a young Volunteer, Dick Willis, which greatly interested him. Willis was working on a building contract in the British military barracks in Mallow, and the information he brought suggested that it could be captured. Willis had carefully noted the movements of the guards and sentries, and the manner in which visitors to the barracks were received.

Willis proposed that he and another Volunteer, Jack Bolster, should be armed with revolvers. They would introduce a third man, also armed, posing as a foreman there to check on the work being done. On a given signal, they would hold up the guard and sentries, giving the Active Service Unit an opportunity to rush the gate from outside.

The question of getting the gate open, said Moylan, was a tricky one. A proposal was made that a member of the Active Service Unit should approach the guard with a letter for the officer in charge. Once the guard had been engaged in conversation, the ASU would charge the gate.

Moylan recalled that there was no lack of Volunteers for the operation and that O'Malley more or less nominated himself to carry the letter. Moylan put himself forward to act as the foreman, but he was overruled by the Brigade Commandant, who said he was not prepared to risk losing a valuable officer on an operation where, in his view, the chances of success were entirely out of proportion to the risk involved. Paddy McCarthy, a great personal friend of Moylan, was chosen to pose as the site foreman, even though he knew next to nothing of the building trade:

> *The foreman was to be a man who had been one of my closest companions in all activities since his escape from Strangeways Prison almost a year before, Paddy McCarthy, who was my first selection for membership of the ASU. He was of that sparse but richly endowed brotherhood, the men who know no fear. For an hour we worked over a draft of a repair specification which I made. I explained to him the meaning of the terms, the methods by which he could at least minimise the danger of showing his complete ignorance of the Building Trade and felt at the end that he was at least sufficiently lessoned to pass muster among a group of men who were doubtless no better informed than he was.*

Moylan then volunteered to be part of the storming party, but again he was to be disappointed by his superior officer, who ordered him to proceed to a district some twenty miles away. He was bitterly disappointed, as were the men he had brought with him from his Active Service Unit. He had, he said: 'hoped to give them the opportunity of being shot over; to utilise the ambush as the finishing touch to the training they had undergone'. Their disappointment was compounded when the Brigade Commandant ordered all of them to hand over their rifles before they left the area.

Moylan and his comrades were disconsolate on the journey home and there was very little in the way of conversation. Before dawn, Moylan reached the safe house where he was staying, the home of Dan Galvin. Galvin and his wife soon joined Moylan in the kitchen, anxious for any news he might have brought with him and fearful that something had gone wrong for him and his unit. The embers in the fire were gathered together and Moylan recalled how he turned the wheel of the bellows and soon the kettle was singing over a glowing fire.

Galvin, a local schoolteacher, and his wife were completely in Moylan's confidence and he often put great store in their advice and wisdom. That morning, Galvin advised him to put his disappointment to one side and look to the future. Moylan slept well into the afternoon and spent that evening attempting to placate the men in his Active Service Unit, many of whom felt undermined and undervalued by being excluded from the attack on the Mallow barracks.

The following day, Moylan and his men proceeded to an unoccupied house, where they began to experiment in the making of explosives and land mines. They knew nothing of chemicals, but Moylan had set a local chemist's apprentice the task of studying the subject and, from his notes, they carried out their first tentative trials. The unoccupied farmhouse became a well-equipped factory with a staff of skilled craftsmen.

As they worked during that first day, they speculated on what might be happening in Mallow. The attack was scheduled for that morning, but news of it did not arrive until night had fallen. The operation was a complete success, with no IRA casualties, though one British Army Sergeant had been shot dead. The arms haul included fifty rifles, two machine guns and a lot of ammunition, and the news was greeted by Moylan's comrades with a tremendous roar of triumph. However, there was a downside, as the town of Mallow was burned and sacked by the British some hours after the raid.

Moylan later received an account of the raid from some who had taken part in it. The plan had been discussed on the Monday and a large map of Mallow was procured before the final arrangements were agreed upon. Dick Willis confirmed that the British officer in charge of the barracks in Mallow was concerned about the inadequacy of the water supply and had spoken to him about it.

Willis assured him that he would speak to the Town Clerk and arrange for a water inspector to call to the barracks on the Tuesday morning to see if a better supply could be tapped into the barracks. The arrangement fitted perfectly with the attack plans, and it was decided that Ernie O'Malley should play the role of Council water inspector.

On the morning of the attack, Paddy McCarthy, posing as a foreman, arrived at the barracks and had a discussion with Willis about the work being done. Bolster, in the meantime, was working outside the window of a room where off-duty soldiers were taking their ease. Ernie O'Malley appeared at the gate, brandishing a letter for the barracks Commander. He was admitted on to the premises, and immediately grabbed the sentry's rifle, which was the signal for the others to move. Bolster then threw open the window where he was working, drew his revolver and yelled at the troops to stay where they were.

Willis and McCarthy now rushed to the guardroom door with their guns drawn and jumped between the soldiers and the rack where the rifles were stored. A British sergeant charged at Willis, who had no option but to shoot him dead. Simultaneously, a number of IRA men poured into the barracks, encountering no resistance. The raiding party seized every weapon and every round of ammunition in the barracks before leaving.

Soon after the Mallow raid, the 3rd Charleville Battalion brought off two engagements with the British, both of which were reasonably successful. In one of the engagements, Commandant Paddy O'Brien from Liscarroll was shot in the face from close range. The wound, according to Moylan, should have been fatal, but O'Brien was back in action within a few weeks, having suffered no more than a fractured jaw and the loss of some teeth. The only explanation for his very lucky escape was that the enemy's gun probably had a defective cartridge.

In a reprisal attack, the British troops stationed at Liscarroll burned a quantity of newly saved hay, the property of local farmers. One of the farmers was a man named Noonan, whose sons were active Volunteers. Some nights after the burning of the hay, the Noonan household was raided by British military. Mr Noonan and one of his sons were badly beaten before the son, a boy of nineteen, was taken out into the yard and riddled with bullets. As he lay on the ground, the officer in charge shot the young man in the face, smashing his jaw and teeth and almost severing his tongue. They left him for dead, but he was saved by the local doctor, a man named Corbett, aided by the local priest, Father Barry. Even though the young Noonan had been hit by ten bullets, he eventually recovered and went on to become the father of ten children.

On 11 October 1920, an ambush was carried out at Ballydrocane, on the main road between Kanturk and Newmarket, with a force of around sixty men under the command of Liam Lynch and Ernie O'Malley. The men set out from their assembly point at 3am in the bitter cold, trudging across rain-sodden fields to arrive at their destination about ninety minutes later. They waited in difficult conditions and the passing hours seemed endless as early-morning workers and schoolchildren passed by, unaware of what was afoot.

Around eleven o'clock, the men heard a motor vehicle approaching and, as it neared the ambush point, a farm cart was propelled into the road. Moylan and his comrades opened fire. The fight was over in five minutes, and while the British showed true grit, they were overwhelmed and the driver of the vehicle was killed. The rifles, equipment and ammunition of the enemy was collected in the aftermath of the fight. Moylan recalled:

I looked at the young driver as he lay dead across the wheel. I am no soldier. I hate killing and violence. The thought ran through my mind, 'God help his mother.'

Around that time, reports came in from Millstreet that the Black and Tans stationed in the town were becoming more and more belligerent. The Active Service Unit was sent into the town under the command of Paddy McCarthy, who asked Moylan for any revolver ammunition he could spare. Moylan had taken his young cousin, Liam Moylan, under his wing, and McCarthy asked to take him to Millstreet. Moylan reluctantly decided that the time had come for Liam to experience an engagement with the enemy and, much to the young man's delight, he set out for Millstreet with McCarthy.

McCarthy was killed that evening in a close-quarters fight. When Liam Moylan returned to the company's headquarters, it was evident that the grim reality of warfare had replaced the youthful enthusiasm of the previous day. Liam, Moylan said:

... had been under fire in fierce hand to hand fighting, had been bespattered by his comrade's blood. No longer would his mind be troubled by the heroics of the unini- tiate. He was now a soldier.

Moylan had a coffin made in Kiskeam and travelled to Millstreet to bring McCarthy's body home for burial, with the aid of the Active Service Unit hiding out in the hills around the town. The coffin was carried along lonely byroads from Millstreet to Kilcorcoran around midnight. In spite of the secrecy with which the funeral had to be veiled, a big crowd was waiting at Kilcorcoran to pay their respects to their dead comrade.

Christmas 1920 was a joyless one for most of the country, and Moylan recounted two sad incidents that took place in his home area. On Christmas Eve, the British raided Gneeveguilla, just across the border in Kerry. There they picked up an old man named Moynihan and took him some distance before shooting him dead and leaving his body by a roadside. Some nights later in Newmarket, an old man called John Murphy took his Christmas candle from his kitchen to his bedroom, where there were no curtains. A military patrol in the street, seeing the light, knocked on his door and called to the old man. He came to the window and the officer in charge shot him dead.

Moylan alluded to the difficulties endured by him and his fellow officers in relation to communications throughout the independence conflict. Several Brigade Council meetings were abandoned owing to British raids. Meetings with fellow officers often necessitated long treks on foot across inhospitable terrain and during inclement weather. Around the 1920 Christmas period, Moylan had cause to visit another officer, Seamus Brislane, a journey of some thirty miles. He set out in the middle of the afternoon and soon the rain began to fall, continuing throughout the journey. He eventually arrived at Brislane's house around midnight, bedraggled, cold and very hungry.

Brislane dragged Moylan to the fireplace and offered him whiskey. As he attempted to find a glass, he dropped the bottle and it broke with a crash on the flagstone in front of the fire. Moylan recalled that there was a groan of anguish from all present in the room. He gazed at the fragments of the bottle on the floor, but rather than be outdone by the accident, he bent down and removed some of the broken pieces of glass. He recalled:

There was a depression in the flagstone worn by the feet of many generations who had lived in the house. It was now full of whiskey. Hygienists and teetotallers may raise their hands in holy horror, I was no Philip Sidney, and my need was greater than theirs is ever likely to be. I went on my knees on the flagstone and drained the depression dry.

On 28 January 1921, Moylan and his men ambushed a Crown forces patrol at Tureengarriffe, armed only with ten rifles. From the viewpoint of observation, he and his unit had perfect cover, but from the viewpoint of protection they had none. The fight, he maintained, had to be fought to the finish. Having trenched the road and taken their positions, Moylan and his men waited for the enemy, who arrived in due course, travelling in two cars. Coming swiftly around a bend, the cars skidded to a halt when the drivers saw the trench. Moylan's men opened fire, and the Tans leaped out of their cars, taking cover behind them.

They fought a good fight and when Moylan called on them to surrender, they replied with a fierce volley of shots. The IRA men opened fire again for a short time before the enemy dropped their rifles. Every one of their number had been wounded, while two of them, including General Holmes, the leader of the patrol, died in the firefight.

Moylan's squad got a fine haul of rifles, automatic shotguns, grenades, revolvers and ammunition, and everything was driven off in one of the cars. The Tans were searched and their personal belongings returned to them. They were then allowed to take their wounded away in the other car. The car used to transport the arms cache was dumped after every item was distributed and all members of the ambush party then marched home, tired and hungry but jubilant. For some of them, it was their first experience of engaging with the enemy and they felt as if they were walking on air.

A few weeks after the ambush, Moylan heard there was a good deal of local gossip about the car they had commandeered, and its hiding place had become something of a tourist attraction. He concluded it should be removed before the British discovered it and he delegated four of his men, whom he called the Musketeers, to drive it away out of the district.

Moylan began to worry that his men might have walked into a trap when retrieving the car. He went looking for them, setting off on a bicycle around 1am. After a number of punctures and many hours of searching, he eventually arrived at Horan's of Caherbarnagh, at 6am. There he was told by Andy Horan that the Musketeers had indeed been in the area with the car, but they had taken it to a wedding. Moylan, astounded at the news, asked where the wedding was, and was told it was being held in Killarney. He recalled:

> I swore to high heaven. Here was a car, the description of which was in every bar-racks, a car in size, power and colour standing out from the ruck of cars like a sore thumb. And these lunatics had driven it into Killarney.

Not only had they driven the car to the Cathedral in Killarney, but they had also taken the bride and bridesmaids with them. The car that was to take the bridal party to the church had broken down, and the chivalrous four, rather than dis-appoint the girl, drove her to the church through the town, which was alive with Crown forces. They parked the car at the Cathedral and later headed the wedding procession on its way back through the town again. Needless to say, the four heroes avoided Moylan for a few days, until his temper had cooled.

British raiding parties were active around Buttevant in February 1921, and Moylan decided to ambush of one of them. He fixed the date for Sunday, 6 Feb-ruary. On the Saturday, he selected the ambush site, around three miles east of Kingwilliamstown. That night, as he prepared to retire to bed in a safe house, he noticed a Mills bomb missing from his belt. Knowing that children often played in the area, he spent some anxious hours looking for it and eventually found it beside a fence.

The following day was a beautiful one, as Moylan and his men assumed their positions at the ambush site. They were, however, disappointed, because the mili-tary patrol changed its route and came nowhere near them.

However, the day was not to be without drama and sadness. In a field beside nearby Knocknagree village, some boys were playing hurling. Suddenly, military lorries approached and two bursts of machine guns sent them scattering in fear. British soldiers kept advancing, firing on the fleeing boys and, when the shoot-ing was over, they were all rounded up. One of their number, seventeen-year-old

Michael J Kelleher, had been shot through the head. Another boy, Michael Herlihy, was shot through the thigh and his brother, Donal, shot in the lung.

Both Herlihy boys recovered, and Michael went on to be a curate in Tralee while Donal eventually rose to the position of Bishop of Ferns. The RIC in the area refused to be associated with the shootings, and the military were forced to return to Knocknagree and hand the body of Michael Kelleher over to his distraught father.

The official report of the incident was published in the *Irish Independent* the following day and claimed:

> *A military patrol saw a body of armed civilians in a field near Knocknagree. Fire was opened and replied to, resulting in the death of one youth and the wounding of two others.*

Moylan commented on the shameful report by quoting from Shakespeare's play *The Taming of Shrew*: 'And now I find report a very liar.'

Around that time, Moylan and his men noticed an increasing use of the railways by British forces. A watch was kept and a report came back that the soldiers seemed to be mostly unarmed during train journeys. It was decided to lay an ambush one mile east of Millstreet Station, at a point where a high embankment made it possible for riflemen lying on each side of the track to have a clear field of fire without endangering each other. A number of armed men were placed at the station at Millstreet, where they were to watch for a train carrying British military. When that train left the station, they were to jump on the footplate and force the driver to bring the train to a stop where their comrades were waiting.

The waiting went on for a week, the signal for action eventually coming on 11 February. The train came to a standstill at the ambush point and, as it was night time, lighted oil torches were thrown into the cutting beside the train, illuminating the carriages containing the British soldiers. They were called on to surrender, but instead they opened fire. The column replied with fire of their own and the soldiers all tumbled out of the carriages. After ten minutes of continuous firing from the column, some fourteen soldiers surrendered and one other lay dead. The column had started the attack with eight rifles and marched away with twenty-three and their ammunition reserve was increased by around 1,000 rounds.

One soldier attempted to escape, rushing up the embankment and eventually running into the rifle muzzle of column member Jer Long. Luckily, Long was an experienced and exceptionally cool Volunteer, and he contented himself with pushing the soldier back down the embankment. It transpired that the man was a Munster Fusilier, who later, after being demobbed, joined a column in Kerry.

One of Moylan's comrades that night was a man called Michael O'Riordan, the eldest of three brothers from Millstreet who served with the Active Service Unit from its inception to the end of hostilities. The story goes that some years later O'Riordan was on holiday in Ballybunion and he went for a swim. Seemingly he got into difficulties, having swum out too far, and was unable to get back to the beach. Two strong swimmers came to his rescue and, after a struggle, they managed to get him back to the shore. One of O'Riordan's rescuers that fateful day turned out to be the same Munster Fusilier who had climbed the embankment and found himself looking into the muzzle of Jer Long's rifle.

Early in March 1921, Moylan made a plan to ambush a patrol consisting of senior British officers and their military guard, which he learned would be returning from an inspection tour in Kerry. After careful consideration, he chose a site at Clonbanin, about five miles from Kanturk. The site was also about five miles from Millstreet, which at the time had a garrison of Black and Tans as well as an RIC presence. The close proximity of Crown forces was a concern for Moylan and it was always in the back of his mind as a possible problem during his preparations and during the attack itself.

Moylan took his men out at 3am on 3 March, and they arrived at Clonbanin at 6 am. The unit was joined by a section of the Kerry No 2 Brigade, under the command of Tom McEllistrim, as well as some men from Charleville, led by Paddy O'Brien. Other men from local companies provided scouting for the force, which had in its possession a Hotchkiss gun captured in the raid on the military barracks in Mallow. Moylan also had his men lay some mines on the road and he ordered the section leaders not to open fire until a mine exploded, which would be the signal for the attack to begin. He decided that if a small patrol passed by, he would let it go in the hope that a much larger one would follow.

At around 10am, Moylan received word from his signallers that the British were coming. Soon three wire-covered lorries appeared, with one man actually playing an accordion and others singing. Moylan recalled saying to himself:

Poor devils, they little know how close to disaster they were. What a horrible thing is war. Here were men against whom we had no personal hatred. Yet, because of the wisdom of a statesmanship that refuses to recognise right except when it is backed by force, a single shot fired by accident, or by a nervous or excited youngster meant swift dissolution for all of them.

No shots were fired, however, even though his men, lying cold and wet in a ditch, very much wanted to shoot the enemy. The lorries travelled on over the crest of the hill and disappeared. Moylan, like his men, for a while thought they may well have missed a glorious chance to strike at the enemy. They continued waiting patiently for their second chance, and at around 2.15pm it came. Three lorries again trundled along the road, followed by an armoured car, spaced at intervals so as to cover a half-mile of the road. Moylan recalled following the progress of the vehicles through his looking glasses:

I watched the coming of the armoured car. The mine in the centre of the ambush position was destined for it. As it passed over the mine, I pressed the switch on the battery. I got a shock that almost knocked me over. It had short circuited.

Despite the mine failure, the other men watching opened up a burst of fire. The leading lorry went into a ditch when its driver was hit and wounded. It was followed by the armoured car and soon the firefight began. Moylan bemoaned his men's shortage of ammunition throughout the fight, which left them at a disadvantage. They also had to contend with the Lewis guns and the heavy Maxim machine gun of the enemy.

Throughout the engagement, Moylan and his men attempted a number of manoeuvers to attain the upper hand, as did the British, all of which resulted in something of a stalemate. Moylan expected British reinforcements to arrive at any moment during the early part of the battle. He was sure the sound of firing would be heard in the nearby garrison towns, and he later learned that they were. A military lorry carrying troops did leave Newmarket, but it hit a fence and overturned a mile from the town. It seems that the soldiers in Kanturk were not inclined to get involved. They buried themselves in the town's public houses before eventually being rounded up.

The reinforcements eventually arrived as darkness fell. According to Moylan, they came in strength: 'the line of lorries was like the parked cars on O'Connell Street'. The arrival of the reinforcements made Moylan's mind up. He and his men began to move away, with the Millstreet and Kerry troops heading to the west. Those from Charleville and Newmarket went north to Kiskeam.

Remarkably, Moylan and his comrades suffered no casualties. Later reports suggested the British had suffered thirteen dead (though official British records show four dead), including General Cumming, and fifteen wounded.

The Clonbanin ambush was undoubtedly the pinnacle of Seán Moylan's military career, marking him out as one of the real military talents of the IRA during the War of Independence. His success did not go unnoticed by his superior officers and, in May 1921, he was promoted to the position of Commanding Officer of the Cork No 2 Brigade. Some days after his promotion, he was captured by the Gloucester Regiment in a raid at Boherbue; he spent the rest of the War of Independence imprisoned on Spike Island in Cork Harbour.

Seán Moylan went on to fight for the republican side during the Civil War, before dedicating his life to politics and service to the State as a member of Dáil Éireann and a government minister. He now occupies a much-admired and revered place in Ireland's modern history.

Chapter 14

Tadhg Kennedy:
A Proud Kerryman and a
True Patriot

I saw the tenants of Lord Cork's estate come through the village of Annascaul
with their hats off, a quarter of a mile away from Moriarty's Hotel where the
agent had his rent office. They were so downtrodden and fearful that, though
they had the rent, they were afraid of being evicted. Occasionally, there were
evictions and Moore Stack and other Fenians held meetings in the village which
were attended by the artisans and the few labouring men.
The farmers daren't put in an appearance there.
(Tadhg Kennedy)

T adhg Kennedy was born in a thatched house in Annascaul, a village
on the main road between Tralee and Dingle, on 20 August 1885. His father was
a farmer's son who served time in Cork as a grocer's assistant before becoming
a shopkeeper himself in Annascaul. He married a local woman and a short time
later found himself imprisoned for twelve months in Clonmel gaol on the back
of an agrarian offence. He avoided being deported only by the intervention of a
local landlord. His companion in the crime was another local man called Patsy
O'Sullivan, and the two remained close friends all their lives.

The Kennedys were Fenians, and Tadhg Kennedy recalled meetings held in the
back room of their house attended by local artisans such as bakers, blacksmiths,

coopers and carpenters, none of whom owned an acre of land. In later years, their sons, including Tadhg, carried on the struggle for Ireland's independence, eventually achieving what their forefathers had longed for.

Tadhg Kennedy received his education in the Christian Brothers in Dingle before going on to Skerries College in Dublin in 1902. Among other notable classmates of his was the tenor John McCormack. Kennedy finished his education in 1905, and spent some months working in Gillingham in Kent, where his uncle, a naval officer, lived. He returned because his father contracted pneumonia, and he then applied for a position with Kerry County Council. He placed first in the examination, out of forty-two candidates, and was appointed to the service on 5 October 1905.

Kennedy took up his new position in October 1905. Within a week of that, he met a young man called Austin Stack, who he had seen play for Kerry against Kildare in the 1904 All-Ireland Final. As it happened, Stack's father was an old friend and Fenian associate of Kennedy's father.

Stack brought Kennedy to the home of Tom Slattery in Rock Street in Tralee, and there he was inducted into the IRB, even though, as Kennedy said in his statement, he 'hadn't the foggiest notion what it was about'. From then on, Kennedy paid his 2d a week to maintain his membership of the secret organisation. However, he was 'not mixed up very much with political matters up to 1913'. During this time, Kennedy was involved in the GAA as a player and as an official, and he was also a leading member of the Gaelic League in Kerry.

Kennedy's friendship with Stack grew, through both the IRB and the GAA. Both men were members of the Kerry County Board, with Stack taking the role of Chairman. Kennedy recalled that he often sat in as Chairman if Stack could not get time off from his work as a clerk in a solicitor's office. Stack was also Chairman of the Management Committee, which oversaw the running of the Tralee GAA Sports Field, now known as Austin Stack Park. Kennedy was also a member of that committee. Stack represented the John Mitchels club on the County Board, while Kennedy represented Lispole, which included the Annascaul area.

Stack had a reputation as a fair and honourable man, who always attempted to do the right thing, in politics and also in sport. That reputation was never more in evidence than in 1912, when his own John Mitchels club played Dingle in the Kerry County Final. John Mitchels won the game, but Dingle lodged an objection on the grounds that one of the Mitchels players, Michael Quinlan, who became Secretary of Kerry County Council, had played in a rugby inter-provincial match some time previous to the county final. Stack chaired the meeting to discuss the objection and, along with Kennedy, voted to uphold it, voting against his own club. The other club representatives on the Committee voted in favour of John Mitchels keeping their title.

Tadhg Kennedy's involvement in republican activism really began when he joined the Irish Volunteers in 1913. With the advent of the Great War and the recruitment drive by the Government and the Irish Parliamentary Party, it did not take him long to make his views known in public. In September 1914, on the same Sunday that John Redmond made his famous recruitment speech at Woodenbridge in Wicklow, Kennedy replied to a speech made at a recruitment meeting in Annascaul. He recalled suggesting that:

> Britain could make the first gesture by granting us independence and we could then decide on making a contribution to an army and a navy who would defend Britain and Ireland against attacks by Germany or any other country.

In that speech, Kennedy also advised the young men listening that they should train and arm so they would be ready to fight in their own army for the cause of Irish freedom.

Stack had a major influence on Kennedy's republican views. He saw Stack as an inspiration to many young men in Kerry and across the country, a man who led by example and by self-sacrifice. Kennedy stated that Stack was convinced the armed struggle was the only way to achieve independence and that it should supersede all other republican activities.

By 1915, Kennedy was immersed in all things Gaelic and republican. In his capacity as a Gaelic League official, he welcomed Padraig Pearse to Tralee to give an opening address at the Feis and Exhibition. Pearse had been editor of the Gaelic League newspaper *An Claidheamh Soluis*, but a short time before arriving in Tralee, he had resigned his position because, it was alleged, he was using the paper for political purposes. Kennedy recalled:

> I was directed to meet Pearse at the train when he arrived from Killarney and warn him that he wasn't to introduce politics into his lecture at the Green. He assured me smilingly that I could tell the committee that they would have nothing to complain about and, in a beautiful setting under the trees in the Green, he delivered an oration which enthralled the large gathering of people who were in attendance.

Like many others, Kennedy was unaware of Roger Casement's landing on Banna strand prior to the Rising. It seemed that Casement just turned up in Kerry unannounced and, because Stack had definite mobilisation instructions from Dublin, he believed it was not his duty to deviate from them to rescue him. Of course, given Kennedy's obvious loyalty towards Stack, it is not surprising that he defended him against criticism from others for his failure to prevent Casement from falling into the hands of the authorities.

Kennedy was rather scathing about Casement, claiming that his appearance in Kerry was an unwanted diversion, which could have jeopardised a successful landing of arms by the *Aud*. He also claimed Casement came to prevent the Rising, and gave a message to that effect to Father Frank Ryan of Tralee. Father Ryan delivered this to the Volunteers leaders in the town before it was passed up the line to the Dublin headquarters.

Kennedy also indicated just how close republicans were to the cache of arms on the *Aud* – while on his way to Dingle by train on Holy Thursday evening, he could see the ill-fated vessel at the entrance to Tralee Bay. He said that he often thought about what might have been.

Kennedy brought the Volunteers from the Dingle peninsula to Tralee in the days prior to the Easter Rising. He had been sent by Stack to Dingle on Holy Thursday evening with a message for Mick Moriarty, the commanding officer of the Volunteers in the town. Before leaving Tralee railway station, Kennedy recalled:

> Stack stressed to me that Headquarters had given specific instructions that we were to be particularly careful that no diversion should be allowed to occur to impede the carrying out of the plan as decided on by them for the Rising.

Stack insisted that Kennedy should begin his return journey to Tralee with the Volunteers unit on Easter Saturday night. He was very adamant that the order be carried out to the letter – Kennedy was to disregard any order issued to him by any superior officer other than himself. Stack was arrested on Good Friday, but Kennedy stuck rigidly to the plan and he and the Volunteers left for Tralee from Annascaul at midnight on Easter Saturday, arriving in Tralee around 8am.

Unfortunately, like for many other rural Volunteers units around the country, the overnight march was for nothing. The rebellion was essentially a Dublin one, with the rest of the country anxiously looking on.

By 1918, republican activity in Kerry had been stepped up considerably and several serious incidents resulted in loss of life. On 16 April that year, there was an attack on the RIC barracks at Gortatlea, just outside Tralee, by a Volunteers unit under the command of Tom McEllistrim, who later became a prominent TD. Like many attacks around the country at that time, it was not authorised by the Volunteers Headquarters in Dublin, but was a local initiative for the purpose of procuring arms and ammunition. Two Volunteers, John Brown and Robert Laide, lost their lives in the incident.

The following June saw another serious confrontation in Tralee, when Tom McEllistrim and John Cronin shot two RIC constables by the names of Fallon and Doyle. Kennedy witnessed the shootings as he stood talking to some people nearby. Martial law was declared in the town in response to the killings, and it brought Tralee and its surrounding area under the microscope of the authorities.

The military quickly set up headquarters in the County Hall. This, on the one hand, made life a little uncomfortable for Kennedy, who had his office in the building. But on the other hand, it provided him with some opportunities to use his intelligence skills to extract useful information.

Kennedy was appointed Director of Intelligence for Kerry No 1 Brigade in 1919, even though he had no training or real experience in that area. He took on the job with enthusiasm and set out for Michael Collins his views on how it should be carried out. Soon after his appointment, he made the acquaintance of Sergeant Michael O'Rourke of the RIC, through their mutual love of the Irish language. In the course of their conversations, O'Rourke confirmed that he was

Crime Special Sergeant at headquarters, dealing with political as well as criminal issues. Kennedy was fairly sure at the time that O'Rourke was unaware he was speaking to a Brigade Intelligence Officer. He asked him what his job entailed and the answer, according to Kennedy, was very enlightening:

I soon realised that the RIC kept a constant watch on the activities of all the national organisations and up to that time were able to keep a 'representative' in the republican secret organisation, the IRB, and so were in a position to know what was going on fairly well.

Kennedy gave Michael Collins a detailed report of what he had learned from O'Rourke.

Collins suggested a widening of the intelligence operation in Kerry, and Kennedy began to make contact with Post Office officials, hotel employees and anyone else he believed would be useful to his work. He had little difficulty in attaining particulars of the military in the area, such as their numbers and armaments levels.

Without any prompting, Sergeant O'Rourke began to supply information, and his first act was to give Kennedy the heads up on a planned raid to capture the Brigade Adjutant, Daniel J O'Sullivan, on a certain morning. O'Sullivan had previously been fined for having a ground sheet in his possession, but had refused to pay the fine.

It became obvious that O'Rourke was anxious to show his willingness to help and even donated £1 to a fund set up by the officers and ranks of the No 1 Brigade to have a portrait of Austin Stack painted and presented to him. Kennedy thanked him for the donation and asked him if he would continue to provide information, a request he readily acceded to. He agreed to supply the key to the code used by the RIC for telegrams, and did so that evening, allowing Kennedy to travel to Dublin the following day to pass it on to Michael Collins. O'Rourke also agreed to supply the new key every time it was changed. He also furnished Kennedy with information on all planned raids from then on until he retired in 1920. As a reward, Kennedy managed to secure the Governor's house in Tralee gaol for him and his family after the British left. The County Council rented the house to him and, after his death, to his widow at a rent of 3/6d per week.

The Tralee Post Office was a constant source of information for Kennedy thanks to the Chief Clerk, Tom Dillon, who had been introduced to Kennedy by Austin Stack. Tralee was the headquarters of the British military and police force in the area, and it was important for the IRA to have access to all telegraph messages that came through the Post Office in the town. Dillon and his colleagues, whom Kennedy recruited gradually into his intelligence circle, became adept at obtaining copies of letters and telegrams destined for the Crown forces.

Local Fianna boys were taken on as telegraph messengers, though one was caught opening and copying a telegram by the Chief Telegraphist, Ned Meyers, and reported to the Postmaster, Mr Senior, an innocent Englishman. Meyers received threatening letters and was advised by Dillon to contact Kennedy, who told him that they 'regarded his offence as a very grave one and expected him to make up for it by supplying them with a copy of every code message which came or went to British forces'.

Kennedy said that, having 'frightened the life out of him', Meyers became a prolific supplier of information and turned out to be as enthusiastic as those he was passing it on to.

Between April and October 1920, Kennedy was based in Dublin on the orders of Collins and was sent by him on two missions to Britain. The first was to London, where he made contact with friendly officers in Scotland Yard, and the second was to Glasgow, to oversee a shipment of arms to republicans in Aberdeen.

During his sojourn in Dublin, Kennedy spent a lot of time in Collins's company and on one occasion they were forced to evade the military and police in a most unusual place. They were in number 22 Mary Street, Collins's headquarters at the time, when news came that the sector around Henry Street and Mary Street was completely surrounded by British forces and a house-to-house search was about to be carried out.

Collins calmly walked with Kennedy down Henry Street to another house, where they went up the stairs and down a corridor until they reached what Kennedy took to be a bookcase. Collins pressed a spring and the bookcase opened up, revealing a darkened room with no windows. They entered, and Collins locked the entrance with a lever mechanism. Not long after, they heard soldiers tramping along the corridor and the sound of rifles as they touched the floor.

The two spent the night in the room. Kennedy recalled that he did not get much sleep, though Collins slept soundly. The room had been constructed by Batt O'Connor, a Kerryman living in Dublin, one of a number built by O'Connor in houses around the city. O'Connor offered to build one for Kennedy in Tralee, but he declined.

Kennedy returned to Tralee in August after the death of his brother, Paddy. Paddy Kennedy had been shot by a British soldier, a Private George from the East Lancs Regiment, and a Black and Tan by the name of Jaspar, at Gurteens, near Annascaul. An inquest was held and a verdict of wilful murder was returned, despite the Coroner, Dr John O'Connell, receiving a telegram from the authorities forbidding the holding of it. It transpired that George and Jaspar were pursuing another man, Jack Kennedy, who had participated in an attack on Crown forces the previous week, when they came across Paddy with two other young lads in a boreen. George more or less shot Paddy, who was only twenty-nine years of age, in cold blood, and it seems that Jaspar did not fire a shot. Paddy Kennedy's death certificate confirmed he 'died of shock and haemorrhage the result of bullet wounds inflicted by a British soldier without cause or provocation or justification on 20th August 1920, when he was foully murdered'.

George was later transferred to another regiment, while Jaspar was captured and executed and his body buried in the sands on Banna Strand, against the wishes of Kennedy. Sometime later, the corpse was exposed by the shifting of the sand and Kennedy had it transferred to England for burial. He also certified the death so that the man's widow and family could claim a pension and compensation from the British government.

The retirement of Sergeant O'Rourke from the RIC was a blow to Kennedy's intelligence operation in Tralee. However, it wasn't long before a replacement arrived on the scene to offer his services. That man was Sergeant Michael Costello, a native of Glin in County Limerick. He had been in touch with IRA Intelligence headquarters in Cork city before he came to Tralee. He was advised by Florrie O'Donoghue, another Kerryman and Cork No 1 Brigade Intelligence Officer, to contact Kennedy when he arrived in the town.

Costello frequented Paddy Quinlan's pub in Bridge Street, and one evening he asked him if he knew Kennedy. As it happened, Kennedy was sleeping every night at that time in the living quarters upstairs. Costello told Quinlan he wished to see Kennedy and had a message from a friend in Cork. Kennedy made an appointment through Quinlan to meet him one evening after the pub closed. In the meanwhile he checked him out and discovered he was O'Rourke's replacement.

On the appointed evening, a squad of Black and Tans entered the pub, but they only wanted a drink. They found Costello on the premises. Kennedy was upstairs in bed, sharing a room with another IRA man, Jack Lawlor, who was also sleeping. They both had to get out on to the roof for safety, in their pyjamas and without boots on a cold, frosty night. When the British left, Kennedy went down to the bar where Costello gave him the note from O'Donoghue. There and then, Kennedy acquired a new and valuable contact in the RIC to work alongside another contact, County Inspector James Duffy.

While Costello was in Tralee, he supplied Kennedy with the telegraph code every month and whenever it was changed in between, as it sometimes was. He also sent word of every raid by the Black and Tans and gave him an update on the attitudes of every member of the RIC in the Tralee barracks.

One man in the barracks, a Sergeant Clarke, was particularly keen to apprehend IRA men. He volunteered to go on every raid carried out by the Black and Tans. He explained one day to Costello that he did so because he believed it would help him gain promotion. He expected, in time, to be made a District Inspector, as did some others who regularly went out with the Tans' murder gangs.

Costello sent word to Kennedy that Head Constable French, Sergeant Clarke and a Tan named Heapy from Sligo were about to raid his digs on a certain night, and were determined to 'do him in'. The raid took place on the indicated night, but Kennedy wasn't there, having moved to the home of Mrs Hudson on Strand Street on the recommendation of Richard Hudson, a local solicitor and secretary of the Freemasons Lodge, who was a school friend of Kennedy. Costello also sent word one evening that Willie McCarthy, the Lixnaw Battalion Intelligence Officer, who was in Tralee on a visit, was about to be arrested and 'done in'. Kennedy recalled:

I located McCarthy at Lawlor's Hotel and warned him and told him to get out of town as quickly as he could. He went to Moore's yard in Pembroke St and was actually in a pony and trap about to go to Ardfert where he had relatives, but at the last moment he decided to go to the Dominican Church to Confession. He returned to Lawlor's Hotel where he was arrested and taken by two Tans to the RIC barracks. He was taken out that night by Head Constable Benson and some Tans and taken into The Green where he was murdered after torture.

Kennedy was in no doubt that were it not for Sergeant Costello, the Tans and the RIC would have meted out the same treatment to him.

Towards the end of the War of Independence, Costello was transferred to Dublin and Kennedy notified Collins of his presence in the city. Costello initially had difficulties contacting Collins, but he eventually managed with the help of a priest, and went on to do further good work for the Intelligence Unit.

After the War of Independence, Costello, through Kennedy's representation, got a job as a clerk in the Board of Works. However, after a time, Costello's boss got to hear of his activities during the conflict and sacked him. Kennedy wrote to Collins and, after an inquiry, the boss, a man by the name of Roe, lost his job and Costello was reinstated and held the job until he died. After his death, his wife qualified as a midwife and Kennedy procured a job for her working with the Board of Health and Public Assistance.

Kennedy acquired another invaluable contact in the RIC when a former school friend arrived in Tralee near the end of 1920. Changes were made in the barracks in the town, with the County Inspector, a man by the name of Heard, being transferred to Dublin and replaced by James Duffy.

Duffy had been in the British Army during the Great War, and left it with a fairly high rank. Born in Tralee, he was the son of an RIC Sergeant. He was educated at Blackrock College and was a schoolmate of Eamon de Valera and Paddy Cahill, a friend of Kennedy and Commanding Officer of the Kerry 1st Brigade. Duffy completed his education in Skerries College on St Stephen's Green, where he became a classmate and a friend of Kennedy. From there, Duffy went to the RIC, while Kennedy went on to the Civil Service.

In early November, Kennedy strolled into the Grand Hotel in Tralee, where he noticed a local man, Michael Walsh, sitting with a stranger in the bar. Walsh, also a former Blackrock College student, called him over and introduced him to Duffy, who, it seems, had been inquiring about Kennedy and Paddy Cahill, anxious to make contact with both of them. Cahill was a member of the Kerry team that won the All-Ireland football title in 1904 and was also on the beaten team in the 1905 final. He was later elected as a TD in the second Dáil in 1921.

Duffy was in plain clothes and obviously off duty. The three of them spent a couple of hours in the bar chatting before Kennedy strolled home with Duffy via the RIC barracks. Before they parted, Duffy asked Kennedy to set up a meeting with Cahill, somewhere near Tralee. Kennedy agreed to contact Cahill, who was in camp out in Fibough, and put the proposition to him. Duffy confirmed that he would guarantee Cahill's safety at the rendezvous.

Kennedy went to Fibough and spoke to Cahill, who agreed to meet Duffy wherever and whenever it could be arranged. Kennedy decided to ask David Moriarty, a longstanding friend and a former Chairman of Kerry County Council, for help in setting up the meeting. He readily agreed and made his home, Ballyard House, a short distance from Tralee, available for the assignation. He agreed to be out of the house along with his wife on a certain night, and Kennedy, Duffy and Cahill would be admitted by the Moriartys' housekeeper.

On the agreed night, Kennedy and Duffy walked out to Ballyard House. They were admitted by the housekeeper and shown to the dining room, where the table was laid with tea and sandwiches as well as a couple of bottles of whiskey. They were soon joined by Cahill and a happy reunion ensued. Cahill, an intolerant teetotaller, chided the other two for drinking the whiskey, but they all enjoyed the evening, reminiscing on past times.

During the evening, Duffy made it clear he was willing to go out with Cahill and serve in any capacity Cahill wished. He said he was unmarried with no one dependent on him, and he was suffering from tuberculosis as a result of gas attacks in the war. He saw no reason why he shouldn't fight for the freedom of his own country, after going through 'hell' for the freedom of other nations, small and big. Cahill and Kennedy decided that his services would be most valuable to the IRA if he remained in his position at the barracks. Duffy agreed, and from that day forward, Kennedy had two very important contacts supplying him with information – the County Inspector and the Crime Special Sergeant. Kennedy recalled:

I did not let either of them know that the other fellow was in it and they were both supplying me with the same stuff and were a check on each other. Costello had a suspicion that Duffy was in the swim as he knew what I was and saw me with Duffy.

Duffy retired soon after, but he persuaded his successor, a man called Blaney, to continue to pass information on to Kennedy. On one occasion the British discovered that Paddy Cahill was in Tralee visiting his mother and was staying with Paddy Cantillon. Blaney sent word through Sergeant Clarke, the very same sergeant who was always keen to apprehend IRA men. He did not tell Kennedy, but inadvertently let it slip to his wife that Cahill was about to be arrested. Unknown to Clarke, his wife passed on the information to Kennedy, who just managed to get Cahill away to safety before Clarke and the Tans arrived at the house. Kennedy later advised Blaney that Clarke was a 'bad hat' and he should give him a wide berth. Blaney decided not to hang around. He took sick leave and went off to the Canary Islands, and never resumed his duties in Tralee.

Paddy Foley was born in Ballycullane near Annascaul, the son of respectable small farmers and reared by his aunt and her husband, Tom Foley. The couple had no children of their own and in many ways spoiled Paddy. Young Foley was a wild lad and was related to Paddy Cahill as well as most of the Volunteers Officers in the district, including Kennedy. Foley's brother, Mick, was a great friend of Kennedy as well as an Annascaul football club teammate. During the Great War, Paddy Foley ran away and joined the British Army, even though he was under age. Tom Foley attempted to get him out of the Army, but failed to do so. Paddy served for the duration of the war, and no one was sure where he ended up after it.

One evening in the summer of 1920, Paddy Foley walked into Kennedy's digs on Nelson Street in Tralee, and stayed the night. Kennedy didn't pay much attention to Foley's arrival home at first, but became suspicious when he started asking about the reception he could expect to receive from the Volunteers in his home place. He stayed in Tralee for about a week, and during that time, some of the

Fianna boys, Kennedy's young eyes and ears around the town, saw him visit the RIC barracks almost on a daily basis. They reported his movements to Kennedy, who saw him go into the barracks himself one day. Kennedy then advised Foley not to go home to Annascaul. However, one Saturday evening, he travelled out by train with Kennedy and had tea with him in the Kennedy homestead. Kennedy again tried to persuade him to clear out, but he wouldn't take the advice. From then on, Kennedy recalled:

> I had him tightly watched. He went to Dingle several times and I found him making inquiries as to who were the officers in the IRA in the area. He stayed with an aunt of mine, Mrs Bowler, in the Main Street, and tried to pump her eldest son, Michael, who reported to me.

Foley visited the local RIC barracks on several occasions. He made contact with the District Inspector, Bernard O'Connor, who, unbeknownst to Foley, was friendly with Kennedy. O'Connor cleverly gave Foley some notebooks in which he could record information he came across during his stay in Dingle, asking him to return them when his work was done.

Kennedy suggested to his cousin Pat Kennedy, Quartermaster of the Dingle Battalion, and Mick Foley that they take Paddy away and detain him somewhere until the war was over. They attempted to do so, but to no avail.

O'Connor arranged to meet Kennedy at Camp Junction, a railway station on the Tralee to Dingle line. There, O'Connor handed over the notebooks to Kennedy, as well as reports compiled by Foley. Kennedy brought them back to Tralee and passed them over to Paddy Cahill. The notebooks contained the names of every officer in the district and every prominent Sinn Féin member. Those named were nearly all relatives of Foley. After Kennedy's name there appeared to be a question mark. Kennedy recalled: 'It was a very painful situation for Cahill and myself as we were both relations of his.'

A decision had to be made about Paddy Foley, and it was made by Paddy Cahill. He gave Kennedy a job of escorting by car some money for railwaymen's pay, apparently to get him out of the district for a few hours. While Kennedy was away, Paddy Foley was taken out to Moriarty's Hotel in Annascaul and tried as an informer or spy. He was found guilty and condemned to death.

Foley was attended to by Father Edmond Walsh, a close friend of Bishop Fogarty of Killaloe. After receiving the last rites of the Church, he was executed at Meenascarthy, which was in the Castlegregory Battalion district. The sentence could not be carried out in the Dingle Battalion district, as almost all the officers there were relatives of Foley.

When the war was over, Mick Foley asked Kennedy for any tangible proof of his brother's guilt. Kennedy recalled:

I took him to his cousin Paddy Cahill, Brigade OC, who produced the notebooks to him and when he saw and read them, he said he would shoot him himself. Cahill also told him that I did my best to save him and, ever since, Mick and I have maintained our friendship and he did his best to ease the tension in the district caused by my friend Paddy's execution. To us, his friends, it was a terrible tragedy and I was very upset by it, more so than my own brother's death at the hands of the British.

Sometime after the reorganisation of the Kerry Volunteers in 1919, someone had the idea of taking a photograph of the Kerry No 1 Brigade Staff. The photo would be taken at the Sports Field in Tralee, now Austin Stack Park, on a Wednesday afternoon. Kennedy promised to be there, but on the day in question he forgot the appointment and went home to Annascaul, as he usually did on Wednesday afternoons.

The remainder of the staff waited at the venue for Kennedy to turn up, but when he didn't appear, they asked Patrick J O'Connell, the then-Chairman of the Kerry County Board, who was there for a meeting with Austin Stack, to stand in for him in the photo. He was about the same height and had a bald forehead like Kennedy. They removed his spectacles and his hat so that he passed reasonably well for the missing Intelligence Officer.

O'Connell was so delighted to be associated with the 'big shots' of the IRA that he bought a copy of the photo, had it framed and hung it up in the living room of his house, at Boherbee just outside Tralee. When the Black and Tans and Auxiliaries arrived in Tralee in 1920, they made extensive searches of houses, the homes of innocent and guilty alike. One night they raided O'Connell's house and there, hanging on the wall, was the photograph of the Brigade Staff, with an inscription written by Pat himself: 'Brigade Staff Kerry 1 Brigade'.

Needless to say, the Auxiliaries were delighted with the photo. They took it to the barracks and, with the help of older RIC sergeants, they were able to pinpoint each member of the Staff with accuracy and allocate their rank. One old sergeant knew everybody and their rank and surmised that O'Connell must be the Brigade Intelligence Officer. They had spent many an hour in the past attempting to find out who held that position, and now believed they had their man.

The Auxiliaries returned to O'Connell's house and hauled him out. They manhandled him, broke his spectacles and took him to the barracks. There they questioned him and beat him badly before throwing him into the coalhouse. Major McKinnon, the Commanding Officer of the Auxiliaries, who was later gunned down while on a golf course in Tralee, was delighted that they had at last caught the infernal Brigade Intelligence Officer.

However, a Sergeant Clancy came into the barracks bar and asked to see the photo. No sooner had he spied O'Connell than he burst into laughter, knowing full well he was not a Volunteer. Stack, he said, would never have had him on his staff, because O'Connell liked a drink and often liked it a little too much. He told McKinnon they had got the wrong man. O'Connell was taken out of the coalhouse and plied with glasses of whiskey for the rest of the evening, so much so that he collapsed and had to be taken to hospital. He spent two months there, recovering from the beating and the inordinate amount of whiskey he had consumed. He never forgave Kennedy for being the unwitting cause of all of his suffering.

Before the Treaty negotiations began in London in October 1921, Michael Collins sent for Kennedy and asked him to accompany the delegation to London. He had a specific task in mind for him, involving conveying dispatches during the negotiations. Kennedy refused the request, feeling that he would be more useful to the movement if he remained in Kerry – he wanted to help ease tensions that had emerged after the resignation of Paddy Cahill as Commanding Officer of the Brigade.

He did, however, accede to Collins's request to travel to Portsmouth to meet a Captain Russell of the Royal Navy. Collins wanted him to ascertain whether there was any substance to the threat by Lloyd George that he would order a blockade of the country if the Irish delegation failed to accept the terms laid down by the British delegation. Russell assured him there would be no blockade of the country, and Kennedy returned to Kerry after reporting Russell's answer to Collins. Kennedy was disappointed with the outcome of the Treaty negotiations, telling Collins that it would not be acceptable to the vast majority of the IRA in Kerry:

> *I said to Mick that I was very sorry that they did not return to Dublin to the Cabinet before they signed and he retorted that it was a pity I didn't go with him to London and advise him what to do under the circumstances.*

Kennedy opposed the Treaty and was arrested on 3 August 1922 and jailed. He remained locked up until the end of October 1922, when General Fionán Lynch visited him and asked him to go to Dublin to help negotiate an end to the Civil War. He agreed to the request, but his efforts were in vain. He continued to have a friendship with Michael Collins during the Civil War, though he fundamentally disagreed with him over the Treaty.

Collins's death and the Civil War caused Kennedy much sadness, especially when he saw former comrades, who had fought gallantly side by side against the British, meet on opposite sides in the conflict. Despite his disappointment over the Treaty, it is clear from his extensive statement that Tadhg Kennedy looked back on his involvement with the IRA during the War of Independence with a great deal of pride.

Chapter 15

Eamon (Ned) Broy:
An Extraordinary
Policeman and
Courageous Republican

*The people felt that the local RIC knew all about them and there was no use
in doing anything illegal and secret because the police were certain to find out.
Of course, to a certain extent, this was true, because it was easy for the police
to know everyone of a small and scattered population. This menace of the small
party of police among a small population was one of those that had to be dealt
with later on during the years 1919 to 1921.*

(Eamon Broy)

One of the more notable individuals to emerge in the revolutionary era
was Eamon (Ned) Broy, a man who went on to achieve outstanding success in a
number of fields over the course of his life. As a young man, Broy was a member
of the Dublin Metropolitan Police, while at the same time being a committed
republican. His statement to the Bureau of Military History is one of the most
important recollections of the country's revolutionary era.

Eamon Broy was born in Rathagan, County Laois, in 1887. He joined the
DMP in January 1911, and recalled that the half-year spent training in the depot
did not constitute service in the force. On the completion of their training, Broy
and his fellow recruits had to take an oath that required them to serve without

fear or favour, but which also had the following unusual proviso: 'I swear that I do not now belong to, and that whilst serving I shall not belong to, any secret society whatsoever, the Society of Freemasons excepted.' The young recruits felt it was a great presumption to have that proviso included, and when they took the oath, Broy and his colleagues neither touched the Bible nor repeated the words. When a police union was formed in 1919, it was successful in removing the offensive section in the oath, as well as having the time spent in the depot prior to taking the oath counted in total service.

Broy was appointed to E-Division, a uniformed service that controlled an area of Dublin between the Grand Canal and the Dodder River. This suited him admirably, as the numerous sports grounds in the area allowed him to train for athletics. Between 1911 and 1914, he won several sprint and high jump competitions in Dublin and in England.

He was transferred to G-Division in 1915, which was run from two offices, one at number 1 Great Brunswick Street (now Pearse Street) and the other at Dublin Castle. G-Division was divided into three sections: the routine crime section, which dealt with ordinary crime – burglary, housebreaking, larceny, etc; the carriage supervision section, which enforced laws and regulations regarding public service vehicles; and the political section, which countered and supervised all national movements directed against the English occupation. The actions and movements of all persons suspected of being disloyal to the British administration were carefully and methodically observed.

The total strength of G-Division, which became the focus of attention for Michael Collins and his Intelligence Unit, was set at about forty, the majority of whom were married men living across the city, while the single men lived in number 1 Great Brunswick Street. The men of G-Division all had at least three years in the uniformed service before their transfer. They were required to pass examinations, written and oral, on subjects including English composition, arithmetic and handwriting, and needed a good knowledge of the streets of the city.

On his appointment, Broy was given political duties and worked in the clerical section. He recalled that all the work was handwritten, but the authorities were introducing modern methods such as typewriters and card indexes. Those assigned political duties often found themselves at railway stations and ports, watching the movements of suspects. At railway stations, they would ascertain the station for which the suspect had purchased a ticket and would then send a cipher to police at that destination. Any suspect travelling to Dublin about whom a cipher wire was received was observed on arrival and shadowed to his destination in the city.

Other men in G-Division would travel around the city, observing the movements of suspects. Their observations were carefully recorded in a set of books in the office. Every detective made his own entry and there was a very large central book, giving the particulars and the histories of various suspects. The information contained in each detective's book was transferred into this book daily.

When political arrests were made, this was done by those on political duty, sometimes with support from those on carriage duty and crime duty. If the number to be arrested was big, uniformed police were brought in to assist, and for very big operations, the British military were brought in. Daily reports were made to Government on the activities and movements of suspects and included notes on who they were associating with. Weekly and monthly reports were also made, giving a general review of the political activity across the city.

When Broy began making the reports, he dispensed with the handwritten versions and presented typed documents. One copy was sent to the Commissioner, at that time Colonel Edgeworth-Johnstone, and another copy went to the Director of Military Intelligence, Major Price. A further copy was sent to the Government and yet another to the Royal Irish Constabulary – many suspects who were in Dublin came originally from outside the city and were therefore of interest to police in rural Ireland.

Towards the end of 1915, G-Division moved from its old headquarters in Exchange Court to the new building at number 1 Great Brunswick Street. Around that same time, the republican movement began to establish a greater influence across the city and the country.

Politics was of great interest to Broy and many of his colleagues, with home rule the preferred option for the younger members, while those in the higher ranks were content with continued rule from Westminster. Though Broy took no part in the Easter Rising in 1916, he was a very close observer of what was unfolding across Dublin during that fateful week. He believed that from around March 1916, the portents were there that something of significance was about to take place.

He recalled the Citizen Army holding manoeuvres and practising street fighting one particular evening in Patrick Street, the Coombe and Francis Street. A large force of detectives attended, but they took no action to disperse the gathering. The next morning, in their individual reports, many of them described the night of action as a mere 'rehearsal of street fighting'. A central report was compiled and several copies were submitted to the usual authorities in the Castle, but no one seemed to attach any great importance to the event.

From 1913, the Volunteers were accompanied on all marches and exercises by detectives or police and when the split occurred between the Irish Volunteers and the National Volunteers, both received the same treatment. Broy vividly recalled the Volunteers in the early days:

> In the beginning and for some time the Volunteers looked self-conscious in their uniforms, most of which were not too well tailored. As the men were of all shapes, sizes and ages, some with beards and others with spectacles, they often presented with a rather 'gawky' appearance as compared with police or British military.

Over time, there was a steady improvement in their appearance and demeanour, and also in the way they paraded. By St Patrick's Day 1916, they looked like real soldiers. With rifles and bayonets, Broy recalled, they had acquired a 'workmanlike and purposeful air comparable to the best British infantry battalions of the time'.

Full reports, he said, were made on all marches, but again no real sense of concern was shown by the authorities.

Police raids were continuously carried out during that time on newsagents and small printing operations and 'seditious literature' was confiscated, with those involved arrested for disloyal activities. Broy believed the Castle authorities did not anticipate a rebellion by the Volunteers, but they did expect resistance to arrests or disarmament. He pointed out that though the British constantly claimed they were fighting a war on the continent for the future of democracy and small nations, they were unwilling to admit that they were occupying Ireland against the wishes of her people.

Broy related a very interesting account of a cipher message being received from the RIC in Tralee, stating that a mysterious stranger had been arrested on Banna Strand and was being taken under escort to Kingsbridge station by train that evening. The train was met by a Detective Inspector and a party of other detectives, and the prisoner was taken by the Inspector and two detectives directly to London.

Nobody, except for the Inspector, knew the identity of the prisoner and it was only revealed when he was securely under lock and key in London that it was Roger Casement. It was feared that someone might inform a railway official or let it slip to a newspaper reporter who the prisoner really was, thereby spurring a rescue attempt by republicans.

Broy recalled some years later meeting a government official who had happened to be travelling on the same train from Tralee as Casement. The official did not know who the prisoner was, but guessed he was someone important, even though he was escorted by just two RIC men. Casement, the official maintained, cried during the whole journey to Dublin. The official was also struck by how easy it would have been for republicans to rescue him, had they been inclined to do so. Why no attempt was made to rescue a man who had done so much to promote the republican cause remains one of the great imponderables of modern Irish history.

Around the time of Casement's capture, a report came in of the tragedy at Killorglin, in which a party of Volunteers drove their car over the pier into the Laune River, resulting in the drowning of Con Keating, Dan Sheehan and Charles Monaghan. Broy stated that his superior officers considered that Providence had taken a hand against Irish republicans and favoured the British Empire.

Broy believed the British should have anticipated the Easter Rising in 1916, but the truth is that they did not. He put this, partly, down to Eoin MacNeill's fateful countermanding order, cancelling all parades for Easter Sunday. When the fighting began the following day, it took the Castle by surprise. Most officials had taken the day off, with many heading to Fairyhouse for the races and others having even gone to England.

The first indication Broy and his colleagues had of the Rising came a couple of minutes after midday, via a telephone call from the Central Police Telephone Office in the Castle. The message conveyed the news that a party of Volunteers, accompanied by an ambulance corps and stretchers, had broken into and occupied some buildings in Marrowbone Lane, and the buildings were being barricaded. Other messages soon came in, confirming the occupation of the General Post Office, Jacob's biscuit factory, the Four Courts and Boland's Mills.

Soon, detectives began to return to the office, all carrying the same story – the Rising was underway. The Chief Constable, Colonel Edgeworth-Johnstone, ordered all members of the Dublin Metropolitan Police off the streets and into barracks. Broy and his colleagues sat around the dining room and compared notes of their experiences of the day.

Further messages came in regarding buildings occupied by the Volunteers and the shooting going on in various places. They heard the news of Constable O'Brien's death as he tried to close the gates of Dublin Castle and of Sean Connolly's death during the attack on the Castle. News soon came through that more people had died in the fighting, and it was a shock to hear that some of them were Volunteers, who had so often marched through the city.

Broy recalled that 'the trams continued to pass up and down Great Brunswick Street for over an hour after the rising had commenced, adding their noise to the sound of rifle fire'.Broy and his colleagues prepared to defend their building if it became necessary to do so, though they were only armed with revolvers. Gradually, Dublin members of the British Army, who were home on leave, began to arrive, some armed with rifles and some without any weapons. Broy recalled that 'the soldiers who had rifles were placed at upstairs windows to defend the building in case of an attack, but no occasion ever occurred for any of them to fire a shot'.

Members of the public called to the detective office during the week of the conflict, mostly seeking information about relatives who had failed to return home from some journey or other. Broy maintained that most of those who came into the office condemned the Rising outright. Broy felt that the Rising was not initially a popular one, and remained so for some days after the fighting ended.

Several loyal citizens of the old unionist type called to enquire why the British Army and police had not already ejected the Sinn Féiners from the occupied buildings.

A field gun arrived outside Broy's office on the Trinity College side of the road. A large crowd of sightseers gathered and some of the men, ex-British soldiers with their trademark large moustaches, were advising the soldiers how best to use the gun. Broy and his colleagues gave up watching the antics on the street and retired to their office to continue playing cards.

After some time, there was a swishing sound in the street and they heard the crowd scampering away as fast as it could. Broy looked out the window and saw one artillery man lying dead on the road, killed by a bullet fired from the corner building of Bachelor's Walk. The artillery gun was then taken to Tara Street and began firing from the Butt Bridge area later that day.

There was widespread looting during the Rising, and Broy recalled seeing some bizarre sights from his office window:

I saw corner-boys wearing silk hats, ladies from the slums sporting fur coats, a cycling corps of barefoot young urchins riding brand new bicycles stolen from some of the shops, and members of the underworld carrying umbrellas. One citizen was carrying a large flitch of bacon on his back, with another man walking behind him cutting a piece off with a large knife.

Though they were told to stay in barracks, members of the ordinary crime department went out into the streets. Despite bullets whizzing about, they arrested looters and soon filled the cells at College Street police station. When the fighting ended, senior detectives went to Richmond Barracks to identify and classify the prisoners, selecting those who were best known as leaders for immediate trial by courts martial. The political record book in Broy's office was taken to Richmond Barracks, to provide evidence of previous interactions between the law and well-known republicans who took part in the Rising.

The executions stunned Broy and many of his colleagues and he recalled speaking to local people around Kilmainham who heard the early morning shots ring out. Many of them had opposed the Rising, but were horrified at the cost the leaders had to pay for their involvement in it.

The police authorities appeared to think that the executions, imprisonments and internments of prisoners had finished off Sinn Féin and the Irish Volunteers for good, and so began cutting down the number of detectives on political duty. Of course, only a couple of years later, the republican movement became resurgent and the authorities in Dublin Castle quickly discovered that the detective force was not near strong enough to suppress it.

An enormous mass of Sinn Féin literature was captured by the military and police from meeting places and homes of Volunteers for weeks after the fighting ended. All of the literature, including maps, was stored in the Brunswick Street detective office, and Broy recalled:

> When the Volunteers began to reorganise in 1917, I gradually returned to them samples or copies of all documents, maps and publications which had been captured, which were of some help to them in picking up the threads of their organisation again.

In the months after the Easter Rising, there were a great many retirements in the DMP, as well as promotions and transfers, leading to a modernisation of the force in general. Broy was left alone for a number of days in an office where most of the documents captured during the Rising were held. He maintained that a person of his short service would not have been left in charge of that office but for the changes being implemented at the time.

Broy never had any real intention of staying in the police force long-term, as he had several invitations to go to America. He regarded himself as just another Irish nationalist who, through circumstance, had found himself in the job he was in. With, as it seemed, unfettered access to many important documents, Broy began to consider whether he could be of value to the republican movement. He calculated that, outside his Superintendent, he also probably had the best knowledge in the DMP of political suspects and their activities.

Despite the obvious danger to himself, Broy concluded that it was his duty to help the republican movement, and he made up his mind to go 'all-out to help them'. He began to investigate how to contact the right people, and decided they would have to be extreme in their views and hate England so much that they too would be prepared to take a chance. He decided that the best place to make contact was through some nationalist-owned shop, where callers would not attract any special attention.

After careful consideration of various possibilities, he decided on O'Hanrah-ans of North Circular Road. Michael O'Hanrahan had been executed after the Rising, and his brother Harry and his two sisters ran the shop. Broy knew he could never visit the shop himself, as members of the DMP lived in the area and he was well-known to the general public as an athlete and a policeman. Very probably, he believed, if he entered the shop it would be reported to his superiors within minutes.

He needed someone who would be prepared to deliver information to the shop for him, and settled on Patrick Tracey (Broy misspelled the name as Tracy in his statement). A committed Sinn Féin member, Tracey happened to be married to Broy's first cousin and was employed as a clerk at Kingsbridge railway terminus. Tracey willingly assented to the plan and agreed that O'Hanrahan's shop was ideal for the purpose.

The first report he made through Tracey was related to the planned arrests of Larry Ginnell and Joe MacDonagh. He told Tracey that no information was to come back to him. From that time onwards, every secret and confidential doc-ument and police code that came into Broy's hands was sent, through Tracey and O'Hanrahan's, to Volunteers headquarters. A man called Gregg Murphy transferred most of the documents onwards from O'Hanrahan's, and some of them, he believed, went to Eamon Duggan and Harry Boland.

The documents he passed on ranged from a slip of paper to 100 pages. Broy recalled passing on a document that discussed the Volunteers' plans to obstruct conscription, and this was one of the few he ever heard anything back about. Tracey informed him that the Volunteers leaders were very concerned that the authorities had knowledge of their plans.

One evening around 6pm in the middle of August 1917, a warrant arrived in Broy's office for the arrest of Eamon de Valera. Broy and Detective Ser-geant Fagan, the only two officers present in the office, were duty-bound to carry out the arrest. Fagan was angry at being required to do this after a hard day's work – like Broy, he was due to go off duty at 7pm. Broy recalled the orders accompanying the warrant were very specific. They were ordered, he said:

... to arrest de Valera, who was stated to be residing at 34 Munster Street, Phibsbor-ough. We were told not to enquire for him at that house, for fear he might happen to be absent and calling there might put him on his guard. We were to watch for him in the vicinity.

Fagan, incandescent with rage over having to extend his working day, agreed with Broy that they would not go to Phibsborough until 7pm. Broy did all he could to reinforce his colleague's angst, in the hope that it might give him an opening to warn de Valera of his impending arrest. Broy knew that Peadar Healy, a Volunteer and veteran of the Rising, lived at 86 Phibsborough Road and he decided he would have to get him to inform de Valera to make himself scarce. However, the problem was how to get to Healy without alerting Fagan.

Just after 7pm, Fagan went into the Mountjoy police station to ring the Superintendent and tell him they had not seen 'that man' and to have a drink, as he considered himself off-duty. He asked Broy to join him, but Broy refused, saying he was teetotal and would stay on outside for a while. When Fagan disappeared, Broy recalled:

I decided to sprint to Healy's and try to get back before Fagan emerged from the station. Peadar Healy was absent from his house but his brother was in. I told him who and what I was, and that de Valera was about to be arrested. I asked him to warn de Valera.

Broy then sprinted back towards Mountjoy police station. As he neared it, he ran into Detective Sergeant Revelle from the Castle, who lived in Phibsborough, and told him they were looking for de Valera. He went into the station with Revelle to meet up with Fagan and, as far as he could ascertain, neither of his colleagues were any the wiser about what he had just done.

As for de Valera, he went underground, much to the annoyance of the police, most of whom thought it strange for him to do so at the very moment a warrant for his arrest had been issued. De Valera later sent a message of thanks to Broy via Peadar Healy. Broy had put his prowess as an athlete and sprinter of some repute to good use for the republican cause.

In May 1918, a large list of names and addresses of those to be arrested as part of the 'German plot' debacle came into Broy's hands. It was obvious to him that arrests were about to happen very soon. Broy gave Tracey a copy of the complete list on the Wednesday in a public house on Benburb Street, forty-eight hours before the arrests were due to take place. Broy recalled:

I got Tracey to copy the particulars in his handwriting, destroyed mine there and then, and instructed Tracey that in the usual manner, he should get O'Hanrahan to copy them and destroy his own hand writing. I told him to tell O'Hanrahan that it was almost certain that I would be able to tell him in advance when exactly the arrests would take place.

Broy met Tracey the following Friday and recalled:

I told him, 'Tonight's the night'. Tell O'Hanrahan to tell the wanted men not to stay in their usual place of abode and to keep their wits about them.

Broy recalled that all detectives were told to stand-to and prepare for the raids. He and another detective by the name of McNamara (a detective officer and one of Collins's men) deliberated on whether they should refuse to obey the order, but they decided that it would be of little use and would probably lead to their dismissal from the force.

To his surprise, Broy was put on telephone duty in the Castle that night by Superintendent Brien. He believed the operation would be a failure because of his actions, and was stunned when he started taking calls from detectives on the raids, confirming the arrests of the parties they had been sent for. He was particularly perplexed when a message came through that de Valera had been spotted, having just left Harcourt Street railway station on a train for Greystones, where he was living. Broy fully expected that de Valera would have gone to ground, having been informed he was to be arrested. As it turned out, he took a telephone call from the Royal Irish Constabulary, confirming that de Valera had been arrested in Greystones.

The raids that night were relatively successful, leading Broy to wonder what had gone wrong with his messages through O'Hanrahan. On the following Sunday afternoon, he met Tracey to find out what had happened. He asked Tracey whether he had actually delivered the message to O'Hanrahan, and Tracey confirmed that he had. Some days later, Tracey confirmed that O'Hanrahan had passed on the messages and he was as perplexed as Broy as to why de Valera, more than anyone else, had been arrested.

As it transpired, de Valera had allowed himself to be arrested that night. A few days after the raid, Broy recalled meeting Superintendent Brien in the office. His boss, looking hard at him, said, 'The Sinn Féiners boasted that their most important men had escaped arrest.'

Broy answered, 'When you have got de Valera, surely you have got enough.'

During this time, Broy was unaware of who ultimately handled the information he passed along, and he certainly knew little of a man called Michael Collins. One evening while at Pat Tracey's house on Millmount Avenue in Drumcondra, he met Greg Murphy, who handled the information as it came out of O'Hanrahan's shop. He suggested to Broy that he should meet Collins and made arrangements for him to do so, at the home of Micheal O'Foghludha on the Cabra Road. To inform himself about Collins, Broy checked him out in the police records. They showed he was a six-footer, a Corkman, very intelligent, young and powerful. There was no photograph of him, showing that he was still a bit of a mystery to the authorities.

On the evening in question, Broy turned up at O'Foghludha's house and waited to meet Collins, who arrived in the company of Greg Murphy. Broy was immediately impressed by Collins and recalled:

The moment I saw Michael at the door, before he had time to walk across and shake hands, I knew he was the man. He was dressed in black leggings, green breeches and a trench coat with all the usual buttons, belts and rings. He was very handsome, obviously full of energy and with a mind as quick as lightning.

They had a four-hour discussion, covering subjects such as the 'German plot' information that Broy had passed on and why de Valera had failed to evade arrest. Collins indicated that de Valera could have escaped the authorities but chose not to do so.

Collins decided the time had come for Broy to have direct contact with him and the members of the Intelligence Unit. They both agreed that if independence was ever to be achieved, it would come about through the use of violence and there would be extreme risk for many in the republican movement.

Broy outlined to Collins the fundamentals of police organisation. He suggested that, as the DMP uniformed service took no part in anti-Sinn Féin activities, unlike the RIC, they should not be alienated by attacks on them. The majority, at least the younger men, were anti-British, and many had relatives in the Volunteers. They did not get involved in political work and for the most part did not regard themselves as Crown forces, although the government did.

Broy described the DMP men as more liberal than their RIC counterparts. They were typically also physically bigger, which tended to make them, in Broy's view, a bit more easy-going. They were not under such close personal supervision by their superiors as were the RIC men, especially those in small rural stations. As a result, the DMP men tended to freely exchange their opinions about home rule and other political issues in the mess halls and elsewhere.

Broy and Collins agreed that the RIC were a danger to the Volunteers in the more isolated rural areas. A ruthless war should be waged on the small stations, they said, attacking the barracks if they were occupied by the police or burning them down if they had been evacuated. The RIC would then be compelled to concentrate on the larger towns, causing them to lose their grip, psychologically and otherwise, on the vacated areas and the people living in them.

Broy advocated a psychological approach in the next stage of the process – Volunteers and their friends and families should impress upon young RIC men that there was now a chance to free the country and that, if they were not prepared to help, at least they should not hinder the cause of independence. The families and friends of RIC men should also be targeted, pointing out to them that it would be a disgrace if the young policemen resisted the Volunteers in the coming struggle. After all those efforts were made and, only then, should a ruthless war be waged on the hard core that remained.

In the case of the DMP, no attack should be made on the uniformed service, and no attack should be made on the members of G-Division who were not on political duty. Broy maintained that the DMP would come to realise that, as long as they did not display zeal against Volunteers, they were safe from attack. In the case of any G-man who remained hostile, a warning should be given to him, such as tying him to a railing, before any attack was made on him.

After their conversation, Detective Officer Denis O'Brien was the first member of G-Division to be dealt with when, on 9 April 1919, he was tied to a railing and warned off. A native of Kanturk, he had been more than usually active in observing and shadowing Volunteers and members of Sinn Féin. He was told that if he did not desist in his work, no mercy would be shown to him the next time.

When he was released by his comrades and taken to the Castle, his Superintendent castigated him for allowing himself to be captured and tied up. This annoyed O'Brien very much, and Broy recalled the clearly agitated detective saying to him and his colleagues, 'I would like to know what anyone else would do in the same circumstances.' He also praised his assailants, telling Broy sometime later that, 'They were damned decent men not to shoot me, and I am not doing any more against them.'

Through their conversations, it began to dawn on Broy that Collins did not really understand the fundamental workings of the detective organisation. They both decided it would be necessary for Collins to go into the office and read the records for himself. From ten o'clock each night until six in the morning, it was usual for one man, and generally not from the political staff, to be on duty in the detective office for a week and that man had the cipher in case a telegram arrived. Sometimes, the duty officer was required to attend court during the week and was excused duty on the night prior to his court appearance.

Meeting Collins one night in April 1919, Broy told him he expected to be standing in for the night duty man on the following night from 10pm to 6am. They agreed that Collins should telephone at midnight to make certain Broy was on duty. He would use the name 'Field' and Broy was to use the name 'Long'.

The following night, Broy, as he anticipated, was on duty, and most of the detectives living in the station went to bed around 11pm. Reports began to come in of shootings in Store Street and other areas, and Broy wondered if fate was taking a hand and scuppering his plan with Collins. He intended to let Collins into the secret office on the first floor where the records were kept, but to get access to it, he would have to get into the bigger political office first. Broy had made himself a master key that opened all doors in the building, including the secret records room.

The uniformed B-Division Inspector on night duty was Daniel Barrett. While the average uniformed officer gave G-Division a wide berth, Barrett was an ignorant, presumptuous man, capable of reporting seeing a light on in the office. It was clear to Broy that Collins would not be able to switch on a light, so candles would be required.

At midnight, Collins telephoned, saying, 'Field here. Is that Long?' Broy replied, 'Yes. Bring a candle.' Around 12.15am, Collins arrived, accompanied by Sean Nunan. Broy showed them the back way and the yard door to Townsend Street, in case they had to make a quick getaway.

No sooner had he done so than a stone came through a window. Broy ushered the two men into a dark passageway and told them to wait near the back door. Looking out onto Brunswick Street, Broy saw a British soldier in the custody of a policeman. He opened the door and inquired of the constable what was wrong. It transpired the soldier was drunk and had thrown the stone. The policeman took him to the police station next door.

Broy returned to Collins and Nunan and told them what had happened. He asked if they had brought candles, to which Collins replied, 'No.' Broy then had to go and look for some. With the aid of his master key, he opened the stores room and found plenty of them as well as lots of matches. Broy recalled:

I brought Michael upstairs. With the master key I locked the main doors of the dormitories, which were on the top floor. The same key opened the political office and opened the secret small room, built into the wall, which contained the records. I gave Collins and Nunan the candles and, getting them to close the door fairly tightly, I left them to carry on their investigations.

On his way back downstairs, Broy heard a heavy knock on the front door. He opened it and found the same police constable, inquiring as to the value of the broken glass. Broy gave him a rough estimate and he left.

Collins and Nunan stayed until 5am. According to Broy, there were a number of reasons for the visit. Collins, he said, wanted to know the background of what he called 'the correspondence' he had received from him, the exact degree of British knowledge as regards the Volunteers, Sinn Féin and other national organisations. He also wanted to ascertain who, of their people, were known to the police and, still more important, who were not known. He wanted to gauge the mentality behind the records, and then use the police secret organisation as a model, with suitable improvements and modifications, for the Volunteers' own systems.

It was obvious to Broy that, sooner or later, the records would be taken to the Castle, because at nearly every hour of the day, the authorities there called asking for particulars, in writing, of certain individuals. As it happened, the records were indeed removed to the Castle not long after the visit of Collins and Nunan.

During the remaining months of 1919 and into 1920, Broy continued to supply invaluable information to Collins and the Intelligence Unit, often giving them a real advantage over enemy agents. However, in January 1921, his outstanding work came to an end, when the suspicions of his superiors were suddenly raised. A Detective Sergeant in his office connected Broy to two typed reports that were captured in a raid on a house in Dawson Street, which Broy had indeed passed on to Collins.

A few days later, Broy was called to the Commissioner's office. He admitted typing the reports when they were put before him, but said he had no idea how they found their way to Dawson Street.

The moment the documents were captured, Broy's usefulness to Collins and the Intelligence Unit was at an end. His subsequent work in the office was constantly scrutinised by his superiors and colleagues. Outside of work hours, he still managed to meet with Collins, mostly at night. Broy was convinced he was going to be arrested, dismissed or even shot, but Collins didn't seem to think he was in any real danger.

Broy was summoned to the Commissioner's office in the Castle in late February and was accompanied by Superintendent Purcell. When they arrived, Broy was asked to wait in an anteroom. Sometime later, as he recalled:

> ... my doubts were soon settled, for Purcell emerged from the Commissioner's office trembling and with his face as white as a sheet. In a quavering voice, he told me I was to be arrested for giving out the documents to the Sinn Féiners. The Inspector, though a loyalist, was also shocked and rendered speechless. I, of course, was not surprised, although I had to express indignation to the best of my ability.

Broy had the option of shooting his way out of the building, but that would have been an admittance of guilt. He chose not to, as he said he hadn't the heart to kill

Purcell or any other policemen. He was searched and had his official gun taken from him, and he was brought to Arbour Hill prison.

He was in prison for two weeks when his solicitor, Philip O'Reilly, who had been chosen to represent him by some influential members of Sinn Féin, visited him. He advised Broy that Collins had devised a plan to extricate him from the prison and he intended to participate in the rescue himself. Broy sent word back, via O'Reilly, not to attempt a rescue for the time being, as he was sure he would be released.

He spent the next two months in prison, before O'Reilly demanded his release or a trial. In April, the 'Summary of Evidence' proceedings began. Philip O'Reilly was initially barred from being present at the hearing, but he eventually overturned that decision by invoking precedent. With the 'Summary of Evidence' proceedings completed, O'Reilly demanded the court martial take place as soon as possible, as his client was anxious to get back to work. Weeks passed, anxiously for Broy, with no further developments.

The Truce was announced in July, and O'Reilly came to the prison to inform Broy that he was being processed for release. Some days later, after five months in solitary confinement, Broy was released into the custody of police at the Bridewell station, where he remained overnight. During his time there, he was visited by many officers who came to greet him and fill him in on all that had happened during his incarceration.

Broy was officially released on bail the following morning and brought by Superintendent Purcell before the Commissioner, Colonel Edgeworth-Johnstone. Then, according to Broy, the Commissioner:

> ... informed me that he was suspending me from the police, that it should have been done on my arrest but had been forgotten at the time through an oversight, and that the Prison Commandant had refused to allow that formality to be completed while I was in custody in Arbour Hill. The result was that I would have to receive full pay up to that date for the time I was in Arbour Hill.

Edgeworth-Johnstone then dismissed him from the police force – much against his wishes, he added – and Broy made his way to the detective office in Brunswick Street to collect his pay.

Soon after his release, Broy went on holiday to the country for a number of weeks to recover his health after five months in solitary confinement. On his return, he spent a good deal of time attending Dáil meetings in the Mansion House. He often ran into his colleagues from G-Division and, to a man, they pledged to help him should the conflict with the British ever resume.

With the fighting over, political manoeuvres were gathering pace. Broy recalled Harry Boland being sent to America, 'to prepare the American people for the acceptance of something short of a Republic'. Before leaving Dublin, there was a going-away party for him in Vaughan's hotel. Collins was there and in great form and he entertained everyone with his reciting of the 'Lisht'.

Eventually, it was announced that an Irish delegation would enter into negotiations with the British government in London, beginning on 11 October, 'with a view to ascertaining how the association of Ireland with the community of nations known as the British Empire may be best reconciled with Irish national aspirations'.

On Collins's insistence, Broy accompanied the Irish delegation to London for the negotiations that led to the signing of the Anglo-Irish Treaty in December 1921. Broy supported the Treaty, and became a Colonel in the Free State army during the Civil War. He joined the Garda Síochána in 1925, becoming Commissioner in 1933 and that same year he became President of the Irish Olympic Council, a position he held until 1950.

The history books record how Broy embarked on a dangerous path after the Easter Rising by joining the struggle for his country's independence. From then on, his work in G-Division enabled Collins and his Intelligence Unit to remain one step ahead of the authorities. Eamon (Ned) Broy's extensive and fascinating witness statement provides us with an absorbing account of republican activities prior to and during the War of Independence. He was, in every way, a remarkable man, an extraordinary policeman and a courageous republican.

Chapter 16

Cumann na mBan: The Unsung Heroines of the War of Independence

The general activities of the branches were scouting and housing the columns, keeping dumps and doing intelligence work. These activities were by no means easy to carry out. Reprisals by Black and Tans were being constantly enacted. Houses were burned, men arrested and beaten. Cumann na mBan were always on the spot to help the sufferers. District Council meetings were held occasionally, so that all branches were linked up. Some members were instructed not to appear at branch meetings, as their homes were safe refuges for IRA men. Such members concentrated on Intelligence work.

(Máire Mhic Giolla Phádraig)

When we think of the War of Independence, the exploits of the Irish Republican Army, the Squad and the flying columns come readily to mind. The courage of the men who took on the might of the British Empire knew no bounds and today we revere them as the heroes they were. Their actions brought the British to the negotiating table for the first time in history and set in motion the process that delivered to the people of Ireland the freedom they craved for so long. While the men of the revolutionary era rightly earned the gratitude of the nation, the women who made a massive contribution to the republican cause during that tumultuous time often do not get the credit they deserve.

From the years before the Easter Rising, republican-minded women rallied to the cause and formed themselves into a formidable force, determined to play their part in the fight for independence. That force was Cumann na mBan, many of whose members committed their recollections to paper when asked to do so by Oscar Traynor in 1947, leaving a fine and comprehensive record of their courageous actions for posterity.

One common factor among the statements of Cumann na mBan members is the enthusiasm all the women displayed for the cause of Ireland's independence. They were more than willing to take extraordinary risks, often placing themselves in great danger. They initially conveyed messages and prepared medical supplies prior to the outbreak of the fighting in 1916, then cared for the wounded and maimed, as well preparing hot meals for the men at the front line.

Many Cumann na mBan members were arrested after the Rising and sent to jails both in Ireland and England. When they were released, they refused to fade away, but reasserted their commitment to the new Republic by involving themselves on many levels during the War of Independence. Again, they continuously placed themselves in danger, not only carrying important messages across the country on behalf of the IRA, but also transporting guns and ammunition, often going to great lengths to evade the military and the police.

The archive of statements made by the women of Cumann na mBan is so extensive that to do it justice it would require a project of its own. In order to illustrate the contribution made by these heroic women, I have tried to select statements that are typical of their experiences throughout the revolutionary era, which went a long way towards defining modern-day Ireland.

* * *

Máire Bean Mhic Giolla Phádraig (Fitzpatrick) lived in Enniscorthy in County Wexford. Born into a longstanding republican family, Fitzpatrick immersed herself in the republican movement from an early age. She formed a branch of Cumann na mBan soon after the national organisation was founded in Dublin, and the first meeting in Enniscorthy was attended by around 100 new members.

Fitzpatrick left school in her early teens and concentrated on organising Cumann na mBan, giving lectures and holding First Aid classes. She also distributed the *Workers Republic* paper in Enniscorthy, and recalled that the *Irish Volunteer* was printed in the town by the *Echo* newspaper company and sent on to Dublin.

She recalled the split in the Irish Volunteers and Cumann na mBan in 1914, and the controversy it created around the country. Wexford was a stronghold of the Irish Parliamentary Party, and John Redmond called a big recruiting meeting for his newly formed National Volunteers in Wexford Town. Fitzpatrick, in the company of Liam Mellows and four or five other prominent republicans in Enniscorthy, rowed the River Slaney to Wexford, where they were met by Hanna Sheehy-Skeffington. Fitzpatrick recalled how:

> *... we were given leaflets to distribute. Wexford was crowded with people for the meeting and we got a very rough handling from the crowd. Mrs Sheehy-Skeffington got so badly beaten that she had to be attended by a doctor. We were stoned out of Wexford, but we had our reward. The Irish Volunteers got more members and we got back most of our women.*

Fitzpatrick and her Cumann na mBan colleagues supported the Enniscorthy Volunteers when they took over the town during the Easter Rising. She cycled to Wexford during the conflict to deliver despatches, carrying a revolver given to her by her brother Sean, and returned to Enniscorthy with a parcel of guns. When leaving Wexford, she met a British Army patrol and had to promise two of the soldiers she would meet them later that evening before they allowed her to pass and continue her journey home.

After the Rising, the Fitzpatrick family was targeted and their home was often raided by the police. Máire recalled a very sad incident that occurred around that time. The police raided her sister's home one day when her twin boys were sleeping in a cot. When one baby was lifted out, a policeman pulled up the mattress and tipped out the second infant on to the floor and killed him.

In the aftermath of the Rising, the Cumann na mBan women looked after prisoners' dependants. Fitzpatrick walked to Courtown one day to deliver a letter to the mother of one Volunteer, Sean Etchingham. The RIC prevented her from travelling by train, so she had no option but to walk the fifty-mile round trip.

Fitzpatrick recalled that all republicans were more determined than ever to continue the struggle during the War of Independence. In May 1920, her brother Sean was forced to go 'on the run' and made his way to Drogheda, while her father was paraded around Enniscorthy by the Black and Tans. In February 1921, Sean was murdered in Drogheda by Crown forces. Marie recalled:

We travelled to Drogheda to view his shattered body which was in an outhouse covered by sacking. He left a wife and a nine-month-old infant. We brought his remains home to Enniscorthy. The funeral was banned. Only a few were allowed to go, but the town closed down and men, women and children turned out. Many were arrested and some were hurt.

Máire Mhic Giolla Phádraig and her family continued to involve themselves in the fight for Ireland's independence and every one of them received service medals from the state.

* * *

Mary Rigney joined Cuman na mBan in 1917, and later became Treasurer and Secretary of Ard Craobh Sinn Féin, so her republican credentials are beyond question. She was chosen by Arthur Griffith to attend on Michael Collins between the months of November and December 1920, at a house owned by a Miss Patricia Hoey on Mespil Road in Dublin. Her duties were to answer the door and cook for Collins, who went under the name of Mr O'Brien if anybody inquired about him.

Rigney said in her statement that Miss Hoey's mother was an 'out and out Britisher', but had no idea who the lodger really was. Rigney recalled that 'Patricia told me that her mother would not hesitate to go around to the Officer on the bridge and offer information about Michael Collins for the £1,000 that was on his head'.

Collins did not sleep in the house, according to Rigney, though there was a bedroom available to him, which he actually furnished himself. During the day, a constant stream of messengers visited him with despatches and Rigney was told by Miss Hoey that she did not have to worry about those men coming and going, as each of them possessed their own latch key in order to avoid any delay on the door step and they had instructions never to knock on the door.

The house could not be surrounded, as it had long front and back gardens, with a high wall at the bottom of the back one. Behind the house was a park that Collins could escape to if the house was raided by the police or military. Rigney recalled sleeping in the basement bedroom intended for Collins, which was a blind in case of a raid and was intended to prove that a man was not lodging in the house.

Collins, according to Rigney, 'worked in the front room and thus had a close view of anyone who might come in by the front gate. Should there be a knock at the hall door I was to answer it.' The door was not to be left open and unattended even for one moment. If Rigney was unsure of who the caller was, she asked him or her to wait. She then closed the door and slipped the latch until she returned to let the caller in. Rigney also did the shopping for the household to prevent any unnecessary callers. She recalled the atmosphere of the place almost 'drove her crazy' because of the friction between Patricia Hoey and her mother, which was only alleviated when the older lady left for London to visit her son.

In the upstairs living room and downstairs kitchen, Batt O'Connor created hiding places in the panelling over the windows for papers, ammunition and guns. Rigney recalled some sliding panels that were not perceptible except to someone who knew of them. She also recalled as one came in from the back garden, there was a door leading into a cubby hole under the stairs. The back wall of the cubby hole had shelves on which were old tins, boxes and cleaning materials. Rigney recalled:

This wall could be opened by pressing a spring and behind it was a large space which was capable of hiding an amount of important papers. In the evening the typist working for Collins put all his papers into the compartment and closed the camouflaged door.

Rigney left the house just before Christmas 1920, and was given a number of papers to take with her. At her home in Clontarf, she tied them up into bundles, putting some into the oven of an old kitchen range that was not used. Some bundles were placed under a heavy trunk, while others were placed in the potting shed, covered by flower pots and other rubbish.

On Sunday, 30 January 1921, Rigney's house was raided around lunchtime and searched in a casual way. At first nothing was found, and the officer in charge was about to order his men out of the house, when one of them came down the stairs and produced two or three revolvers that he had found in the attic. The officer then turned to Rigney and said, 'Now, we'll tear the house to bits.'

Rigney had her Sinn Féin branch roll book in the house, but had managed to place it in a wardrobe in a bedroom occupied by an aged aunt before answering the door to the soldiers. She requested they not go into the bedroom, on the pretence that it would upset the old woman greatly, and they agreed. Rigney recalled:

I went to my aunt's door to assure her that she need not worry as the officer had promised not to interfere. While I was speaking in a loud voice to her I quietly opened the wardrobe door, lifted the little roll book and stuck it into the front of my blouse.

Rigney then picked up the family dog in her arms to cover it. When the search was completed, she was ordered to accompany the soldiers to Dublin Castle for further questioning. She refused, saying she would not travel alone in a lorry with soldiers, and so a car was summoned from the Castle to take her there.

As they waited for the car, the little dog in Rigney's arms shifted and the book was exposed. The officer in charge saw it and said, 'You need to be searched.'

She replied, 'You have no women searchers with you and you can't lay a hand on me.'

Going to the top of the stairs, she called her sister Margaret and handed over the dog, at the same time slipping the roll book to her and whispering the name Pat, meaning Miss Hoey. Her sister knew immediately that the book should be brought to her as soon as possible.

At this point, the car arrived to take her to the Castle. On the journey, she reflected on how the revolvers had come to be in the house, as she had no idea they were even there. It later transpired they belonged to an IRA volunteer called Bob Young, a regular visitor to the house, whom Rigney had long been suspicious of. He had walked into the house during the raid and Rigney later thought it odd that an IRA volunteer should do so, at a time when the British authorities were out to capture anyone connected with the movement. She also thought it strange that he was not questioned there and then by the military.

After some questioning in the Castle, Rigney was taken to Mountjoy jail. Here she was searched, but of course nothing was found on her person. From there she was taken to the North Dublin Union and on 12 February was court martialled. She was sentenced to two years' hard labour, commuted to nine months, which she served in Mountjoy.

Margaret (Peg) Broderick-Nicholson was a Cumann na mBan Section Commander in Galway between 1917 and 1921. As well as involving themselves in drilling and First Aid lectures, the women in Galway also engaged in the continuous interruption of British recruitment meetings during 1917 and 1918. They did that by moving through the crowds singing nationalist songs until the meetings either collapsed or they were ejected.

Peg was asked by Volunteers officers to take up intelligence work, which involved keeping an eye out for RIC patrols and carrying despatches. She was also entrusted with distributing bundles of the Volunteers newspaper *An tÓglach*.

After the 1918 general election and during 1919, the women began to drill and carry out exercises in the countryside. Peg Broderick-Nicholson recalled one particular exercise held during a Field Day in Barna, where they were being instructed by an officer from the Volunteers brigade called Sheils. As they marched back through Barna, they met a Volunteers scout, who said he thought there were a few RIC men outside the barracks, waiting for the women to pass by. Broderick-Nicholson recalled:

When we reached the barracks, I noticed a sergeant with six or seven men, who then made a charge out to arrest the Volunteers Officer. We immediately pounced on the police. I remember getting up on one policeman's back and getting my two hands round his throat. He wriggled to knock me off and let his grip on the prisoner relax.
Another RIC man then intervened and pulled her off. She grabbed the second fellow's cap and beat him on the head with the hard peak, but then the first man swung around and struck her with his revolver on the side of the head, just above the ear. She was stunned and in shock, staggering against a wall, when someone shouted, 'This is no time for fainting.' She shook herself out of her torpor,

but by that time Sheils had been dragged into the barracks. Some RIC men came out of the barracks shooting into the air to frighten the women. Broderick-Nicholson recalled:

> We collected all the stones, of which there were plenty, and broke every window in the barracks. We then reformed and commenced our march back very 'brónach' indeed.

Around that time, Broderick-Nicholson was attached to the Brigade Staff to carry out intelligence duties, such as delivering despatches and moving revolvers and ammunition from place to place. She carried despatches from General Sean MacEoin to Brigadier Tom Reddington and vice versa.

In the autumn of 1920, the RIC and the Black and Tans attempted to burn down her family home by saturating every door and the whole ground floor with petrol. The house was saved by the intervention of neighbours, despite the Black and Tans firing shots above their heads. Peg's brother was arrested, and the family had an anxious wait before he was released.

Some days later, the Black and Tans raided again, and Peg was called down from the top of the stairs in her night attire. 'Surely I am allowed to dress myself,' she said. They replied, 'No, come down as you are.' She came down and snatched a coat from the hall stand. Her mother shouted after her, 'Be brave, Peg.' She recalled:

> I thought at first, they were going to shoot me, but they took me out and closed the door, then grabbed my hair, saying 'What wonderful curls you've got' and proceeded to cut off all my hair to the scalp with a blunt scissors. I might say they did not handle me too roughly, which is strange to say. There was no further comment until they finished, when they pushed me towards the door and said, 'Goodnight.' All spoke with English accents.

Peg had her head shaved the following day in order to allow it to grow properly again. She later learned that at least one RIC man had previously been seen pointing her out to the Black and Tans.

Undeterred, Peg Broderick-Nicholson continued her Cumann na mBan duties and spent some time 'on the run', sleeping in different houses. She maintained her practice of visiting Galway jail to see Volunteers prisoners from country districts, whose folk, she said, were always anxious about them. She often got parcels through the guard – one particular soldier suspected her of smuggling goods into the prison, but he never gave her away. His stock comment was, 'Are you a mother, an aunt or a sister of some of them today?'

Always willing to obey orders, there was one task Peg did not feel comfortable with, which was enticing British soldiers down to the docks so that they could be relieved of their arms by Volunteers, one of whom, an officer, happened to be her brother.

Peg Broderick-Nicholson was a typical Cumann na mBan girl, determined to play her part in the struggle for her country's independence. She was fearless and willingly placed herself in danger for the cause, and Ireland is forever in her debt.

If Cumann na mBan was active in the west of the country, the organisation was equally, if not more, conspicuous in the south. The statement submitted to the Bureau by Bessie Cahill (nee Harrington) of Ballymacelligott offers a fine insight into the activities of republican women in Kerry. The county was a republican stronghold at the time and almost every family could claim to have a member in either the Volunteers or Cumann na mBan.

Bessie Harrington joined her local Cumann na mBan branch, which had about twelve members, in 1915. The numbers grew rapidly and much work was done with the Volunteers in the months leading up to the Easter Rising in 1916. One of her first recollections revolved around Robert Monteith, who was brought by the Volunteers to Ballymacelligott after he landed on Banna Strand with Roger Casement. Cahill vividly recalled: 'Monteith was suffering from exposure and he was so bad that Lena McEllistrim had to massage his hands until circulation returned.'

Monteith was moved from house to house during his stay in the area, and this represented the beginning of the Cumann women's work with men 'on the run'.

After the Rising, there was a lull in republican activities, but the women continued their work preparing kits for the Volunteers in anticipation of a reactivation of hostilities. In April 1918, Gortatlea RIC barracks was attacked and two Volunteers, John Brown and Richard Laide, were killed. The other men who carried out the attack were forced to seek shelter and Cumann na mBan were called upon to assist them. This made the Ballymacelligott branch the first in Ireland after the Easter Rising required to look after active Volunteers on the run.

In June 1918, two RIC men in the area were fired upon by Thomas McEllistrim and John Cronin, and a period of intense police activity followed. Despite the stepping up of police activity, Cumann na mBan continued to train as well as organise dances and concerts to raise funds for the republican cause.

In March 1920, Kathleen Ahern, a Cumann na mBan member, travelled to Dublin accompanied by Volunteer John Byrne to collect guns and ammunition, all of which were brought safely back to Ballymacelligott. Raids were now coming thick and fast in the area, and Cumann na mBan women were employed in carrying despatches from place to place.

The Black and Tans arrived in the area around this time and began to cause mayhem. On 11 November 1920, a party of Black and Tans, together with some British military, arrived at Ballydwyer Creamery and fired indiscriminately on the workers and suppliers around the premises. One worker was shot dead and another wounded. One supplier was shot dead and Jack McEllistrim, an active Volunteer, was wounded. He was removed to hospital in Tralee that night by members of Cumann na mBan under the supervision of Lena Brosnan. Another wounded man could not be removed except by ambulance as he was wounded in the stomach. He was attended to by Bessie along with four other women of the branch during that night. She recalled:

> At the first crack of dawn, I cycled into Tralee for a doctor. I located Doctor Coffey at about 8am. He willingly consented to come out to the wounded man.

On her return from Tralee, she called into the hospital to see Jack McEllistrim. While there, she was ordered by Jim Bailey and Thomas McEllistrim, who later became a TD for Kerry, to get Lena McEllistrim and a companion to take Jack to hospital in Cork. This was done, and a day or two later, the other man was moved to hospital in Tralee.

On the night of 24 December 1920, a party of Auxiliaries visited the house of John Byrne at Ballydwyer Creamery. Byrne was, by then, a wanted man, but he was not there at the time. Unfortunately, two other Volunteers, John Leen and Maurice Reidy, had arrived at the house only a short time before the Auxiliaries. John Leen was shot on the spot, while Reidy was shot dead after he pleaded for time to say a prayer. The women in the house, Mrs Byrne (nee McEllistrim) and her sister Hanna, pleaded in vain for the lives of the two men. They were locked in a room until the raiding party removed the bodies into the yard. The women were then taken out to a car and told they were being taken to the home of the local priest for the night.

Bessie Cahill was visiting the McEllistrims' house that night and one of the girls there saw the flames coming from the Byrne house across the fields. For Cahill, the night was to be forever etched into her memory:

I took my bicycle and went to the Creamery at Ballydwyer. As I approached, a neighbour told me what happened. I went into the yard and found the bodies in an outhouse.

Cahill then went on to the priest's house and together with Mrs Byrne, Hanna McEllistrim and another woman, Bridie Carmody, they returned to the burning house and the bodies of Leen and Reidy. They were joined by Leen's uncle and aunt and a few other neighbours. Cahill managed to find a candle and she recited the Rosary. She recalled:

We remained with the dead the greater part of the night. We attended first Mass and, after Mass, Nurse Hayes joined us and we returned to the scene of the tragedy where Nurse Hayes and I washed the bodies and laid them out on tables which we procured the previous night.

After the shooting of Leen and Reidy, the Auxiliaries maintained a presence in the area, led by a Major McKinnon. They spent much of their time travelling around and shooting indiscriminately. McKinnon became a hated figure and it was no surprise that he was eventually shot dead on the golf course in Tralee by Con Healy.

That night, the Auxiliaries returned to Ballymacelligott and burned fifteen houses, including that of the local priest. In May 1921, Cahill was sent to Cork to accompany Jack McEllistrim, who was still recovering after his shooting the previous November, back home.

Arriving at Gortatlea railway station, they ran into some British military and Black and Tans. With the help of the stationmaster, Mr Crowe, Cahill managed to get McEllistrim into the stationmaster's house without being seen. McEllistrim had a fractured arm and would not have been able to lift his arms had he been caught and ordered to do so. Some of the other passengers were not so lucky and were searched and harassed.

On the eve of the Truce in July 1921, Richard Shanahan, John Flynn and Jack Prenderville were shot dead in Castleisland. On the day of their funeral, Bessie Cahill performed her final task of the War of Independence when she, along with Hanna McEllistrim, took the rifles for the firing party on a side-car to Castleisland.

* * *

Louise Gavan Duffy was born in France in 1884, into a strongly Catholic and nationalist Irish family. She had a real interest in all things Irish, including the language, which she learned to speak fluently. In 1917, she set up the first Irish language school in the country, but before that, she became involved in the Easter Rising. However, she made it clear at the time, and in later years, that she was very much against the Rising taking place.

In her statement, she recalled the growing activity during the early months of 1916, and that a 'feverish feeling existed', especially in Dublin, that something big was about to happen. She had joined Cumann na mBan in 1914, and by the time of the Easter Rising in 1916, was well and truly imbued with the republican spirit.

Louise Gavan Duffy did not hear that the Rising had begun until late in the morning of Easter Monday. She was told by a girl called Maggie Irvine, who was staying in the same house as her on Haddington Road. Irvine was also a Cumann na mBan member and later married Joe Doherty, a prominent Volunteer from Derry.

Once she heard the news, Gavan Duffy made her way down Northumberland Road, where she saw a wounded man being taken away. It was, she said, 'her first introduction to the bloodshed of 1916'. She continued her journey, going down Westland Row and on into Pearse Street around mid-afternoon. She then crossed O'Connell Bridge and went to the GPO, where she asked to see Pádraig Pearse, as she knew him well. She recalled:

I was brought into the post office and I saw Mr Pearse. He was as calm and as courteous as ever. I now think it was very insolent of me because I said to him that I wanted to be in the field but that I felt the rebellion was a frightful mistake, that it could not possibly succeed and it was therefore wrong. I forget whether he said anything to that or whether he simply let it go. He certainly did not start to justify himself.

She told him she did not want to carry messages from post to post and he suggested she work in the kitchen, which she agreed to.

She reported to Desmond Fitzgerald in the kitchen at the top of the building, and was put to work with other Cumann na mBan women, including Mrs Fitzgerald, who soon left, after bidding her good byes to her husband. Gavan Duffy went to work washing up and cutting bread for buttering and spent much of the week carrying out kitchen duties.

When she and the other women were not working, they rested and she slept on a mattress in one of the corridors. There were a few prisoners in that area of the building – a British officer, who basically sat there during the duration of the fighting, and a number of soldiers in British uniform who had been taken prisoner on the street at the beginning of the rebellion. They were 'quite cheerful' and not anxious about their well-being.

It wasn't until the Friday that Gavan Duffy began to get a little concerned about their situation, as she saw flames outside the windows. She and her companions heard some explosions before they were told to evacuate the building with the wounded. Before the women left, they took messages from the men to bring to their friends and relatives. Gavan Duffy recalled:

I had a notebook but I was afraid to write anything in it, I only wrote their names and addresses. The messages were not exactly goodbyes but that they were alright, they had been in the post office all week and that they were leaving now and not to worry about them.

She recalled taking a message from one man, by the name of Turner, who had three sons fighting in the Rising, two of whom were with him. Gavan Duffy reckoned he was about sixty years old. She eventually managed to take the message to his wife at an address in Summerhill. Gavan Duffy was impressed at how unperturbed she was by her menfolk being away fighting for the week.

Once out of the GPO and into Henry Street, somebody carried a Red Cross flag in front of the group. They went from Prince's Street to Abbey Street via a narrow laneway, and there they met a detachment of British soldiers. Father Flanagan, who was with the group, pointed to the Red Cross flag and the wounded men and indicated that they were taking the men to Jervis Street hospital. The British accompanied the group to the hospital. The wounded men were taken away and the women, numbering about seven or eight, were told they could lie on the floor in the waiting room for the night. Next morning, they were given tea and bread before being allowed to leave.

On the Sunday, after Mass and breakfast, Gavan Duffy visited Jacob's biscuit factory in the company of Min Ryan. Tomás MacDonagh was not there when they arrived – most likely he was in negotiations with the British at that time. They were brought up to see Major John McBride and sat in a room conversing with him for a while. MacDonagh came back soon after and Gavan Duffy told him it was all over and, in her opinion, the rebellion should never have taken place, because it could never have succeeded. MacDonagh reprimanded her, saying, 'Don't talk to my men if that is the way you are feeling. I don't want anything to be putting their spirits down.'

The two women then left for St Stephen's Green, where those who had occupied the College of Surgeons for the week were being rounded up and marched off. They looked, according to Gavan Duffy, deplorable and depressed and utterly despondent. It was the moment, she recalled, when she fully realised the Rising was over and her initial fears that it would all be in vain were, very sadly, confirmed.

Chapter 17

Áine Ceannt:
The Quintessential
Republican Woman

During the week before Holy Week, there were several alarms in the city. On one
occasion a ceilidhe was in progress and word came to the men that there was to
be a raid for arms, I believe at the place where the arms were stored. The Volun-
teers immediately left the hall and stood on guard until the danger passed. I had
hoped to go to this ceilidhe, but my husband refused to go as he did not wish to be
at a social event when there was any likelihood of arms being
seized by the police or military.

(Áine Ceannt)

When Áine Ceannt gave her statement to the Bureau of Military History in May 1949, she was in a position to look back on Ireland's revolutionary era with a great deal of authority. Apart from being the widow of Éamonn Ceannt, one of the executed leaders of the Easter Rising, Áine Ceannt was a true republican hero in her own right. She supported her husband as he willingly gave his life for the cause of Ireland's independence and devoted much of her own life to the same ideal.

Frances O'Brennan was born on 23 September 1880, the youngest of the four daughters of Frank O'Brennan and his wife Elizabeth (née Butler). Frank O'Brennan died about four months before Frances was born and, like her siblings, she knew very little about their father except that he had been a Fenian. On her mother's side, the family were related to Most Reverend Dr Tobias Kirby, who had been the Rector of the Irish College in Rome for over fifty years.

The young Frances was educated in the Dominican College on Dublin's Eccles Street and in 1905 married Éamonn Ceannt. A few years later, she changed her name to Áine, which she claimed was the Irish for Fanny, her home name, and from that time on, she signed all documents as Áine B.E. Ceannt, i.e., Áine Bean Eamoinn Ceannt.

Áine Ceannt joined Cumann na mBan upon its foundation in 1914 and was an original member of its Central Branch. After the Easter Rising, she was appointed Honorary Treasurer and later became one of its four Vice-Presidents, a post she held until she retired in 1924. In October 1917, she was co-opted as a member of the Executive Committee of Sinn Féin and again stayed in the post until her retirement.

That same year, she was also elected as a member of the Dublin Board of Guardians, and the following year successfully contested the local elections, winning a seat on the Rathmines Urban District Council. When the Sinn Féin courts came into being, she was appointed a District Justice for the South City area, before moving to Rathmines and Rathgar.

During the War of Independence, the Labour Department of the Provisional Government appointed her to preside at arbitrations around the country, and she proudly recalled that she managed to settle many disputes.

When the Anglo-Irish Treaty was signed in December 1921, she attended all the subsequent meetings of the Sinn Féin Executive and presided at a Convention of Cumann na mBan to consider the document. By an overwhelming majority, 419 to 63, the women voted to reject the Treaty, making Cumann na mBan the first republican organisation to do so. Áine Ceannt took an anti-Treaty stance during the Civil War, but she consented to being a member of Sinn Féin's Peace Committee, which endeavoured to find a way to end the conflict.

In section two of her statement, Áine Ceannt provides a very perceptive and enlightening commentary on Ireland during the years preceding the 1916 Rising. She rightly pointed out that after the Parnell and Kitty O'Shea love affair scandal of 1889, and the subsequent split in Irish nationalism, there was little interest in politics among the young people of Ireland for the following decade and a half. In her opinion, there were far too many political divisions in the country and so the younger generation instead found a commonality in the Gaelic League and in learning the Irish language. They were also brought together by their love of Irish music and songs as well dancing and Irish games. The first signs of a revived interest in politics came in 1905, with the emergence of the Sinn Féin Party, founded by Arthur Griffith. She said:

> *That body advocated a policy of self-reliance, the election of a parliament of men who would sit in Ireland. The policy was the King, Lords and Commons of Ireland. This organisation did not take on very well throughout the country, but Dublin was a strong centre, some of the most advanced thinkers being members.*

Her comment seemed to indicate that any future move towards some form of independence was destined to have its roots in the capital city, which would lead the way for the rest of the country. However, progress towards independence was to remain on the slow side for at least another decade, as the idea of home rule continued to be favoured by a majority across the country. This was championed by the resurgent Irish Parliamentary Party, under the leadership of John Redmond, whose popularity reached its zenith between 1912 and 1914 with the passing of the Third Home Rule Bill and the promise of the restoration of the Dublin parliament.

That popularity was very evident in March 1912, when a large meeting was held on O'Connell Street in support of the Bill, which was before the parliament in London at the time. Ceannt recalled at least one stand at the meeting being reserved for Irish speakers who wished to address the gathering. She remembered Eoin MacNeill and PH Pearse speaking – this, as far as we know, is the only time Pearse was recorded as supporting home rule in public.

When the text of the Home Rule Bill was issued, the Sinn Féin National Council stayed silent and made no public pronouncement on it. According to Ceannt, the party was fully convinced that the Bill would never be enacted and that in time the Irish people would reject it.

The enthusiasm for home rule and maintaining the Union had also been in evidence a year earlier, during the royal visit. England's King George V and Queen

Mary arrived for a State visit, accompanied by Princess Mary and Prince Edward. Ceannt recalled that a body called the United National Societies Committee was formed to coordinate public opinion opposing the visit. The committee, she said:

> ... met at Sinn Féin Headquarters, No 6 Harcourt Street. On that committee, to my knowledge, were The O'Rahilly, Sean McDermott, Sean Fitzgibbon and Éamonn Ceannt. They would all be Sinn Féiners or members of the National Council. To one meeting PH Pearse came, accompanied by Tomás MacDonagh, and that was the first time that Pearse, to my knowledge, took any interest in Irish affairs outside the Gaelic League.

Ceannt conceded that the committee was not very successful in persuading the people of Dublin to get out on the streets and show their opposition to the visit, simply because the majority were very keen to see the monarch and his family. The streets were decorated and flags flew everywhere as thousands lined the route into the city from Dún Laoghaire.

With no hope of stopping the visit, Ceannt recalled that members of Sinn Féin decided to leave the city for the day and made their way by train to Bodenstown to visit the grave of Wolfe Tone. When they arrived back into the city that evening, some of the Sinn Féiners were attacked on the quays by the wives of British soldiers.

During the royal visit, some Sinn Féin members in the city did organise a protest meeting in Foster Place. They were not arrested and the only incident of note involved Helena Molony, the prominent republican, feminist and labour activist. Ceannt recalled how Molony:

> ... threw a stone at an illuminated portrait of the King which was displayed outside Yeats's in Grafton Street, and, of course, she was arrested. She got the option of a fine, which she refused to pay, but somebody paid it for her. She was let out – as a matter of fact, she was put out.

There was strong opposition to the Third Home Rule Bill in Ulster, and Ceannt recalled the publication of a document known as the 'Ulster Solemn League and Covenant' on 28 September 1912. This was signed by thousands of unionists, men and women, and many of them signed it in their own blood, vowing to oppose home rule. Four months later, in January 1913, the Ulster Volunteers were formed with the avowed intention of holding Ulster for Britain.

In August 1913, the Dublin Strike and Lockout began when about 20,000 workers, mainly members of the Irish Transport and General Workers' Union, took on around 300 of the city's employers. Led by Jim Larkin and supported by James Connolly and the Labour Party, they hoped to win better working conditions. The bitter dispute lasted until January 1914, when the workers, beaten and deflated, returned to work, many under worse terms than when the strike began.

A public meeting was held in the Rotunda Rink, in the grounds of the Rotunda hospital, on 25 November 1913, with a view to forming an organisation to rival the Ulster Volunteers. Ceannt recalled the occasion vividly, saying:

> ... *overflow meetings were addressed by Sean McDermott and others. There was a special platform reserved for the ladies. The numbers of men attending were quite unexpected and it was evident that the physical force movement appealed to the manhood of Ireland, where the more constitutional movement of Sinn Féin, although revolutionary in character, did not make the same appeal.*

With the Home Rule Bill due to become law, the government in London anticipated opposition from the unionist community in Ulster. British troops based in the Curragh were ordered to deploy to Ulster in March 1914 to quash any resistance from the Ulster Volunteers. Ceannt recalled that the officers in the Curragh mutinied, refusing to go to Ulster to enforce the weakening of the Union. Ceannt noted that no genuine disciplinary measures were ever taken against the officers.

She also recalled that around a month later, on 26 April, a cargo of guns was run into Larne in County Antrim. Without any interference from the authorities, the Ulster Volunteers distributed them around the province in anticipation that they would be needed to forcefully oppose the imposition of home rule on the island of Ireland.

Áine Ceannt was informed on 25 July 1914 that a cargo of guns was due to land that day at Kilcoole in County Wicklow, and that arrangements had been made to receive them. That afternoon, her husband, while adjudicating at a pipe band competition, was informed that the landing would not take place. However, as the cars that were to collect and distribute the guns were already on their way to Kilcoole, the drivers had no option but to continue their journey as if they were all out for an afternoon jaunt around the Wicklow countryside.

The actual gun running took place the following day, a Sunday, when Erskine Childers's yacht the *Asgard* landed at Howth harbour. Dublin members of the Irish Volunteers attended to help with the distribution of the 1,500 Mauser rifles and then marched back into the city. Ceannt recalled:

> When they reached Howth Road the men were intercepted by the police, supported by the military. Many of the men were being bayonetted so Éamonn Ceannt fired from his Mauser and injured one soldier, Lance-Corporal Finney, in the ankle. This shot caused the soldiers to run ... The Volunteers dispersed, retaining their guns. On the way back to the city the soldiers, the King's Own Scottish Borderers, fired on the people at Bachelors Walk killing four and wounding fifty. This enraged the population, with the result that the Regiment had to be confined to barracks until it was got out of the country. An enquiry into the whole incident was held, and many of the police who had refused to disarm the Volunteers, knowing that the Ulster Volunteers had been permitted to receive their guns, were suspended. They were subsequently reinstated.

Ceannt recalled that the funerals of the Bachelors Walk victims were attended by almost everyone in Dublin, and she claimed that the sympathy they invoked served to enhance the republican cause. She also confirmed that a second cargo of guns was successfully landed at Kilcoole some weeks later, on 2 August, just two days prior to the outbreak of the Great War.

Áine Ceannt confirmed that by 1915, her husband had been appointed Director of Communications by the IRB Military Council. As part of his brief, he put in place a postal system called An Post Gaelach. Various houses across Dublin offered to be reception depots for letters. The sender would leave the letter and a penny, the current postage, at one of these depots, and the postman would collect the letters and the money and deliver all the letters within a certain radius of Dublin. If he failed to deliver a letter, he would return it.

Áine Ceannt recalled that the IRB Military Council started to meet in her home in Dolphin's Barn in January 1916. She remembered meeting Tom Clarke, Sean McDermott and PH Pearse and, though she had no recollection of him, she surmised that Joseph Plunkett was also in attendance at their first meeting in the house.

On 19 January, James Connolly disappeared, and it transpired that he and members of the IRB Military Council were holed up in a brick works in Dolphin's Barn. The Council members had heard whispers that Connolly and his Irish Citizen Army were planning a workers' revolution, which they believed would undermine their own rebellion plans. In effect the Military Council 'kidnapped' Connolly in an attempt to persuade him to hold off on his workers' revolution.

Connolly, forward-thinking as he was, had instructed his next-in-command, Michael Mallin, that if at any time he disappeared and did not turn up within three days, the Citizen Army was to go out and take Dublin Castle. Áine Ceannt recalled her husband's reaction to Connolly's disappearance. He said:

'We can't let the Citizen Army go out alone, if they go out, we must go with them. Three of us are going to see Mallin to ask him to hold his hand.' I think Éamonn said McDermott was one, but I am not sure of the names of the three. Éamonn said, 'I am going now to see what was the result of the deputation that went over to the Citizen Army, asking them to wait a few days. In the meantime, I have ordered all the officers of the Fourth Battalion to report here, and on my return, it will be either to give them orders for ordinary manoeuvres, if the situation has cleared, or, alternatively, to tell them their places for the fight.' When he returned, at about half past ten, he dismissed the men rather quickly and told me that Connolly had re-appeared. At the next meeting of the Military Council, held at our house, Connolly was present and was a member of that body from that day forward.

From that moment on, Áine Ceannt had no doubt that a rebellion against British rule in Ireland was a matter of months, if not weeks, away, and that her husband was certain to be in the thick of it.

On 17 March, the Dublin Battalion of up to 2,000 men was inspected by Eoin MacNeill at College Green. They had assembled at St Michael's and St John's Church for a special military Mass at nine o'clock. On that occasion the honour of serving the Mass and of providing the Guard of Honour fell to Éamonn Ceannt's Fourth Battalion. His wife vividly recalled the day in her statement:

The Volunteers, with rifles and fixed bayonets, swung into College Green from O'Connell Street and formed a hollow square. I viewed the scene from the top of a tram-car at where King Billy's statue used to stand, and below me, on the street,

I noticed, as an interested spectator, Viscount Powerscourt. I mention this because immediately after the Rising in 1916 Viscount Powerscourt was appointed Provost Marshall. After the inspection the various Battalions returned to their headquarters. The Fourth Battalion marched to Dolphin's Barn where they formed up, were addressed by their Commandant, and sang the Soldier's Song before being dismissed.

On Monday of Holy Week, Éamonn Ceannt informed his wife that he was taking a week off from his work as an accountant with Dublin Corporation. It was as if he was readying himself and his family for what was about to take place. Áine recalled that on Tuesday, when they were retiring to bed, Éamonn took out his Mauser pistol and placed it beside their bed ready for use, remarking, 'We are living in stirring times. If we live through this night, we will have drawn first blood.'

When they awoke the next morning, Áine Ceannt thanked God that the night had passed peacefully. That day, Wednesday, was an exceptionally wet one. Éamonn Ceannt left home early, and Áine went into the city to buy stores for his knapsack in preparation for the coming manoeuvres. She walked along College Green and passed the feminist and republican activist Hannah Sheehy-Skeffington and her son Owen. Mrs Sheehy-Skeffington was of course unaware then of the terrible tragedy about to befall her and her family just a week later when her husband, Francis, would be murdered by Captain John Bowen-Colthurst of the Royal Irish Rifles Regiment.

Áine Ceannt recalled that Thursday was a busy day in Volunteers circles. In the early afternoon, an important meeting was held in Woodstown House, Dundrum. This was the home of John (Eoin) MacNeill, Chief of Staff of the Volunteers, and his brother James, later to be Governor General of the Irish Free State between 1928 and 1932. At this stage, MacNeill was still setting his face against the proposal to use the Volunteers as the army of insurrection, and he was being supported in that stance by others in the leadership, such as Bulmer Hobson. Áine recalled that her husband told her he walked home from Dundrum with Thomas MacDonagh, who remarked, 'Hobson is the evil genius of the Volunteers and if we could separate John MacNeill from his influence all would be well.'

It is evident then from Áine Ceannt's statement that the IRB Military Council was doing all it could to convince Eoin MacNeill and the Irish Volunteers leadership to allow their men to become the foot soldiers of the rebellion. Another meeting of the Volunteers was held in the city later on Holy Thursday, and from around eight o'clock in the evening, several people called to the Ceannt household to see Éamonn. He later told his wife that he had sent the visitors down the country as couriers with instructions for the impending rebellion. She recalled:

Con Keating, the wireless operator, who was subsequently drowned in the River Laune, and another man had been to the house some days before, and received from Éamonn a lamp which was to be used to signal the Aud. I believed they also travelled South on Thursday. They also got a ship's V/S [visual signalling] lamp, which they brought to Tralee. The latter lamp was in the care of the Volunteers, and was buried by them when the boat failed to get in.

Áine recalled drawing her husband's attention to a report in the newspaper on Good Friday morning as they ate breakfast. The report confirmed that a collapsible boat had landed on a beach in Kerry and that there had been an arrest of one man and another had escaped. Éamonn, it seems, made no comment.

Later, at the Good Friday afternoon devotions that the Ceannt family were attending, a Volunteer entered the church and looked around until he saw Éamonn. He whispered something to him and then left. There can be little doubt he was confirming the loss of the *Aud* and the 25,000 rifles it was carrying, which were destined to arm the Volunteers for the rebellion. Most likely he also confirmed that the arrested man was Roger Casement. That evening, the couple took a walk in the Phoenix Park and sat on a seat overlooking the river. Éamonn Ceannt was particularly silent, and it was obvious to Áine that the enormity of what was about to unfold over the following week was occupying his thoughts.

On Easter Saturday, Éamonn and Áine travelled out to Dalkey to visit a friend whom Éamonn intended to ask for the loan of field glasses. Áine recalled that as they sat on the top of the tram, he whispered to her, 'The man who landed in Kerry was Roger Casement and the man who got away was Monteith. If they catch Monteith they'll hang him.'

Casement and Monteith had been in Germany attempting to raise an Irish Brigade from Irishmen who were fighting in the British army and had been captured as prisoners of war. They had also negotiated the shipment of arms being carried on the *Aud*.

Éamonn and Áine had lunch in Dalkey and left for home around four o'clock. That evening, Éamonn confirmed to his wife that the Rising was set to begin at six o'clock the following evening. His headquarters would be the South Dublin Union. He said:

> *'We Volunteers, an armed body, could not let this opportunity pass without striking a blow while England is at war. We would be a disgrace to our generation, and so we strike tomorrow at six o'clock. I shall not sleep at home tonight in case of accidents, but will stay with John Doherty at James's Terrace.'*

Éamonn then wrote letters to his two brothers, to be delivered the following day by An Post Gaelach. Once the letters were written, he went out to confession, before leaving home for Doherty's around ten o'clock.

Áine retired to bed at midnight, but was woken at 2am by knocking on the hall door. She opened the bedroom window and looked out to see who was there. A man speaking in Irish asked for her husband, so Áine went down to see who it was. It turned out to be Cathal Brugha, who was due to act as Éamonn Ceannt's second-in-command at the South Dublin Union. Áine told him where he could find her husband and he immediately went on his way. Within half an hour, Éamonn returned home with all his equipment, guns and ammunition. Áine recalled:

> *I was astounded, but he merely remarked: 'MacNeill has ruined us – he has stopped the Rising.' Keyed up as I was for the fight, I started to make suggestions, but Eamon replied: 'The countermanding order is already in the hands of the paper. I am off now to see if anything can be done.'*

He went to Liberty Hall to see Connolly and to the Metropole hotel to see Joseph Plunkett. He saw neither of them, as they were both sleeping and both had left instructions with their armed guards that they were not to be disturbed. Ceannt returned home at 5.30, and Áine gave him some hot milk. He slept until 8.30, when she woke him to tell him a Military Council despatch had arrived.

He read the despatch before leaving the house for Liberty Hall. He returned at 1pm, to be met by many of his men and he ordered them to return home and await further orders. Áine recalled:

> After dinner Éamonn suggested we go as far as Howth. I remember him standing silently staring at the Pier where two years previously the famous gun-running had taken place. Éamonn slept at home that night, remarking: 'I may thank John MacNeill that I can sleep in my own house – the cancelling of the manoeuvres will lead the British to believe that everything is all right.'

Áine Ceannt's role as the wife of an Irish revolutionary leader in 1916 required a stout heart as well as a steely determination to stand full square beside her husband, and she was not short of either of those attributes. Easter Monday saw her up early with her husband as he prepared for the momentous day ahead. Éamonn put on his uniform and collected his equipment. Áine recalled that he had a lot to carry, including a large bag full of ammunition. She helped him with his Sam Browne belt and adjusted his knapsack, which was exceptionally large, protruding out beyond his shoulders. While she was dressing him, she asked him how long he expected the fight to continue, and he replied:

> 'If we last a month the British will come to terms. We have sent out messages throughout the country, but as the men have already received at least two other orders, it is hard to know what may happen. Turning to Rónán [their Son] who was watching us, he kissed him and said, 'Beannacht leat a Rónáin,' and the child replied, 'Beannacht leat a Dhaide.' 'Nach dtiubhraidh tú aire mhaith do'd mháthairín?' he asked. 'Tiubhrad, a Dhaide,' said Rónán, and so, they parted for ever. I would have wished to go to Emerald Square to see the men march off, but Éamonn asked me not to and so I embraced him, bade him God speed and he went out.

Áine Ceannt and her son Rónán stayed with Cathal Brugha's wife Caitlín during the week of the Rising, as her husband was concerned that their own house in Dolphin's Barn was likely to be in the line of fire during the fighting. Áine and her host waited anxiously all week for news about the fighting and their husbands. Mrs Brugha's sister was also in the house, along with a friend who had been marooned in the city once the fighting started.

Early on Friday morning, the household was woken by a military raid. The soldiers were somewhat puzzled to see so many women and no men in the house, but Caitlín Brugha explained that her husband was a commercial traveller and was down the country.

That evening, Caitlín's brother, Father Kingston, arrived with the news that Cathal Brugha had been wounded, though he made light of the reported injuries. Áine recalled that though they could see fires burning in the city during Saturday, they noticed that there was very little shooting to be heard. They decided to make their way to Rathmines, where some people told them there was a truce, but they knew very little else.

Áine Ceannt went to Mass in Rathgar church on the Sunday and there she met a woman who told her that a Proclamation had been issued and that Éamonn Ceannt's name had been signed to it. This, Áine recalled, was the first she knew of the Proclamation. That day, she and Caitlín Brugha awaited news of their husbands, but it didn't come.

The following day, Monday, both women met some priests in Rathmines, who told them that the captured Volunteers were to be interned and the leaders were to be tried by field general court martial. This came as a major shock to Áine.

Her fears were heightened the following Thursday when news broke of the executions of PH Pearse, Tom Clarke and Thomas MacDonagh. She heard better news later that day, when it was reported in the press that a sentence of three years' penal servitude was to be imposed on her husband and three others. She recalled:

> I did not know who the other three were. When I read this I was delighted, but at the same time I thought it very hard that MacDonagh, who to my mind had not been so deeply involved until the last moment, should have suffered execution.

The following day, Friday, Áine visited her own home, to find it had been completely ransacked by British soldiers. While there, she heard the sad news that one of her neighbours, a young woman, was so frightened when she saw the soldiers and their guns that she had a seizure and died.

During all that time, Áine recalled that she had essentially been living under the delusion that her husband would not be executed. However, her sister-in-law brought her back to reality when she told that her four other leaders – Willie Pearse, Ned Daly, Michael O'Hanrahan and Joseph Plunkett – had been executed. Naturally, Áine's concern was heightened again by that sad news, and she redoubled her efforts to discover the whereabouts of her husband.

On Saturday, a family friend, Johnny Foley, who had been Secretary to the Lord Mayor for many years, went on her behalf to the Mansion House to see if he could get any news of Éamonn Ceannt. However, he had no great success. He was informed, however, that if he and Áine went to Richmond barracks, they would be admitted. The following day, Sunday, they set off after breakfast, accompanied by Éamonn's brother, Richard.

At the barracks, they were met by the Provost Marshall, Viscount Powerscourt, who was, as Áine recalled:

> … *very amiable but he did not know what sentence these 'gentlemen' got, but consented to give me a note to the Governor of Kilmainham, which permitted me to interview my husband. I arrived at Kilmainham, was shown in, and found Éamonn in a cell with no seating accommodation and no bedding, not even a bed of straw.*
>
> *The first thing I noticed was that his Sam Browne belt was gone, and that his uniform was slightly torn. A sergeant stood at the door while we spoke, and we could say very little, but I gathered from Éamonn that he had heard about the supposed three years sentence and he felt it would worry me. I said to him that the Rising was an awful fiasco, and he replied, 'No, it was the biggest thing since '98. They told me here that the railway lines were up.' Those were Éamonn's words.*
>
> *The rest of our conversation was personal. He gave me Cathal Brugha's watch to give to Mrs Brugha, and some money which he had on him. I left Éamonn after getting a promise that he would send for me no matter what was going to happen.*

The following day, Sunday, was a very wet one, and Áine Ceannt spent it with her son at her sister-in-law's house. The damp weather did little to improve her or the household's mood and the sense of foreboding only increased as the hours passed. In her statement, Áine poignantly recalled the moment her life was changed forever:

At about ten o'clock there was a knock at the door, and an Army officer arrived with a note to say that my husband would like to see me and his sister. We went out to the car and there we found that this soldier had already collected Richard Kent and Michael Kent, brothers. It was a night of fierce rain, and as we travelled along accompanied by a policeman, we came across various patrols, where the policeman put his head out and shouted: 'Command car. King's Messenger.' We reached Kilmainham and had about twenty minutes interview with my husband. He was in a different cell, and been given a couple of boards, on which I presume he rested. He also had a soap box, a chair, a candle and pen and ink. He told me he had sent for Father Augustine to come to him. On our way out, Richard, the youngest Kent, spoke to the Commandant, who said to him, 'There is no reprieve. Go back and tell your brother.'

I remained up all night with my sister-in-law, and each hour we knelt down and said the Rosary. From three o'clock I remained praying until half past five, when I knew that everything would be over if the executions were to take place. At six o'clock curfew was lifted, and we made our way down to Church Street. It was a glorious summer morning and when we arrived at the Priory, I asked for Father Augustine. He sent down another Friar who told me that Father Augustine had only come, celebrated Mass and had gone to his room, but that if I wished he would get up and come down to me. I said no, that I only wanted to know the truth, and this priest said, 'He is gone to Heaven.'

Éamonn Ceannt gave his life for the cause of his country's independence, but he did so safe in the knowledge that he had the full support of his family and, most particularly, his loyal and loving wife. She publicly and privately stood by him and encouraged him on every step of his revolutionary journey, all the time displaying the most immense courage, knowing that, on any given day, she could be parted from him forever.

That parting came on 8 May 1916. One hour before his death, Éamonn Ceannt wrote his final letter to the woman he loved dearly:

2.30am8/5/16

My dearest wife Áine.

Not wife but widow before these lines reach you. I am here without hope of this world and without fear, calmly awaiting the end. I have had Holy Communion and Father Augustine has been with me and will be back again. Dearest 'silly little Fanny'. My poor little sweetheart of – how many – years ago. Ever my comforter, God comfort you now. What can I say? I die a noble death, for Ireland's freedom. Men and women will vie with one another to shake your dear hand. Be proud of me as I am and ever was of you. My cold exterior was but a mask. It has served me in these last days. You have a duty to me and to Rónán, that is to live. My dying wishes are that you shall remember your state of health, work only as much as may be necessary and freely accept the little attentions which in due time will be answered upon you. You will be – you are, the wife of one of the Leaders of the Rebellion. Sweeter still you are my little child, my dearest pet, my sweetheart of the hawthorn hedges and summer eves. I remember all and I banish all that I may be strong and die bravely. I have one hour to live, then God's judgement and, through his infinite mercy, a place near your poor Grannie, and my mother and father, and Jem and all the five old Irish Catholics who went through the scourge of similar misfortune from this Vale of Tears into the Promised Land.

Adieu, Éamonn

After her husband's death, Áine Ceannt continued to live her life fully committed to the cause of her country's independence. The executed leaders of the Easter Rising all had wives, mothers and sisters to call upon for support and encouragement, and Éamonn Ceannt clearly showed in his final letter that he felt himself very much blessed by having, in his life, a woman who understood and approved of all he was fighting for.

Postscript:
The Legacy of the Civil War and the Road to Recovery

The Witness Statements Archive provides a unique window into one of the country's most tumultuous eras. It was a time when the majority of the people were united in one common goal, namely, the pursuit of independence and the establishment of a sovereign Irish state, free from British rule. In order to achieve that goal, it was necessary in 1916 and, from 1919 to 1921, to take on the might of the British Army as well as other Crown forces such as the Royal Irish Constabulary and the detested Black and Tans. The conflicts during those years brought suffering, death, injury and destruction, but also a sense of comradeship and loyalty among the Irish people, who were determined to see the fight through to a successful conclusion.

When a truce was agreed by Eamon de Valera and Lloyd George in July 1921, a joyous cheer rang out across the country, as well as a collective sigh of relief. For the first time in history, the people of Ireland had managed to bring the British to the negotiating table to discuss the future of the country and the ideal of independence.

The months following the cessation of hostilities brought a sense of hope and anticipation across the country as political leaders on both sides of the Irish Sea sought to find a solution to the 'Irish question'. Those months saw a new political elite emerge in Ireland, dominated by men like Eamon de Valera, Michael Collins and Arthur Griffith. They had come to realise that the only way forward for the country was through negotiations rather than further warfare. The fighting men of the IRA had proved themselves a formidable force, which the British could never hope to defeat in the field, but their day was over, their task completed. In an era when the statesmen of Europe were negotiating new political, social and economic structures, it was only right that the politicians on both sides of the Irish Sea should do the same, in order that a new and independent Ireland could take her place in the emerging international community of nations.

Between October and December 1921, the pace of negotiations quickened in London. The Irish delegation, led by Arthur Griffith and Michael Collins, pitted their wits against the experienced and formidable British delegation led by the wily 'Welsh wizard', Lloyd George. That time was not without its controversy, as de Valera, the universally accepted leader of the Irish people, decided to absent himself from the negotiations, claiming that by being detached from them, he would be in a better position to pronounce on the agreement that finally emerged from Downing Street.

When the Treaty did become public, de Valera rejected it, as did many others, causing a major rift in republican leadership and deep divisions among the public. Friendships were broken and family members fell out over the contents of the agreement. The main bone of contention was that it did not deliver on the independent republic that had been fought for in the revolutionary era.

Men and women who stood beside each other during the Easter Rising and the War of Independence now found themselves on opposite sides of the Treaty divide. Those who accepted it, like Collins and Griffith, recognised that it fell short of the republic they wanted, but saw it as an important stepping stone towards a completely free and independent island of Ireland. Those who rejected the Treaty, like de Valera, saw it as an abandonment of all that had been fought for. Though a majority were in favour of the Treaty, seeing it as bringing peace to the country, differences in public opinion could not be bridged. Despite the best efforts of politicians and others, the republican movement, which had been so united during the Easter Rising and the War of Independence, also fractured, with devastating consequences.

As the people of the twenty-six counties grappled with the complexities of the Treaty, the unionists of Ulster looked on in consternation, fearful of what might happen to their province and the Union. Northern Ireland was created in May 1921, and the unionist government in Stormont and the majority of the people jealously guarded their status within the United Kingdom. James Craig, the Unionist Party leader and Prime Minister, refused to take any part in the Treaty negotiations, maintaining that whatever emerged from them would be an agreement between two other states. Yet, such was his, and his Cabinet's, concern over the discussions in Downing Street, he made sure he was kept fully informed and up to date by certain members of the British delegation.

When the Civil War broke out, Collins assumed the position of Commander-in-Chief of the National Army. The Army steadily gained the upper hand over the anti-Treaty forces, the 'Irregulars', throughout the summer of 1922. Though it caused him great personal pain and sorrow, having to confront former friends and allies, he was committed to the Treaty, believing it represented the best way forward for his beloved country.

As the Civil War raged on through the summer of 1922, Collins's stature grew among friends and foes alike. With the untimely death of Arthur Griffith in early August, the burden of leadership fell even more heavily on the shoulders of Collins. Those close to him worried about whether he would survive the ordeal and deliver peace to the country. Unfortunately, it was not long before their worst fears were confirmed.

Collins's physical and mental health was in a fragile state during the last week of his life, and he was less than convinced that he would survive the conflict. Despite his depressed state of mind, he insisted on making a tour of his native County Cork. Convinced that his own people would do him no harm, he ignored the advice of his senior officers not to undertake the inspection trip. At around 7pm on 22 August, Collins and his convoy were ambushed by anti-Treaty forces at Béal na mBláth. Despite being urged by Emmet Dalton, one of his close confidants, to order the convoy to speed up and break through the ambush, Collins decided to stop and confront the enemy.

A gunfight ensued, lasting, according to Dalton, for around twenty minutes. Collins was the only fatality, taking what was probably a ricochet bullet behind his ear. When Dalton and Sean O'Connell found him, he had what Dalton described as a 'fearful gaping wound at the base of his skull and behind his right ear'.

There seems to be, even to this day, no definitive agreement on who fired the shot that killed the probable future leader of the Free State. Many historians believe it may have been fired by Dennis (Sonny) O'Neill, an anti-Treaty volunteer and former British Army marksman. This view was corroborated by Liam Deasy, commander of the ambush party, when he later said 'we all knew it was Sonny O'Neill's bullet'.

Collins's body was driven back to Cork and from there it was taken by ship to Dublin. He lay in state for three days in Dublin City Hall, where he was viewed by many thousands of heartbroken mourners. The funeral Mass was held at the Pro Cathedral, and some 500,000 people lined the streets of Dublin as the cortege made its way to Glasnevin Cemetery.

The war finally ended on 24 May 1923. When the fighting was over, Richard Mulcahy, who succeeded Collins as Commander-in-Chief of the National Army, put the number of Free State forces dead at 540, though the government estimated it as 800. On the anti-Treaty side, there is even less certainty, but the number is probably greater than the Free State dead. There are no definite figures for civilian dead either, but some historians estimate the total number of deaths in the conflict at about 4,000, which, given the size of the population at that time, is horrific.

Those who lost their lives included prominent individuals like Harry Boland, Cathal Brugha, Liam Mellows, Rory O'Connor, Liam Lynch and Michael Collins. The fledgling Free State was therefore denied the talents of individuals who would have contributed enormously to its early development, and none more so than Michael Collins. He had reached iconic status by the end of the War of Independence, and his stature was enhanced when he dominated the Irish delegation that negotiated the Anglo-Irish Treaty between October and December 1921. He was set fair to lead the Free State once Dáil Éireann had ratified the Treaty in January 1922.

As soon as the fighting was over, WT Cosgrave called a general election. The pro-Treaty element of Sinn Féin split into a new party called Cumann na nGaedheal, with Cosgrave as leader and Kevin O'Higgins as his deputy. They promised a return to peace, stability and law and order, which was just what the majority wanted after years of conflict and suffering. The party was returned to Dáil Éireeann with sixty-three seats, while Sinn Féin abstained with its forty-four seats because its candidates refused to take the Oath of Allegiance required under the Treaty. The Labour Party, under the leadership of Thomas Johnson, took fourteen seats with the Farmers' Party returning fifteen TDs and independents seventeen. Many of the Sinn Féin candidates were still in jail during the campaign because of their role in the Civil War, and during the campaign itself de Valera was arrested and jailed.

With Cosgrave at the helm, many people felt the country was in safe hands. Though lacking the charisma of Collins, the quiet and unassuming Dubliner took over the running of the country at a time when chaos and no little bitterness reigned. He set out some important aims for his government, including the restoration of law and order and the establishment of democracy. Conservative by nature, the forty-two-year-old had no ambition to introduce any dramatic reforms. In his view, what the country needed was a period of calm and quiet to allow people to reflect on the turbulent past few years and plan for a peaceful future.

He surrounded himself in Cabinet with like-minded men, all of them younger than him, to steer the fledgling state through its first decade of existence. Kevin O'Higgins would prove to be a formidable deputy leader and Minister for Home Affairs. Richard Mulcahy brought all his military acumen to the post of Minister for Defence. A youthful Patrick Hogan took on the post of Minister for Agriculture, while Desmond Fitzgerald, father of future Taoiseach Garret Fitzgerald, became Minister for External Affairs. The nation's finances were entrusted to Ernest Blythe, whose conservative attitude to economics ensured that not a penny went astray, and the education of the younger generation became the responsibility of Eoin MacNeill.

History would prove to be less than complimentary regarding many of the policies this government implemented, but it must be acknowledged that these young men assumed power at a difficult time. They faced multiple urgent difficulties, ranging from balancing the finances to restoring law and order in a country that had experienced nothing but lawlessness over the previous few years.

The Civil War had had a devastating effect on the country, leaving a challenging financial legacy for the incoming government to deal with. It was estimated that the material damage inflicted was around £30 million, which came on top of the £17 million it cost to finance the war. The damage to property during the conflict far outstripped the damage caused by the War of Independence.

The expenditure problem was not helped by the fact that the collection of taxes and rates had been badly hampered in the areas that had experienced the heaviest of the fighting. This created a problem in the short and medium term for Ernest Blythe, as he struggled to manage the nation's finances. Despite the difficult fiscal situation, Blythe always insisted on balancing the books. Some economists and commentators criticised Blythe during his tenure as Finance Minister for his lack of radicalism, while others felt that his conservative approach was the correct one as the new State was attempting to establish itself as an economically viable and independent entity.

A very pressing issue for the Cumann na nGaedheal government to confront was the question of law and order. The country was emerging from many years of conflict and the rule of law was not always adhered to. Even though the fighting had officially come to an end, there were still elements in society who were not prepared to accept the legitimacy of the new government or any laws it passed. To counteract this threat, the government successfully set up the Garda Síochána, and this essentially unarmed force was quickly accepted by the people. The arrival of the new police force was complemented by the introduction of a relatively stable and efficient courts system, which had no difficulty in sentencing those found guilty of crimes against the State and society to fines or time in prison, and in seventy-seven cases, death.

For many republicans, however, the Free State offered little personal opportunity, and they found themselves excluded from many sections of society. Many felt they had little choice but to emigrate, which denied the state the services of some very talented people. And this feeling of exclusion was not just felt in an individual sense. Areas of the country like Kerry in the south and Mayo in the west felt alienated from the hub of national activity and decision-making. Opposition to the Treaty had been vociferous in both of these counties as well as in other smaller pockets around the country, and many living in these areas felt they were being made to pay the price for the stance they had adopted during the conflict.

War is always terrible and divisive, but civil war is surely the most horrific of all. Ireland's Civil War left a scar on the psyche of a very young nation that has taken many decades to heal. On 15 April 1922, an editorial in the *Kilkenny People* summed it up well:

> *Ireland is big enough for great things and great movements, but is too small for Civil War. Civil War means death and destruction. It means the material ruin of the nation and the moral degradation of its people.*

One hundred years on, the Free State is no longer in existence and the death and destruction that shattered the unity of its people is a distant memory. Time has indeed been a great healer, even if the healing has been at a slower rate than most would have wished. The divisions over the Treaty have now being consigned to the history books and, 100 years on, the Ireland of today is in a much better place. We can now look at the Witness Statements archive as a stand-alone record of an important chapter in the totality of Ireland's coming of age.

Éamonn Duggan, 2021

References

Chapter 2

Statement of Michael Staines (Witness Statement number 284)

Chapter 3

Statement of Sean Murphy (Witness Statement number 1598)

Statement of Patrick Coakley (Witness Statement number 45)

Chapter 4

Statement of Monsignor Michael Curran (Witness Statement number 687)

Chapter 5

Statement of Joseph V Lawless (Witness Statement number 1043)

Chapter 6

Statement of Nicholas Laffan (Witness Statement number 703)

Statement of Patrick Ahern (Witness Statement number 1003)

Statement of Patrick J Whelan (Witness Statement number 1231)

Statement of George Fitzgerald (Witness Statement number 684)

Statement of Michael Healy (Witness Statement number 1064)

Statement of Joseph Kinsella (Witness Statement number 476)

Chapter 7

Statement of Patrick O'Dwyer (Witness Statement number 1432)

Statement of Sean Fitzpatrick (Witness Statement number 1259)

Statement of Liam Hoolan (Witness Statement number 1553)

Statement of James Leahy (Witness Statement number 1454)

Chapter 8

Statement of Daniel Corkery (Witness Statement number 1719)

Statement of Denis Lordan (Witness Statement number 470)

Statement of Patrick O'Brien (Witness Statement number 812)

Chapter 9
Statement of Kitty O'Doherty (Witness Statement number 355)
Irish Times, 6 May 1961
Statement of Kathleen Lynn (Witness Statement number 357)
Statement of Rose McNamara (Witness Statement number 482)

Chapter 10
Statement of Father Aloysius (Witness Statement number 200)

Chapter 11
Statement of Frank Thornton (Witness Statement number 510)

Chapter 12
Statement of Vincent Byrne (Witness Statement number 423)

Chapter 13
Statement of Seán Moylan (Witness Statement number 838)
Irish Examiner, 12 November 2007

Chapter 14
Statement of Tadhg Kennedy (Witness Statement number 1413)

Chapter 15
Statement of Eamon Broy (Witness Statement number 1280)

Chapter 16
Statement of Máire Mhic Giolla Phádraig (Witness Statement number 1344)
Statement of Mary Rigney (Witness Statement number 752)
Statement of Peg Broderick-Nicholson (Witness Statement number 1682)
Statement of Bessie Cahill (Witness Statement number 1143)
Statement of Louise Gavan Duffy (Witness Statement number 216)

Chapter 17
Statement of Áine Ceannt (Witness Statement number 264)

Postscript
Kilkenny People, 15 April 1922